HOW TO BE A CONSISTENT WINNER
IN THE MOST POPULAR CARD GAMES

BOOKS BY JOHN R. CRAWFORD

How to Be a Consistent Winner in the Most Popular Card
   Games

Crawford's Contract Bridge

Samba (*Three-Deck Canasta*)

How to Play Samba

Canasta

How to Play Calypso

HOW TO BE
A CONSISTENT WINNER
IN THE MOST POPULAR
CARD GAMES

BY

JOHN R. CRAWFORD

Dolphin Books
Doubleday & Company, Inc.
Garden City, New York

HOW TO BE A CONSISTENT WINNER IN THE MOST POPULAR
CARD GAMES *was originally published by Doubleday & Company in 1953. The Dolphin Books edition is published by arrangement with the publisher.*

Dolphin Books edition: 1961

CONTENTS

INTRODUCTION

I have played nearly every kind of card game in nearly every part of the world. Always I have played for money, and sometimes for a lot of money. I have had a chance to observe, in action, nearly every type of card player.

Some of these have studied their favorite games for a long time and know a lot about them, and yet they lose. Why? Usually it is because of just a few habitual mistakes that they make over and over. Yet they could correct these mistakes quite easily if they knew what they were.

In this book I have tried to analyze the mistakes that the average *good* player makes most often and finds most costly. Usually a player can easily avoid such mistakes if he knows the few basic—and generally simple—principles that govern them. Pay attention to these principles and you will speedily change into a consistent winner.

This is not a book for beginners. I assume that the reader knows at least the mechanics of playing. But I have also included the laws of each game, to supply the procedure of play for those who do not know it, and to settle whatever arguments may arise.

I have been fortunate in having the co-operation of several great card authorities, and I gratefully acknowledge the assistance of:

OSWALD JACOBY, my toughest opponent at all games, and author of excellent books on Poker and Canasta.

WALDEMAR VON ZEDTWITZ, one of the greatest Bridge players and analysts of all time.

GEOFFREY MOTT-SMITH, who gave generously of his vast store of knowledge of games.

B. JAY BECKER, who was of great assistance in Pinochle analysis.

HARRY HARKAVY, a sensational player of Hearts, a great Bridge master.

C. E. WILSON, the leading authority on Auction Pitch.

JACK J. DREYFUS, who knows Gin Rummy percentages as well as he knows stock-market percentages (he is senior partner of Dreyfus & Co.).

ROGER R. BALDWIN, HERBERT MAISEL, WILBERT E. CANTEY, and JAMES P. McDERMOTT, whose mathematical research revolutionized the playing of Blackjack.

ALLAN WILSON, a Blackjack expert as well as a computer scientist, who carried the new science of Blackjack many steps farther.

The United States Playing Card Company, whose "Official Rules of Card Games" (adopted by the Association of American Playing Card Manufacturers) is the basis of the laws I have used.

Most of all I want to express my deep appreciation to ALBERT MOREHEAD, whose many books on card games have earned him the title of "the modern Hoyle," and without whose encouragement and advice I could never have written this book.

JOHN R. CRAWFORD

BRIDGE

TEN THINGS EVERY WINNING BRIDGE PLAYER MUST KNOW

1. It pays to bid a vulnerable game when the odds are 8 to 5 against you; when not vulnerable you need a 50–50 chance.

2. It pays to go down 400 or 500 (depending on vulnerability) to prevent an opposing game.

3. It is worth going down as much as 200 to prevent an opposing part score.

4. To bid a little slam you need a 50–50 chance; to bid a grand slam you need at least 2 to 1 in your favor.

5. An opening major-suit bid should show at least a five-card suit or a strong four-card suit.

6. Bid your strength whenever possible—the suit you want to have led.

7. Don't overcall at the two level unless your trump suit is at least five cards long and very strong.

8. Don't make a light third-hand bid if you can't stand a lead in the suit.

9. Bid more cautiously when you suspect a misfit.

10. Take a moderate set rather than risk having a big contract made against you—it's insurance.

CONTRACT BRIDGE

All the authorities have always said, "If you want your Bridge books to sell, write for beginners. There just aren't enough players who are interested in the finer points." I intend to disregard their advice, and I hope this book will disprove their theory.

In spite of their advice to sugar-coat everything and make it palatable for beginners, I don't intend to do it. I'm sure you have other Bridge books.

The advice I give you will follow the theories I follow myself. At least they have proved effective enough to give me the best Bridge record in the world for the last fifteen years. Furthermore I don't think they are theories that any Bridge player can't follow as easily as I do.

To begin with, however, I must make it clear where I stand on the most discussed and most disputed points of the day.

Point-Count Valuation All the point-count systems, Goren or any other, in nine out of ten cases will arrive at the same result. So will mine. However, I believe it to be slightly simpler and in some cases more accurate.

My high-card count is the same one you are undoubtedly using: Ace 4, King 3, Queen 2, Jack 1.

Add 1 point for a fifth trump, and an additional 1 point for each trump over five.

Add 1 point for a four-card side suit or 2 points for a five-card side suit, but do not count more than one side suit in the same hand.

You will note that this gives a value of only 1 distributional point to the 4-4-4-1 hand pattern, whereas Goren gives it 2 points. It gives only 2 points to the 5-4-4-0 pattern, whereas Goren gives it 3 points. I don't think these hands deserve any higher valuation than I give them until your partner has responded. They are hands that can lead to serious misfits, if your partner has nothing but a long suit and it coincides with your singleton or void. Slightly undervaluing such hands at the start guards you against making some dangerous borderline 12- and 13-point bids.

Every point-count system has to have a slightly different schedule of points for raises and for revaluation of a hand that has raised. I have gone over the various suggestions and my conclusion is that they are all about 90% correct and in the other 10% will result in some degree of overvaluation or undervaluation. In my experience it is a mistake to try for 100% accuracy in Bridge valuation; in the effort a writer has to make so many exceptions to his basic point count that it confuses the student, and by the time he gets through there are still numerous hands that the system doesn't quite fit. I am content to take any one of the popular methods and rely on the law of averages to make it fit most hands, and on intelligence to recognize the hands that it doesn't fit.

Opening One-Bids In recent years bidding has become more competitive than it used to be, with both sides bidding and with many more pre-emptive bids. Therefore, the trend is to sound opening bids, for your partner must often depend on you to have sound values and not the very light hands experts were opening seven or eight years ago.

Rather than the opening-bid requirements that are usually published, I recommend the following:

13 points *may* be opened;
14 points *should* be opened, but it is not obligatory;
12 points may be opened only on rare occasions;
This is just about the minimum 13-point bid:

♠ x x   ♡ A K J x x   ◇ K J x   ♣ x x x

You have a nice solid major suit and a convenient rebid over any response. It is all right to bid one Heart.

This kind of 13-point hand I would pass:

♠ x   ♡ A Q x   ◇ K 10 x x x   ♣ Q x x x

The hand has no body and no good rebid. It may open the way to an opponent's Spade bid which you cannot outbid.

With 12-point hands the pass is the rule, the bid the exception. Here is a frequent holding:

♠ A K x x x   ♡ A x x   ◇ x x   ♣ x x x

Generally speaking, this is a better pass than a bid. With a very conservative partner I might stretch a point and open. The redeeming features are the three sound tricks and the fact that the strength is in the majors; if the suit were a minor I wouldn't open it with any partner. (Of course, I would open it in third or fourth position, major or minor.)

The typical 12-point opening bid is a hand like this:

♠ A Q 10 x x x   ♡ x   ◇ A x x   ♣ x x x

With the strong six-card major suit you always have a good rebid and you can't lost control of the bidding. Any 12-point hand without a six-card suit is doubtful.

I wouldn't open the following hand though it contains 14 points (even after you deduct 1 point for the Aceless hand) and is a compulsory bid in the most popular systems:

♠ ——————   ♡ K x x x   ◇ K J x x x   ♣ K Q x x

Of course, with my point-count (described in the preceding section) this is only a 13-point hand, since the 5-4-4-0 pattern adds only 2 points to the high cards, and 1 point is deducted for the Aceless hand. But the following hands, which count 14 points by my count as well as others, are still passes to me in first or second position:

♠ Q x	♠ A J
♡ x	♡ x x
◇ A J x x x	◇ K x x x x
♣ K J x x x	♣ K J x x

These both fit the "cumpulsory" minimums of other authorities, but they are not easy to rebid; they are very

awkward to handle if the opponents compete; they have no
support for the major suits; and they are short in quick tricks.
But hands with 14 points *in high cards,* or even with 13
points in high cards if the points are not mostly made up of
Queens, must be opened. An exception would be:

♠ K J x   ♡ Q J x   ◇ Q J x x   ♣ Q J x

or any similar hand where your points are in the lower honors
and you have no uncounted distributional points.

I want to stress the fact that every opening bid must have
two genuine defensive tricks. By a defensive trick I mean an
Ace or King-Queen in the same suit as one trick, Ace-King
in the same suit as two tricks, Ace-Queen in the same suit
as one and a half, and King as half a trick.

Which Suit to Bid   When the authorities first suggested that
you should bid a higher-ranking four-card suit ahead of a
touching five-card suit, it was a great departure from the
rigid rules of the past, and Bridge players adopted it eagerly.
I am afraid it became so popular that it is now overdone.

Your partner should always play your first suit as being
as long or longer than your second suit. This may not always
be true, but if your first suit is not as long as your second suit,
it will have extra high-card values to make up for it.

Also, whenever you make a bid, this question should be
in the back of your mind: "If the opponents play the hand,
my partner will lead my suit. Is that what I want?" You may
occasionally have to bid a suit that you don't want your
partner to lead, but you should avoid it when you can. I have
seen good players bid one Spade on the following hand, but
I wouldn't do it:

♠ A 10 x x   ♡ A Q J 10 x   ◇ Q x   ♣ x x

Even when they are willing to bid a Heart on that hand,
they usually would bid a Spade on this one:

♠ K Q x x   ♡ K Q 10 x x   ◇ A x   ♣ x x

I would bid a Heart on either hand. You have a perfectly
sound Heart rebid, and you don't have to show the Spades

unless your partner can respond one Spade to one Heart,
or unless your partner shows a lot of strength.

It isn't when your partner shows strength that you get in
trouble on these borderline hands. Suppose your partner holds
a hand like this:

♠ x x x   ♡ x x x   ◇ J x x   ♣ A Q x x

If you bid one Spade on either of the preceding hands, he
would respond one No Trump. Now when you bid two
Hearts, your partner should surely bid two Spades—obviously
a very poor contract, while two Hearts would have an
excellent play.

I don't go so far as some players who insist that an opening
bid in a major suit must be a five-card suit. It is an excellent
principle, and I would make every effort to have a five-card
suit, but I am satisfied with a good four-card suit. But not the
minimum biddable suits of most of the authorities, such as
bidding one Spade or one Heart on each of the following
holdings: the Q-10-x-x, Q-J-x-x, K-x-x-x, A-x-x-x, or K-J-x-x.
Opening bids in such major suits should be avoided if at all
possible. To me a sound major suit is at least the A-Q-J-x
or K-Q-J-x. Borderline major suits are the A-K-x-x, A-Q-x-x,
K-Q-x-x, A-J-10-x; these may be opened if absolutely necessary. Rather than a weaker suit, I would bid a three-card
Club or Diamond suit.

Everyone knows that with two four-card suits that are
touching (Spades and Hearts, Diamonds and Clubs, etc.) the
rule is to bid the higher-ranking. But I would completely
depart from the accepted rule and bid the lower-ranking suit
on hands like these:

♠ K x x x   ♠ K x

♡ A K J 10   ♡ A x x x

◇ x x x   ◇ K Q J x

♣ A x   ♣ J x x

I would bid one Heart on the first hand and one Diamond
on the second. The worst that can happen to you is that on
rare occasions you will have to rebid your good four-card
suit.

What the average player forgets is that 90% of the time your choice of opening bids doesn't affect your rebid. The customary precautions are taken to protect you against the other 10%. On the first hand above, you can't have any rebidding problems unless your partner's response is two Clubs, and then your Heart suit is good enough to rebid. (Over two Diamonds, you bid two No Trump; over one Spade you bid two Spades; and over one No Trump you simply pass.) On the second hand it is again two Clubs that can present the only possible problem, and neither two Diamonds nor the slight overbid of two No Trump would be dangerous.

It is not only to protect my rebid but also to show my strength that I choose the shorter suit on hands like this:

♠ x x	♠ A K Q x
♡ A K J 10	♡ J x x x x
◇ J x x x x	◇ K x
♣ A x	♣ Q x

I would bid one Heart on the first hand, one Spade on the second. But I do this only when the four-card suit is strong, the five-card suit is not rebiddable, and the hand as a whole only fair.

Third-Hand Bids   I don't believe in sub-par opening third-hand bids unless they have a purpose. That purpose, 90% of the time, is to direct the opening lead.

It may be true that 12 points and perhaps even less are enough in third position, but before bidding such a hand you must ask yourself whether you are prepared to have your partner lead the suit. If the answer is no, you must pass. The following hand may be strong enough for a third-hand bid, but because of the weakness of the suit it is better passed, especially with equal vulnerability:

    ♠ Q x x x x   ♡ A x x   ◇ J x x   ♣ A x

Practically no one makes what I consider the proper third-hand bid on the following hand:

    ♠ x x   ♡ J x x x x   ◇ A K Q   ♣ Q x x

The hand is strong enough to bid, but a Heart bid might

cause a disastrous loss in the defense. I would bid the hand, but I would bid one Diamond on it. Then, of course, I would pass any response (except two Hearts).

Any one of the following hands is a third-hand bid for me in certain circumstances:

♠ x x	♠ x x	♠ x x x	♠ A K Q J
♡ A K J x x	♡ x x x	♡ x x x	♡ x x x
◇ Q J x	◇ K J x	◇ A K Q x x	◇ x x x
♣ x x x	♣ A Q J 10 x	♣ x x	♣ x x x

The first two I would bid whether vulnerable or not, and regardless of my partner. The two at the right I would bid unless I were vulnerable and had an unreliable partner.

That last one may shock you, yet I would bid it even if vulnerable, with a partner I could trust. Granted that there is some risk, I stand to gain so much by making sure of a Spade lead that I would take the chance. Besides, my bid might keep the opponents out of three No Trump (they can't possibly have a Spade stopper, and how do they know I don't have five Spades?), and this might be the only game contract they could make, even if a Spade is opened.

Spade Trouble No books and few experts worry enough about Spades—the Spades you don't have. No matter how good your hand, if you haven't defense against Spades you must worry about losing control.

When the opponents seem sure to have the Spades, your defense is usually a pre-emptive bid of some sort.

♠ x x　　♡ A K Q J 10 x　　◇ K　　♣ K J 9 x

Any rules will tell you this hand is too strong for a three Heart bid, but that was the bid made on it, fourth hand, with both sides vulnerable and the bidder's side 60 on score. Without the score, four Hearts would be the proper bid. In the actual case, the player made four Hearts and his opponents could have made four Spades—but with five Spades each, they never got into the bidding. Neither had a good enough suit for a vulnerable overcall at the three level.

The danger of missing a slam on the hand above was not very great, when partner had passed. But on the next hand there was a distinct possibility, and the player still thought it worth while to bid four Hearts rather than risk having the Spades come in against him for a cheap sacrifice—or even for a superior score:

♠ ———   ♡ A K Q 10 x x x x   ◇ x   ♣ A J x x

The third-hand four Heart bid shut the opponents out. As it happened, they could have made six Spades!

Of course, I wouldn't dream of opening either of these hands with anything but a one Heart bid if I were first or second hand. The danger of losing a slam outweighs the danger from the Spade suit.

When you are missing both majors, the urgency of guarding against Spade trouble is even greater. With only minor-suit strength you have practically no control. To me the following is a clear-cut situation:

♠ x x   ♡ ———   ◇ A x x x x x   ♣ K x x x x

Your partner opens with one Diamond and the next hand doubles. I can't imagine any other bid than five Diamonds— unless it's six Diamonds. Your opponents will have to guess. If they do bid, it will be a shot in the dark. If they double, you can hardly go down more than two—and every now and then, on a hand like this, they will guess the wrong lead and you will make your bid.

Responses to Opening Bids   The authorities fought for years to convince the public that a one No Trump response isn't any weaker than a single raise. One Spade—pass—two Spades, they said, is no stronger than one Spade—pass—one No Trump; it just shows different distribution.

The authorities finally won their argument, so now most of the average-to-advanced Bridge players give a single raise on practically nothing.

Well, I think the public is wrong now, and the authorities were wrong all the time. I believe one Spade—pass—two Spades should be a fair hand, encouraging partner to bid again, and that one Spade—pass—one No Trump is quite weak and doesn't necessarily show any type of distribution. It may even include a singleton.

If my partner bids one Spade, I would respond two Spades on either of these hands:

♠ K x x x	♠ Q x x x
♡ x	♡ A x x
◊ Q x x	◊ x x
♣ Q x x x x	♣ K x x x

I wouldn't dream of responding two Spades on either of the following hands; I would bid one No Trump:

♠ Q x x	♠ J x x x
♡ x x	♡ x x x
◊ K x x x	◊ A x x
♣ J x x x	♣ J x x

An equally big mistake made by the average player is to respond in the two-range on too weak a hand. Players worry too much for fear they will give the wrong picture of their distribution, and they don't worry enough about giving the wrong picture of their strength, or of the ability of their suit to stand a lead. After your partner's opening bid, you need an average hand or better—preferably 11 or more points, and never less than 10 points, of which at least 9 should be in high cards—to bid two of a suit over your partner's opening bid.

If my partner bids one Spade, I would bid one No Trump on any of these hands:

♠ x x	♠ x	♠ x
♡ x x x	♡ Q x x x x	♡ x x
◊ J x x	◊ J 10 x x	◊ A 10 x x x
♣ A K x x x	♣ A x x	♣ K 10 x x x

When you bid two over one, you should nearly always be prepared to make a second bid. I don't mean that you would feel that you must make a second bid if you were North in a bidding situation like this:

SOUTH	WEST	NORTH	EAST
1 spade	Pass	2 clubs	Pass
2 spades	Pass		

Even here I would make an effort to rebid, though on some

hands I might pass. But if your partner had made some reasonably encouraging rebid like two Diamonds or two Hearts, or a very encouraging rebid like two No Trump, you would be disappointing him—and disturbing the entire structure of modern bidding—if you could not find another bid.

Sometimes you can't afford to pass. That's when you have a weak hand with no defense and a pass would be an invitation to the opponents to enter the bidding and very often reach a game and make it. Suppose your partner opens with one Diamond and you hold either of the following hands:

♠ K x x x x	♠ x x x
♡ x x	♡ Q J x x x
◊ 10 x x x	◊ x x
♣ x x	♣ Q x x

I wouldn't dare pass either of these hands in a tough game. I would bid one Spade on the first and one Heart on the second. Neither hand has any defense against a game the opponents might bid. If you can avoid it, never wave a flag at the opponents, and say, "I'm weak."

But I would pass the following hand if my partner bid one Spade:

♠ x x   ♡ J x x x   ◊ Q x x x x   ♣ Q x

The hand actually has some defense. There is the doubleton Spade and a probable Heart trick if the opponents bid Hearts; stoppers in two suits and a high card in the third one if they bid No Trump. I still don't call it a good hand, but it offers some hope, and when you have some hope of beating the opponents you shouldn't make dangerous bids.

Neglected Responses In my opinion bidding today has become over-refined. We "approach" contracts that there is no reason not to bid immediately.

One of the most informative but most neglected bids today is an immediate double raise of your partner's major suit. Suppose your partner bids one Spade and you hold either of the following hands:

$$♠ Q 10 x x \qquad ♠ K 10 x x$$
$$♡ x \qquad\qquad ♡ x x$$
$$♢ A J x x x \qquad ♢ A K Q J$$
$$♣ A x x \qquad\quad ♣ x x x$$

Nearly everyone nowadays would respond two Diamonds to the one Spade bid on either of these hands. Afterwards they say, "Well, I wanted to show my suit." But it is not important to show your suit when you know in advance what the contract is almost sure to be, and sometimes it is very costly to do so.

On the hand at the left you should bid three Spades (a forcing bid) and not bother to show your Diamonds. You are not strong enough to think about a slam unless your partner can make a slam try over three Spades, and there is plenty of time to show your Diamonds if he does.

On the hand at the right a two Diamond bid might shut off the only opposing lead—and not an unlikely lead at all—that will make a four Spade contract a lay-down. In addition it allows the opponents to come in too cheaply.

Equally important and perhaps even more neglected is the two No Trump response to your partner's opening bid. Years ago this used to be quite a common bid. Today players seldom make it because, they say, "After all, a suit response is forcing; why should I rush things?" They forget that the object of bidding is to withhold information from the opponents just as much as to give information to your partner, always provided your bid is an accurate expression of the genuine strength of your hand. To make the usual two Diamond response to one Spade on the following hand is, in my mind, pointless:

$$♠ J x \qquad ♡ K J x \qquad ♢ A Q 10 9 x \qquad ♣ K x x$$

Where are you going to play this hand when your partner bids one Spade? Not in Spades, unless he can rebid them twice. Not in Diamonds, unless it turns out to be one of those once-in-a-blue-moon cases. This hand is going to be played at No Trump. If that is the case, why bid Diamonds and warn the opponents that the Diamond suit is the one suit

they must not lead? The proper response on this hand is two
No Trump. It gives complete information to your partner
and the least information to the opponents, and that is a good
definition of the perfect bid.

And incidentally, that is the principal reason for raising
your partner's No Trump bid on a hand like this:

♠ x x   ♥ x x x   ♦ A K J 10 x x   ♣ x x

You know that if your partner bids one No Trump, this
is a good three No Trump bid and a terrible two or three
Diamond bid. You raise the No Trump because you think
three No Trump can be made, you don't want to warn the
opponents about the opening lead, and you want to shut out
a possible lead-directing overcall.

Bidding Your Strength   I believe in bidding your strength
in responding the same as in opening the bidding, provided
you don't give a false picture of your hand by doing so.

I do not subscribe to the theory that a one-over-one
response has to be stronger than a one No Trump response.
It might even be weaker. A one-over-one response is the
cheapest bid you can make and it does not show more strength
than one No Trump.

However, with a weak hand you must at least reserve the
thought that the opponents may play the hand and your
partner will have to lead. You don't want him to lead a suit
you can't stand. Suppose your partner bids one Club and you
have this:

♠ Q 10 x x   ♥ 10 x x x   ♦ A Q x   ♣ x x

The expert response is one Diamond. Not one No Trump,
when you have two four-card major suits. Not one Spade,
which could shut out a Heart rebid by your partner. And
certainly not one Heart on such a terrible suit. The Diamond
response leaves the way open to any possible rebid your partner may want to make, and at the same time you are bidding
your strength. If it turns out that your partner must make
the opening lead, Diamonds are the suit you want.

The foregoing hand may seem quite cut-and-dried to

students of the game, but I must say that I have yet to meet the player, outside of the very tough expert circles, who handles the following hand correctly:

♠ K J x   ♡ x x x   ◇ A K x   ♣ Q x x x

Your partner bids one Spade. This is much too good a hand for a two Spade response. Therefore all knowledgeable players agree that a temporizing bid must be made. But they make the mistake of responding two Clubs. The bid on this hand is two Diamonds. You are interested in showing where your strength lies, not that you happen to have a four-card length in a suit that is never going to become trumps anyway.

Rebids by Opening Bidder The same mental block that causes players to go wrong on the previous hand afflicts them on this one:

♠ x x   ♡ x x   ◇ A K J x x x   ♣ A K x

You open the bidding with one Diamond; your partner responds one Spade.

At this point conservative bidders will rebid two Diamonds and bold bidders three Diamonds, but both types overlook the only useful rebid you can make, which is two Clubs. If you are going to make a game on this hand (again, barring freaks and slams, which will take care of themselves) it will be in No Trump. No rebid but two Clubs will give your partner the information he may vitally need to bid No Trump; and you, with a worthless doubleton in the off-suit, cannot safely bid it yourself. The only danger in the two Club rebid is that your partner might pass it (which rarely happens), and if he does, you probably don't have a game and you may make your bid.

The most common failing I have observed is in rebidding a suit because the suit itself seemed to justify it, whereas the hand doesn't. The average player seems unable to learn the advantage of playing borderline and balanced hands at No Trump. You can often eke out seven tricks at No Trump when you could not make eight tricks in a suit, and the 40-point score is usually just as valuable as a 60-point score.

Either of the following hands is commonly misbid:

     ♠ A Q J x x   ♠ K x x
     ♡ x x   ♡ A K J x x
     ◇ A x x   ◇ J x
     ♣ Q x x   ♣ K x x

On the hand at the left you open one Spade, and on the hand at the right one Heart; in each case your partner's response is one No Trump. And in each case you should pass.

A lot of players don't realize how good a hand it takes to make game when your partner has responded one No Trump. You should figure that without about 17 points you won't have a good play. When you can pass a balanced hand at one No Trump, having no chance for game, you are usually in the contract that gives you your best chance to get on score.

However, with a singleton or two unguarded doubletons, you should usually take out the No Trump response.

     ♠ x x   ♠ A J x x x
     ♡ A Q 10 x x   ♡ x
     ◇ x x   ◇ K x x
     ♣ A K x x   ♣ A J x x

On either of these hands, having bid one Heart on the first hand, or one Spade on the second, and having received a one No Trump response, I would bid my second suit, two Clubs.

The foregoing discussion has applied only to one No Trump responses. It should apply equally when the response is two No Trump. Here it is not a matter of finding the cheapest contract, since game must be reached anyway. It is a matter of the meaning of the bid, which is ordinarily misunderstood.

This is very common bidding:

SOUTH	WEST	NORTH	EAST
1 heart	Pass	2 no trump	Pass
3 hearts			

South's bid should have only one meaning: "Partner, I don't think this hand should play at No Trump."

It should not mean "I am giving you a choice and showing five Hearts." On any of the following hands, if you open one Heart and your partner responds two No Trump, your rebid should be three No Trump, not three Hearts:

♠ Q x	♠ Q x	♠ x x
♡ A K 10 x x	♡ A Q J x x	♡ A K Q J x
◇ x x x	◇ A x x x	◇ A x x
♣ A x x	♣ J x	♣ x x x

On the third hand, particularly, the greater ease of making nine tricks outweighs any possible consideration of the value of the honors.

The time to bid three Hearts is when you have a six-card or longer major suit, or an unbalanced hand. In these cases you rebid your suit. Then, if your partner rebids No Trump, you pass if you have the tops in your suit, and insist on the suit contract if you lack the tops.

♠ x x	♠ A x x	♠ x
♡ A K 10 9 x x	♡ A K J 10 x	♡ Q J 10 x x x
◇ Q x	◇ Q	◇ A Q x x
♣ A x x	♣ Q x x x	♣ K x

On any of these hands, if I opened one Heart and my partner responded two No Trump, I would bid three Hearts. But on the first two hands, if my partner persisted in No Trump I would pass. On the third hand I would bid four Hearts.

Raising Partner's Suit   When you open the bidding and your partner responds in a major suit, the theory is that a single raise in his suit is no stronger than a one No Trump rebid. Maybe this has some merit, but I don't find that it works in practice. I think the raise in your partner's suit has an encouraging sound, in addition to which it takes you to a contract at which you must win eight tricks, whereas if you rebid one No Trump, you would need only seven. When I open the bidding and then raise my partner's one-over-one response to two, I want him to know that I have better than an opening bid and very good trump support—which means four trumps, or three good trumps and a singleton, or three very good trumps and a doubleton.

♠ A K x	♠ K x x
♡ x x x	♡ A Q x x x
◇ Q J x	◇ K x
♣ A x x x	♣ x x x

On the hand at the left I open one Club, on the hand at the right one Heart. Suppose my partner's response is one Spade; in either case my rebid is one No Trump.

These are hands on which after opening with one Heart, I would raise my partner's one Spade response to two Spades:

♠ K x x x	♠ A K x
♡ A Q x x x	♡ A Q x x x
◇ x x	◇ x x
♣ K x	♣ K x x

The first hand is a minimum, but it has four good trumps. The second has three strong trumps and is well above the minimum opening bid.

Misfits Nearly every experienced Bridge player has learned to fear a misfit. He knows that a two-suiter is strong if his partner fits either suit, and the weakest hand in the world if his partner has a two-suiter in the other two suits.

He reacts to this knowledge in different ways. The pessimist, when his partner makes an opening bid and he himself holds a two-suiter in two other suits, will immediately fear a misfit. He may pass the opening bid because of his pessimism. True, this keeps him out of trouble, but his side may have a slam. The optimist, with the same hand, never doubts that his partner will be able to fit one of the two suits. He makes sure to bid both suits at least once, and usually he manages to bid them twice. By this time, if it is a misfit, his side is too high.

The pessimist and the optimist are both wrong, of course, as you could have foreseen when I started this discussion. The happy medium is to bid once even when you fear the misfit, because your partner's second suit (if he has one) and your second suit may coincide. But stop fast when you see the possibility of a misfit, and when it would be dangerous to keep on bidding until you find out.

This topic permits me to bring up a subject that is of the utmost importance to players who have learned the "rules" of point-count bidding. I hate to disillusion millions of Bridge players, but I have to say that 26 points don't always make a good game. These bidding standards are based on ordinary occurrences. A good player must rise above the law of averages. The general rules for bidding game, whether it is 26 points or an opening bid facing an opening bid, are based on the probability that some sort of suit fit will be found, or that the hands will be played at No Trump. When you know this is not so, you must pass as quickly as possible.

♠ A J 9 x x x   ♥ x   ♦ A Q x   ♣ K x x

You open with one Spade and your partner responds two Hearts. You bid two Spades and he bids three Hearts. At this point you should pass.

It is true that you have 16 points and your partner shows at least 10, but there is no game. He could not raise Spades and he could not bid two No Trump. It would be foolhardy for you to bid No Trump when he may have nothing but a Heart suit that you do not fit, and the chances are overwhelming that the hand will play better in Hearts than in Spades. If he has a Heart suit like the K-J-10-x-x-x-x, his Hearts will be worthless to you, and as trumps they will mean five tricks to him. Meantime your high cards will be worth just as much at a Heart contract as they would be at a Spade contract.

A rebid in a new suit, especially at the three level, shows such strength that you must not risk it on a borderline hand that is a possible misfit.

♠ J   ♥ x x   ♦ A J x x x   ♣ A 10 x x x

When your partner opens one Spade, you respond two Diamonds; the strength of your hand justifies it. When your partner rebids two Hearts, you must fear a misfit, but it still would be destructive pessimism to pass. You can't quit with good hands because of an imaginary danger. But you don't rebid three Clubs. It is too strong a bid. Your rebid should be two No Trump, which is not so strong.

Now if your partner bids three Hearts, you must give up and pass. He would have bid three No Trump if he could have, and he would have jumped to four Hearts if he was sure of a game. To stop too soon on possible misfits would cost many games; to keep on bidding too long means many penalties. The answer is to find the happy medium.

The object is to find a bid that is reasonably safe and keeps the bidding open, but does not paint too rosy a picture of the strength of your hand.

♠ x   ♡ x   ◊ Q J 10 9 x x   ♣ A J x x x

On this hand, too, you respond two Diamonds to your partner's bid of one Spade. But if your partner bids two Hearts (or two Spades, for that matter) you do not bid three Clubs. It is too strong a bid, being virtually forcing to game in the present method of play. You prefer the weaker sounding rebid of three Diamonds. This is safe if partner must pass, and does not shut off game possibilities if he actually has some Diamond support or a strong enough hand to bid three No Trump.

When your hand is very strong, you must not let the fear of a misfit prevent your bidding it normally.

♠ x   ♡ J x   ◊ A K x x x   ♣ A Q J x x

You respond two Diamonds to your partner's Spade bid, and your rebid is three Clubs when he bids two Hearts (or two Spades). This is such a strong hand that you will have a probable game even if your partner has a similar sort of two-suiter in Spades and Hearts. You can probably make game someplace, despite the absence of a good fit in any one of the four suits.

Bridge Mathematics   How many times have you heard people say, after missing a game, "But we were vulnerable. I was afraid to take a chance"? This is usually the opposite of how they should have felt.

When neither side is vulnerable, you should usually not bid a game unless you have an even chance to make it.

If you are vulnerable against nonvulnerable opponents, you can take a slight chance—you can bid a game even if the odds are about 6 to 5 against your making it. But if both sides are vulnerable, you should bid a game even if the odds are 8 to 5 against making it. This means you should bid a game when you can make it with a 3–3 break in a suit (the odds are 64 to 36 against this).

Here is the most important laws-of-percentage chart in Bridge. The distributions of the cards of a suit in the other two hands when the number of cards the declarer can see in his own hand and dummy is:

Declarer and Dummy Hold in Suit	Opponents' Cards in Suit Will Be Divided	
6 cards	4–3	62%
	5–2	31%
	6–1	7%
	7–0	Less than ½ of 1%
7 cards	4–2	48%
	3–3	36%
	5–1	15%
	6–0	1%
8 cards	3–2	68%
	4–1	28%
	5–0	4%
9 cards	3–1	50%
	2–2	40%
	4–0	10%
10 cards	2–1	78%
	3–0	22%
11 cards	1–1	52%
	2–0	48%

A small slam should be bid when you have an even chance to make it.

A grand slam should be bid when the odds are 2 to 1 in favor of making it. For example, the following is mathematically a good seven Heart contract for East-West:

	♠ A x x x		♠ x x
	♡ A Q x x	N	♡ K x x x
W	◇ J 10	E	◇ A K Q x x
	♣ A Q x	S	♣ K x

All they need is a 3–2 break in trumps.

However, when you bid a grand slam and go down, even if an unlikely break is responsible, it has a poor effect on yourself and your partner. For that reason, if you stop at a small slam in a close case like the East-West hands shown above, don't feel regretful. However, if West held the A-Q-10-x of Hearts, so that the only possible loss would be to five Hearts, or four Hearts to the Jack at his left, he should definitely be in the grand slam. He would then have about a 4-to-1 chance to make it.

Don't Be Afraid to Go Down Most Bridge players have an unreasonable antipathy to being set. They are wrong.

Bridge is a bidders' game.

The toughest kind of opponent is one who is continuously in the bidding.

If you don't regularly get into the bidding, you are unlikely to be a winning Bridge player. True, every now and then you will go down, and sometimes you will be doubled. True, every now and then you will bid a trick too high and be set when you could have stopped and set the opponent. But more often, if you bid your hands to the hilt, the opponents will stop bidding sooner than they should. I can state as a general principle: When in doubt in a competitive hand, bid one more.

Players most often go wrong when they fail to compete for part scores. A part score is worth much more than most people think. Take a bidding situation like this:

SOUTH	WEST	NORTH	EAST
1 club	1 spade	2 clubs	Pass
Pass	2 spades	3 clubs	?

You are East, holding:

♠ J x x x   ♡ Q x   ◇ Q x x x x   ♣ x x

You should bid three Spades. When your partner could bid two all alone, nothing much is going to happen to you. You have no reason whatsoever to think you can set three Clubs.

An overcall, as you know (or as you will know when I get into the subject), shows a stronger suit than an opening bid or a response guarantees. As the suit is stronger, the trump support required for a raise can be correspondingly less. Suppose the bidding begins:

SOUTH	WEST	NORTH	EAST
1 heart	1 spade	Pass	Pass
2 hearts	Pass	Pass	?

You are East, holding:

♠ K x   ♡ x x x   ◇ A x x x x   ♣ Q x x

If you pass, you probably let them make two Hearts. You should bid two Spades. The contract is unlikely to be doubled; you have enough high cards to justify a raise, and King and one will usually be sufficient support for a suit in which your partner has overcalled.

All too often I have heard players say, after their opponents have made a part score, "Well, partner, we couldn't go anyplace. We would have been down if we had bid again, and after all, they didn't bid game." This is very fallacious reasoning. If you can go down one to stop a part score, you have a good result even if you were vulnerable and doubled.

To stop the opponents from making a part score, you should bid up to the point at which you think you will be down two if not vulnerable, and down one if vulnerable.

If they let you play it, most of the time you will not be doubled.

If they take it away from you, you cannot have lost by pushing them one trick higher, and occasionally you will beat them just because they are one trick higher.

Finally, every now and then your hands will fit better than you expected, or they will drop a trick in defense, and you will make your contract. This will be a clear profit, and a large one on your bid.

The guiding principle is this: It is worth 200 points to save a part score.

It is worth 400 points to save a game when no one is vulnerable, or when you are vulnerable and the opponents are not.

It is worth 500 points to save a game when the opponents are vulnerable and you are not.

And it is worth 600 points to save a game when both sides are vulnerable.

Barring honors, there is no 400- or 600-point set on a sacrifice bid, so I will give you a practical application of this. When you can afford to take a 400-point set, you can overbid enough so that it depends on a finesse whether you go down 300 or 500, not vulnerable, or 200 or 500, vulnerable.

When you can afford to take a 600-point set, you can bid so that it depends on a finesse whether you go down 500 or 700, not vulnerable, or 500 or 800, vulnerable. But these are at best "break even" figures and I would not take the chance unless there were also a chance of going down only one.

Of course, if you have a hope of beating the opponents you don't take chances unless their score, if they make it, will be very big, and your loss is bound to be small. For example:

SOUTH	WEST	NORTH	EAST
1 spade	2 hearts	Pass	2 spades
3 diamonds	Pass	4 spades	5 hearts
6 spades	Pass	Pass	7 hearts!

East holds:

♠ ———   ♡ A Q J x x   ◇ K x x   ♣ A J 10 x x

East does not expect to make seven Hearts, and perhaps you, with East's two Aces and a King, would expect to beat six Spades. But with both sides vulnerable you are fairly sure that you cannot lose more than 500 points at seven Hearts, and may go down only 200; you have no real assurance that you can beat six Spades (particularly since your partner had a chance to double, and didn't). Six Spades, if made, will score nearly 1500 for the opponents—more if you double.

Perhaps you believe you can beat six Spades, but are you willing to lay such odds on it? If not, you take out cheap insurance by bidding seven Hearts.

This is an actual hand, on which East doubled and six Spades were made; his side could have made seven Hearts if a Spade or a Club had been opened, and would have gone down only one if a Diamond had been opened.

The same principle applies in more commonplace situations:

SOUTH	WEST	NORTH	EAST
1 heart	1 spade	2 hearts	2 spades
4 hearts	Pass	Pass	?

East holds: ♠ Q x x x x   ♡ K J 10   ◇ K J x x   ♣ x

You might beat four Hearts, but you can't be sure of it, and it is very likely that you won't be down more than one at four Spades, while you might make it. You bid four Spades as insurance against the big swing you would have against you if four Hearts were made and you could have made four Spades.

Opening Two-Bids With most partners I prefer an opening two Club bid as the only forcing bid, with all bids of two Spades, two Hearts and two Diamonds pre-emptive bids. However, I have nothing against the usual custom of making every opening two-bid in a suit a forcing bid. The one thing I want to express is my opposition to an Ace-showing response to two-bids. I think when information about Aces is important, the Aces can always be shown later; information about trump support or a good suit opposite the two-bid cannot be.

Looking over the average player's use of two-bids, I believe that most mistakes are not due to making two-bids on hands that are too weak (though many players do), or even on waiting for a 75% sure slam before making a two-bid (which many other players do). The great fault usually lies with the partner of the two-bidder, who refuses to look beyond his own horrible hand and realize that it can have hidden values, when his partner, who opened with a two-bid, is so strong. For example:

SOUTH	WEST	NORTH	EAST
2 spades	Pass	2 no trump	Pass
3 hearts	Pass	3 spades	Pass
4 clubs	Pass	4 spades	Pass
5 spades	Pass		

In the bidding up to this point South avoided a mistake that I have seen hundreds of players make. South's hand was:

♠ A K J x x   ♡ A K J x x   ◇ ————   ♣ A Q J

He did not waste time on a Blackwood bid, which could not have given him any information of value. He did not jump to six Spades, as most players would. He made a simple slam try of five Spades, which was the scientific bid—it left it up to his partner to make the decision. It is a player's duty to show when he has great strength. Equally it is his partner's duty to bid any values he has, even when they seem at first glance to be nothing to get excited about.

North's hand: ♠ Q x x x   ♡ x x   ◇ x x x x x   ♣ x x

His proper bid is six Spades over five; from his two No Trump response and simple preference bid of three Spades, South could not possibly have relied on finding him with four Spades to the Queen and two doubletons, and yet South was willing to go to five Spades all alone. When your partner can bid for eleven tricks on his own hand, and you have as much support as North had, you have a slam bid.

Furthermore if North had held a hand like this:

♠ Q 10 9 x x   ♡ x x   ◇ x x x   ♣ x x x

he should not have been content with a simple preference bid of three Spades. He should have jumped to four Spades over three Hearts. He had already shown his lack of high cards by bidding two No Trump in the first place.

A good bid for North on either of these hands would have been an immediate jump to four Spades—if he and his partner were playing that this jump raise shows strong trump support without any Ace, King, or singleton. This is a very good convention, but it is not very widely played, and it is very dangerous to use it with a partner who may not understand it.

Part-Score Bidding I have discovered that most Bridge players do not appreciate the value of a part score. They do not fight hard enough to get one themselves; they do not fight hard enough to keep the opponents from getting one.

As I have said before, it is worth 200 points to keep the opponents from getting a part score. No Bridge book I have seen recognizes that the value is so high, but some expert players that I know would place it even higher.

Bidding practices change considerably when there is a part score, and vary according to which side has a part score. However, in any part-score situation, when you have a choice of bids, you should choose the one that is most pre-emptive. If you have the part score, you want the bid to go uncontested. If the opponents have it, you don't want to make it easy for them to enter the bidding. The higher ranking your bid is, the better its pre-emptive effect: one Spade is better than one of any other suit, and one No Trump is better than one Spade.

♠ K Q x x   ♡ A x x x   ◇ x x   ♣ A Q x

On this hand you would bid one Club if there were no part score, but with a part score you bid one Spade or even one No Trump (in spite of only 15 points and the two small Diamonds). You should avoid bidding a three-card minor, especially Diamonds, when you are on score.

In responding to your partner's bid you bid in the two-range much more freely.

♠ x   ♡ K J 10 9 x   ◇ x x x   ♣ K x x x

Your partner opens one Spade. Without a part score you would bid one No Trump; with a part score you bid two Hearts. *Whenever your bid puts you high enough to complete the game, your partner should pass if his hand is at all suitable.*

Each of these hands is bid differently in a part-score situation from a blank-score situation. Suppose you have 60 on score and your partner has opened with one Spade:

```
    ♠ x              ♠ x x
    ♡ x x x          ♡ x x
    ◇ K x x x x x    ◇ J x x x
    ♣ K J x          ♣ A K 10 9 x
```

With the part score you should respond two Diamonds on
the one at the left and two Clubs on the one at the right. You
would bid one No Trump on either if you had no part score.
Since your partner should pass whatever you bid, if it is
enough to give you game, you must be careful what you bid.
Don't bid a suit you are not willing to play with two small
cards in your partner's hand.

```
    ♠ Q x x          ♠ Q x
    ♡ A J x x x      ♡ A x x
    ◇ x x            ◇ Q x x
    ♣ K x x          ♣ K 10 x x x
```

If your partner opens one Spade, and you have 60 on score,
you should not bid two Hearts on the hand at the left, or
two Clubs on the hand at the right. On the one at the left
bid two Spades; on the one at the right one No Trump. You
cannot bid your suit because you are not prepared to have
your partner pass it.

The corollary to the foregoing principle—and something
that is much abused—is this: Trust your partner. If he makes
a bid that will put you out, pass. You must consider two
small cards in his suit as sufficient support, unless you have
an overwhelming suit of your own that can't go wrong.

```
    ♠ A K Q 10 x x   ♠ A K 10 x x
    ♡ A x x x        ♡ A x x
    ◇ x              ◇ K x x
    ♣ x x            ♣ J x
```

You have 60 on score. On either of these hands suppose
you open one Spade and your partner responds two Clubs.
On the one at the left, you bid two Spades. But on the one at
the right you pass! It isn't because your Club support of the
J-x is better, but because your Spade suit isn't good enough.

You would equally pass your partner's two Club response on the following hand:

♠ A K x x x   ♡ A K x x   ◇ x x   ♣ x x

Having bid one Spade, and having received a two Club or two Diamond response, you don't bid two Spades and you don't bid two Hearts. You pass.

A two-suiter should be rebid, but you must know when to quit:

♠ A K x x x   ♡ A J x x x   ◇ K x   ♣ x

You bid one Spade, your partner responds two Clubs, and your rebid is two Hearts. But if his response had been two Diamonds, you would have passed—again assuming, of course, that your part-score is 60.

♠ x   ♡ x x   ◇ K J x x x x   ♣ A x x

You hold this hand and your partner opens one Spade with a 60-point part score. You respond two Diamonds. If he now bids two Hearts, you pass without giving it a single thought. You don't want to play Diamonds if your partner has a void or singleton; and if he had two Diamonds, he would have passed.

Overcalling Problems   Bridge players learned the hard way that they shouldn't make dangerous overcalls. Twenty years ago an expert could clean up in the average game just by doubling his opponents' vulnerable overcalls. Somehow it took the average player years of 800- to 1400-point sets to learn not to make vulnerable overcalls too weak. The great advance in the standards of average and advanced players over the course of these years is most evident in their over-calling habits.

But this lesson, like some others, they have learned too well. Most average and advanced players, and quite a few experts, are weakest in the overcalling department. Their overcalls are either too weak or too strong.

These are the most important reasons for overcalling:

To tell your partner what to lead.

To compete with the opponents for a part score.

To set up a possible sacrifice against an opposing game.

To reach game yourself.

No one before has seemed able or willing to give direct requirements for an overcall. I propose to do it here for the first time. These are the minimum and maximum requirements in terms of points, counting distributional points as well as high-card points (see Page 12):

ONE-LEVEL OVERCALL   Minimum   8 points
Maximum 14 points

If not vulnerable, a one-level overcall may be as low as 8 points.

If vulnerable, a one-level overcall may be as low as 10 points.

In neither case should the hand contain more than 13 points.

TWO-LEVEL OVERCALL   Minimum 13 points
Maximum 16 points

The weaker of these hands, with 13 points, is the borderline requirement for an opening bid. If not vulnerable, you need a bare opening bid to overcall; if vulnerable, you need a sound opening bid to overcall. In either case the overcalling suit must be good and the hand must have some defensive strength.

In applying the above point requirements for overcalls keep in mind the four purposes that I stated above. If your hand does not seem to fit one of them, you should choose to pass rather than overcall; if your hand does fit one or more of them, stretch a point to overcall.

I would not overcall a one Diamond bid with one Heart, not vulnerable, on even the following 9-point hand:

    ♠ J x   ♡ Q 10 x x x   ♢ K x x   ♣ J x x

I don't particularly want a Heart lead, I am not in a good position to compete for a part score if the opponents have Spades, I can't see much hope of a successful sacrifice if they bid game, unless my partner is good enough to come in by himself, and I am not optimistic enough to think we are going to make a game.

I would make a nonvulnerable overcall of one Spade over

one Heart on any of the following hands:

♠ A Q x x x x	♠ K Q 10 x x	♠ A K Q x
♡ x x	♡ x	♡ x x x
◇ x x x	◇ Q x x x	◇ x x x
♣ x x	♣ x x x	♣ x x x

The third hand may shock some players. I admit that, generally, an overcall shows a five-card suit or longer. But this third hand, with the A-K-Q of Spades, so admirably serves the first purpose in overcalling—to tell partner what to lead—that the overcall should be made.

The basic principle in overcalling on a dangerous hand is this:

You are almost never doubled at a low level—especially at the one-level—unless the opponent holds trump tricks. Therefore, if your suit is good enough, you can take more of a chance than if your hand is good but your suit is poor.

♠ x x	♠ x x x
♡ A K Q J x	♡ Q x x x x
◇ x x x	◇ A K x
♣ x x x	♣ A Q

I would much rather overcall one Spade with two Hearts on the hand at the left than on the hand at the right, though the one at the left doesn't fulfill the requirements and the one at the right does. A two Heart contract will almost never be doubled if you hold the hand at the left; the exception would be a very bad break that gives an opponent something like five Hearts to the ten. Any number of Heart combinations, with a smattering of strength outside, might cause an opponent to double a two Heart overcall that you make on the hand at the right. If you want to bid this hand (and often you should) a double is safer than an overcall.

When you overcall at the two-level, your suit *must* be good, and you must have at least five cards in it. It is important to have Tens and Nines; an opponent will double on a holding like the K-10-6-3 or K-9-8-4, when he wouldn't double on the K-6-3-2. These are sound two-level overcalls if not vulnerable:

```
    ♠ x                    ♠ x x
    ♡ A Q 10 9 x x         ♡ A J 10
    ◇ K 10 9 x             ◇ x x x
    ♣ x x                  ♣ A K 10 9 x
```

The following hands are sound two-level overcalls when vulnerable. It will be obvious from these that a vulnerable overcall at the two-level shows a very strong hand:

```
♠ x x              ♠ x                ♠ x
♡ x                ♡ x x              ♡ A K J x x x
◇ K x x x          ◇ K Q J 9 x x      ◇ K x x
♣ A K J x x x      ♣ A x x x          ♣ Q x x
```

An overcall should never be made when you hold strength (like the K-10-x-x) in the opponents' suit; it should seldom be made if you hold as many as three low cards in the opponents' suit, unless your own suit is very strong. Take the following hand:

```
♠ x x x     ♡ A K x x x     ◇ x     ♣ A x x x
```

This is not a good two Heart overcall over one Spade, especially if you are vulnerable. If you had a singleton Spade and three Diamonds, it might be a fair risk.

You should not, of course, have too good an overcall. That is the reason I placed maximums as well as minimums on the requirements. The following 18-point hand would be a terrible overcall over one Spade:

```
♠ x x     ♡ A K Q 10 x x     ◇ A Q x x     ♣ x
```

On such a hand you must show strength by doubling. Otherwise your side is very likely to miss a game.

Reopening the Bidding   Players have learned laboriously to double, instead of overcalling, when the opponents open the bidding and they have strong hands. Unfortunately the most neglected bid in Bridge is still the double by the opening bidder when his opponents have overcalled and his partner has passed. This is a typical bidding situation:

SOUTH	WEST	NORTH	EAST
1 spade	2 diamonds	Pass	Pass

South should not merely rebid two Spades on a hand like

this, though I am afraid most players would:

♠ A K Q x x x   ♡ A Q   ◇ x x   ♣ K J x

It is more important to show the strength of a hand than to show the length of a suit, even when you have a one-suit hand like the one above. South should double on this hand. If he merely bids two Spades, he is not encouraging a weak raise by partner. He doubles first to show strength, and later rebids his Spades over any response. However, his partner can pass this double if his principal length or strength is in Diamonds, but he did not have enough high cards to double two Diamonds when it was bid.

The importance of showing strength by doubling is emphasized by the fact that you must often stretch a point to reopen the bidding for fear the opponents will get a part score too cheaply. For example, in the same bidding situation, you would reopen by bidding two Spades on this hand:

♠ A K Q x x   ♡ K x   ◇ x x x   ♣ K x x

It is obvious that there is absolutely no comparison between this hand and the one above.

When short in the opponents' suit, you have every reason to fear that the opponents will make their part score. When you reopen the bidding to compete for a part score, it is usually safer to double than to bid on a "fair" hand, especially when your trump suit is weak.

♠ A Q x x x   ♡ K 10 x x   ◇ x   ♣ A Q x

As in the bidding situation last shown above, you opened with one Spade, it was overcalled by two Diamonds on your left, and your partner and right-hand opponent passed. This hand is no powerhouse, but you want to compete for a part score. The double is much safer than a two Spade rebid (and you should not consider a two Heart rebid, which partner may pass if he has a singleton Spade, a small doubleton Heart, four Diamonds and six Clubs). By doubling here you give yourself the best chance to find a suit fit. Don't worry for fear that your partner will pass the double; high cards have their greatest defensive value when they are distributed among several suits, as yours are in this case. You'll probably beat two Diamonds, and if you don't the loss won't be serious.

When your suit is weak and you cannot support any suit that your partner might bid in response to your double, you must not compete for a part score. You have to pass and let them play it. I would not reopen the bidding on either of these hands:

♠ K J x x x	♠ A Q x x x
♡ K x	♡ x x
◇ x x x	◇ x x
♣ A Q x	♣ A Q x x

In each case you opened with one Spade, it was overcalled with two Diamonds at your left, and your partner and right-hand opponent passed.

Two Spades is dangerous on either, because most of the other Spades may be stacked against you in an opposing hand; you can't double because you can't stand a Heart bid; and I am sure you are too good a player for it to be necessary for me to say how suicidal a three Club bid would be on the hand at the right. Yet I have often seen players make just this bid.

Doubles of Overcalls For years, now, writers of Bridge books and newspaper articles have been pounding away at the subject of doubling overcalls. Most good Bridge players are gradually learning the advantage of doubling an opposing overcall of two Diamonds or two Clubs.

The ideal time to double an opposing overcall is when you are short in your partner's suit. Suppose your partner opens with one Spade, next hand bids two Clubs, and you hold:

♠ x   ♡ A K 10 x x   ◇ Q x x   ♣ K 10 x x

This is a doubling hand. You should not be deterred by the five-card major suit. If your partner happens to have a singleton Heart you may not have a game anywhere. Yet you can collect a juicy penalty from two Clubs.

The hand above is much better for a double of two Clubs than a hand with five or six Clubs and little or nothing else, like this:

♠ x x   ♡ x x x   ◇ Q x   ♣ K 10 8 x x x

If the opponents rescue (which is very likely) you cannot double anything else they may bid, and you cannot support further bids by your partner. Your partner has a right to depend on you for some general strength when you double so early. If you pass the overcall, and then your partner re-opens the bidding by doubling, you will be in a fine position to pass for penalties.

Another time not to double is when you have length in your partner's suit, even though your holding in the opponent's trump suit is good. When your partner has bid one Spade, this hand has a better Spade raise than a double of a two Club overcall:

♠ Q x x x   ♡ x x   ◊ Q x x   ♣ A J 9 x

You know, of course, that on a double of a two Club or two Diamond overcall, the partner is not supposed to stand for it if his hand isn't suitable. But do you, like most players, take such doubles out very often? Remember, most hands are suitable.

You bid a Spade, it is overcalled by two Clubs, and your partner doubles. You hold one of these hands:

♠ A K 10 x x	♠ A Q x x x	♠ A J x x x
♡ A J x	♡ K x x	♡ K Q 10 x
◊ x x x	◊ x x	◊ A Q x
♣ x x	♣ Q x x	♣ x

Most players would take out the double on any one of the three. On the first because the Spade suit is pretty good and the Clubs are weak, on the second because they opened a sub-minimum hand and think you shouldn't stand for a double when you have less than you promised, on the third because of the singleton Club.

Yet the fact is that on any one of these three hands you should pass like a shot. Two cards of the opponents' suit are plenty on any kind of hand; three to the Queen are super-excellent; and even a singleton should be no deterrent to passing if you have plenty of defensive strength outside. Your partner usually doesn't double if he thinks your side is likely to have a game that will be worth more than the penalty.

The type of hand on which you take out your partner's double is more like one of these:

♠ K Q J 10 x x	♠ A Q x x x
♡ A Q x x	♡ K Q J x x
◇ x x	◇ Q x x
♣ x	♣ ———

Neither hand offers much defense against Clubs. The first one is almost sure to make a two Spade contract, even if it can't make a game, and you should not risk your sure score when it appears likely that a doubled contract can be made against you. On the hand at the right, you are pretty sure your partner can't fit Spades, but he hasn't said anything about Hearts, and there is still an excellent chance of a Heart game. At the same time your void makes it likely that the opponents have a Club fit in spite of your partner's double, and they can probably make their contract. You can't abandon a possible game so lightly, and particularly you can't do it when a pass would probably result in a loss.

Doubles of Other Bids The most costly of all mistakes is failure to double often enough.

How many times have your opponents gone down two or three or even four tricks, and you have said, "We should have doubled"? Almost always you are right—you should have doubled.

Expert players make a fortune by doubling at the right time. I can't count the number of times I have doubled three No Trump just because I didn't like the bidding. Once in a while they have made it, but much more often they went down with a penalty ranging from 300 to 800 points. A 300-point penalty means you have gained 200 points by doubling. An 800-point penalty means you have gained 500 points by doubling. You can't afford to neglect profits like that.

This is bidding that you hear a dozen times in every session of Bridge:

SOUTH	WEST	NORTH	EAST
1 spade	Pass	2 clubs	Pass
2 spades	Pass	2 no trump	Pass
3 no trump	Pass	Pass	Pass

Generally a hand bid like this is about an even chance to make. If the cards break favorably, they will make it; if they don't, they will go down; and if there is a bad break, or if the declarer miscalculates, he may easily go down two or three.

Your chance of beating them is best if the cards held by yourself and your partner are fairly evenly divided between your two hands, and you have a great advantage because you know whether the cards of your side are placed favorably or unfavorably for declarer.

Suppose the bidding is as given above, and I am East with this hand:

♠ x   ♡ Q x x   ◇ Q J 10 x x   ♣ A Q 10 x

I will always double and I will usually show a profit, sometimes a big one. I have a good suit to open, I have the Clubs behind the Club bidder, and whatever Spades the opponents lack will be in my partner's hand over the Spade bidder. If I had the same cards in different suits, like this:

♠ A Q 10 x   ♡ Q x x   ◇ Q J 10 x x   ♣ x

I would not double. My Spades are on the wrong side of the Spade bidder, and whatever my partner has in Clubs is under the Club bidder.

Sometimes it is necessary to double in order to get the proper lead. In this connection I want to explain something on which Bridge books tend to be somewhat vague. It is tremendously important for partners to understand what suit should be led when one partner makes a close double and the other partner has the lead.

If I double three No Trump, and my side has not bid any suit, I want my partner to lead the dummy's first-bid suit (assuming, of course, that it has not been rebid or supported).

Here is an example:

SOUTH	WEST	NORTH	EAST
1 heart	Pass	1 spade	Pass
1 no trump	Pass	2 no trump	Pass
3 no trump	Pass	Pass	Double

Being East, I want my partner to lead a Spade. I may have a hand something like this:

♠ K Q J 9 x   ♡ 10 x x x   ◇ A x   ♣ x x

If my partner leads a Spade, we are almost sure to beat three No Trump. If he leads anything else, we cannot have a very good chance. I must double if I want to beat it, and I ask him to co-operate by leading the dummy's first bid suit. This doesn't shut off the few chances you get to double when the opponents overbid ridiculously and you have a big hand. In such cases you can probably beat them no matter what is led. But bidding is pretty accurate nowadays, especially No Trump bidding since point-count valuation came in, and you don't get many chances to double a bid that is totally unjustified. It is much more valuable to reserve the double for cases when it takes the proper lead to defeat the contract.

When my partner and I have both bid, and I double three No Trump with him on lead, I want him to lead his own suit and not mine. After all, one of the oldest principles of Bridge is: "Lead your partner's suit." My suit is the one I should expect if I don't double; therefore when I double I am asking him not to lead my suit.

Doubles of Slams A double of a three No Trump bid is often for a lead; a double of a slam almost always is. You have to trust your opponents enough to know that they know how good their own hands are, and if they bid a slam they expect to make it against a normal lead and normal breaks. To double them on the grounds that they have miscalculated is insulting, and, worse, it is expensive.

The time to double is when you know something about the hand that they don't—and, more important, that your partner doesn't. By doubling you tell your partner about it.

A double of a slam tells your partner not to make his normal opening lead, but to make some unusual lead; there are no invariable rules, but very often this is the first suit bid by the dummy.

Consider this bidding situation:

SOUTH	WEST	NORTH	EAST
2 spades	Pass	3 diamonds	Pass
3 hearts	Pass	3 spades	Pass
6 spades	Pass	Pass	?

Sitting East, if that were the bidding, I would not double on this hand:

♠ x x   ♡ K J x   ◇ K Q x   ♣ A K x x x

I have an unusually good hand on the bidding, but the strength of my hand is all in high cards. South knows he is missing these high cards just as well as I do. If I were to double, he might very likely redouble and make seven. He could be void of Clubs, my Hearts are under his higher ones, and I am not even sure to get a Diamond trick, because North probably has the Ace, and South may not need anything else. But I would double six Spades on this nearly worthless hand:

♠ x x x   ♡ x x x x   ◇ ——   ♣ x x x x x x

This time it will be my partner and not I who has the King of Hearts if declarer lacks it, and in my partner's hand it will win a trick. I am in a position to trump a Diamond lead, and if I don't double, my partner will probably make the "normal" opening, the only unbid suit, which is Clubs. With a Club opening, I can't see any chance at all of beating six Spades. With a Diamond opening, we have a chance. True, he still may redouble and make it, but he won't get any overtrick if my partner leads the Diamond I ask for, so my risk by doubling is 300 points. If my double succeeds in defeating the contract, the gain to us will be as much as 1600 points, that is, 5 to 1 in my favor, and for such odds I will take the chance.

LAWS OF CONTRACT BRIDGE

(Condensed from The Laws of Contract Bridge, copyright, 1948, by The National Laws Commission of the American Contract Bridge League.)

Preliminaries

1. Number of Players Four, two against two as partners. Five or six may take part in the same game, but only four play at a time.

2. The Pack 52 cards. Two packs, of contrasting back designs, are invariably used. While one pack is being dealt, dealer's partner shuffles the other pack for the next deal.

3. Rank of Suits Spades (high), Hearts, Diamonds, Clubs.

4. Rank of Cards A (high), K, Q, J, 10, 9, 8, 7, 6, 5, 4, 3, 2.

5. The Draw A shuffled pack is spread face down on the table and each player draws one card but not one of the four cards at either end. A player who exposes more than one card must draw again. No player should expose his card before all have drawn.

The player drawing the highest card deals first. He chooses his seat and the pack with which he will deal; next-highest is his partner and sits across the table from him; the two others take the other two seats. If two players draw cards of the same rank, as ♡6 and ♣6, the rank of the suits determines the higher card.

6. Precedence When five wish to play, the draw establishes order of precedence. Example: North draws ♣A, South ♠K, East ♣5, West ♡2 and a fifth player draws ♢2. North and South play as partners against East and West. After the first rubber the fifth player plays and West sits out; after the next rubber West reenters the game and East sits out, and so on until North has sat out a rubber, after which the fifth player sits out again.

7. The Shuffle The player on dealer's left shuffles the cards and places them at the dealer's left. The dealer (after shuffling again if he wishes) sets the cards down at his right to be cut.

8. *The Cut* The player at dealer's right must lift off a portion of the pack (not fewer than four cards nor more than forty-eight) and set it down toward dealer. Dealer completes the cut.

9. *The Deal* Dealer deals thirteen cards to each player, one card at a time, face down, in clockwise rotation beginning with the player at his left.

10. *Rotation* The turn to deal, to bid and to play always passes from player to player to the left.

The Auction

11. *Calls* After looking at his cards, each player in turn beginning with dealer must make a *call* (pass, bid, double or redouble). If all four pass in the first round, the deal is passed out and there is a new deal by the next dealer in turn. If any player makes a bid in the first round, the bidding is opened.

12. *Passing* When a player does not wish to bid, to double or to redouble, he says "Pass."

13. *Bidding* Each bid must name a certain number of tricks in excess of six (called *odd tricks*) which the bidder agrees to win, and a suit which will become the trump suit, if the bid becomes the contract; thus: "One Spade" is a bid to win seven tricks ($6 + 1$) with Spades as trumps. A bid may be made in No Trump, meaning that there will be no trump suit. The lowest possible bid is one, and the highest possible bid is seven.

Each bid must name a greater number of odd tricks than the last preceding bid, or an equal number of a higher denomination. No Trump is the highest denomination, outranking Spades. Thus, a bid of two No Trump will overcall a bid of two Hearts, a bid of four Diamonds is required to overcall a bid of three Hearts.

14. *Doubling and Redoubling* Any player in turn may double the last preceding bid if it was made by an opponent. The effect of a double is to increase the value of odd tricks,

overtricks and undertrick penalties (see Scoring Table, on Page 56) if the doubled bid becomes the contract.

Any player in turn may redouble the last preceding bid if it was made by his side and doubled by an opponent. A redouble again increases the scoring values.

A doubled or redoubled contract may be overcalled by any bid which would be sufficient to overcall the same contract undoubled; thus, if a bid of two Diamonds is doubled and redoubled, it may still be overcalled by a bid of two in Hearts, Spades or No Trump and by a bid of three Clubs, or by any higher bid.

15. Information as to Previous Calls Any player in turn may ask to have all previous calls made in the auction restated, in the order in which they were made.

16. Final Bid and the Declarer When a bid, double or redouble is followed by three consecutive passes in rotation, the auction is closed. The final bid in the auction becomes the *contract*. The player who, for his side, first bid the denomination named in the contract becomes the *declarer*. If the contract names a trump suit, every card of that suit becomes a *trump*. Declarer's partner becomes *dummy*, and the other side become *defenders*.

The Play

17. Leads and Plays A *play* consists of taking a card from one's hand and placing it, face up, in the center of the table. Four cards so played, one from each hand in rotation, constitute a trick. The first card played to a trick is a *lead*.

The leader to a trick may lead any card. The other three hands must follow suit if they can, but, if unable to follow suit, may play any card.

18. Opening Lead; Facing the Dummy Hand The defender on declarer's left makes the first lead. Dummy then spreads his hand in front of him, face up, grouped in suits with the trumps at his right.

19. Winning of Tricks A trick containing a trump is won by the hand playing the highest trump. A trick not containing a trump is won by the hand playing the highest card of the suit led. The winner of each trick leads to the next.

20. *Dummy*   Declarer plays both his and dummy's cards, but each in proper turn. Dummy may reply to a proper question but may not comment or take an active part in the play; except that he may call attention to an irregularity and may warn declarer (or any other player) against infringing a law of the game; as by saying, "It's not your lead," or asking, "No Spades?" when a player fails to follow suit to a Spade lead. See Dummy's Rights, paragraph 53.

21. *Played Card*   Declarer plays a card from his own hand when he places it on the table or names it as an intended play; from dummy, when he touches it (except to arrange dummy's cards) or names it. A defender plays a card when he exposes it, with apparent intent to play, so that his partner can see its face. A card once played may not be withdrawn, except to correct a revoke or in the course of correcting an irregularity.

22. *Taking in Tricks Won*   A completed trick is gathered and turned face down on the table. Declarer, and the partner of the defender winning the first trick for his side, should keep in front of him all tricks won by his side, so arranged that it is apparent how many tricks that side has won, and the sequence in which they were won.

23. *Claim or Concession of Tricks by Declarer*   If declarer claims or concedes one or more of the remaining tricks, or otherwise suggests that play be curtailed: Play should cease, and declarer, with his hand face up on the table, should forthwith make any statement necessary to indicate his intended line of play. A defender may face his hand and may suggest a play to his partner. If both defenders concede, play ceases and declarer is considered to have won the tricks claimed. If a defender disputes declarer's claim—see paragraph 72.

24. *Claim or Concession of Tricks by a Defender*   To claim or concede any part of the remaining tricks, a defender should show his hand, or part of it, to declarer only. A

defender's concession is not valid unless his partner also concedes.

25. Trick Conceded in Error The concession of a trick which cannot be lost by any play of the cards is void.

26. Inspecting Tricks During Play Declarer or either defender may, until his side has led or played to the next trick, inspect a trick and inquire which hand played any card to it.

The Scoring

When the last (thirteenth) trick has been played, the tricks taken by the respective sides are counted and their number agreed upon. The points earned by each side in that deal are then entered to the credit of that side on the score sheet. See the Scoring Table on the next page for the point values.

Any player may keep a score. If only one player keeps score, both sides are equally responsible to see that the score for each deal is correctly entered.

Each side has a *trick score* and a *premium score*.

27. Trick Score If declarer made his contract, the trick-point value of the odd tricks he bid for is entered to the credit of his side in its trick score (called "below the line").

28. Premium Score Odd tricks won by declarer in excess of his contract are *overtricks* and are scored to the credit of his side in its premium score (called "above the line"; see illustration). Honors held in one hand, premiums for slams bid and made, for winning the rubber, and for undertricks are scored to the credit of the side earning them, in its premium score.

29. Undertricks When declarer wins fewer odd tricks than he bids for, his opponents score, in their premium score, the undertrick premium for each trick by which he fell short of his contract. (See Scoring Table.)

30. Slams If a side bids and makes a contract of six odd tricks (all but one trick) it receives the premium for a *little slam;* seven odd tricks (all the tricks), the premium for a *grand slam.*

31. Vulnerable A side which has won its first game toward the rubber becomes *vulnerable*. It is exposed to increased undertrick penalties if it fails to make a contract, but receives increased premiums for slams, and for overtricks made in doubled or redoubled contracts.

32. Honors When there is a trump suit, the A, K, Q, J and 10 of that suit are honors. If a player holds four trump honors in his hand, his side receives a 100-point premium whether he is declarer, dummy or a defender; five trump honors in one hand, or all four Aces at a No Trump contract, 150-point premium.

33. Game When a side amasses 100 or more points *in trick points* (whether these points are scored in one or more hands), it wins a game. Both sides then start at zero trick score on the next.

34. Rubber When a side has won two games, it receives the premium for the rubber—500 points if the other side has won one game, 700 points if the other side has not won a game. The scores of the two sides are then totaled, including both trick points and premium points, and the side which has scored the most points has won the rubber. The players then draw again for partners and seats and a new rubber is begun.

35. Scoring See Scoring Table, Page 56.

IRREGULARITIES

36. New Shuffle and Cut Before the first card is dealt, any player may demand a new shuffle and cut. There must be a new shuffle and cut if a card is faced in cutting.

37. Changing the Pack A pack containing a distinguishable damaged card must be replaced. The pack originally belonging to a side must be restored if reclaimed.

38. Redeal There must be a redeal if, before the last card is dealt, a redeal is demanded because a player is dealing out of turn or with an uncut pack. There must be a redeal if the cards are not dealt correctly, if a card is faced in the pack or elsewhere, if a player picks up the wrong hand and looks at it, or if at any time (until the end of play) one hand is found to have too many cards and another too few (and the discrepancy is not caused by errors in play).

When there is a redeal, the same dealer deals (unless the deal was out of turn) with the same pack, after a new shuffle and cut.

39. Missing Card If a missing card is found, it is deemed to belong to the deficient hand, which may then be answerable for exposing the card and for revoke through failure to play the card in a previous trick. But if a missing card is found in another hand, there must be a redeal; or in a trick, the law on defective trick (paragraph 70) applies. If a missing card is not found, there must be a redeal.

40. Surplus Card If a player has a surplus card due to an incorrect pack or incorrect deal, there must be a redeal. If the surplusage is due to omission to play to a trick, the law on defective trick (paragraph 70) applies.

41. Drawing Attention to an Irregularity Any player (including dummy if he has not forfeited his rights) may draw attention to an irregularity and give or obtain information as to the law covering it. The fact that the offending side draws attention to its own irregularity does not affect the rights of the opponents.

42. Enforcing a Penalty Either opponent (but not dummy) may select or enforce a penalty. If partners consult as to selection or enforcement, the right to penalize is canceled.

43. Improper Remarks and Gestures If by remark or unmistakable gesture a player other than declarer: discloses his intentions or desires, the nature of an unfaced hand, the presence or absence of a card in an unfaced hand; or improperly suggests a lead, play or line of play; or improperly directs attention to a trick before his partner has played to it; the offender's side is subject to penalty as below. If the offense occurred:

(a) During the auction, either opponent may require the offending side to pass at every subsequent turn; and if that

CONTRACT BRIDGE SCORING TABLE

	Odd Tricks Bid and Won in	Undoubled	Doubled
TRICK POINTS FOR CONTRACTORS	Clubs or Diamonds, each	20	40
	Hearts or Spades, each	30	60
	No Trump { first	40	80
	{ each subsequent	30	60

Redoubling doubles the doubled points for Odd Tricks.
Vulnerability does not affect points for Odd Tricks.
100 Trick Points constitute a game.

		Not Vulnerable	Vulnerable
PREMIUM POINTS FOR CONTRACTORS / DEFENDERS	Overtricks		
		Trick Value	Trick Value
	Undoubled, each	100	200
	Doubled, each		
	Making Doubled or Redoubled Contract }	50	50
	Undertricks		
	Undoubled, each	50	100
	Doubled { first	100	200
	{ each subsequent	200	300

Redoubling doubles the doubled points for Overtricks and Undertricks, but does not affect the points for making Doubled Contracts.

PREMIUM POINTS FOR CONTRACTORS / HOLDER	Honors in { All Honors	150
	One Hand { Four Trump Honors	100
	Slam Bid { Little, not vulnerable 500, vuln.	750
	and Won { Grand, not vulnerable 1000, vuln.	1500
	Rubber { Two game	700
	Points { Three game	500

Unfinished Rubber—Winners of one game score 300 points. If but one side has a part score in an unfinished game, it scores 50 points. Doubling and Redoubling do not affect Honor, Slam or Rubber points. Vulnerability does not affect points for Honors.

©—The National Laws Commission.

side becomes the defenders, declarer may require or forbid the opening lead of a specified suit.

(b) During the play, declarer or either defender (as the case may be) may require the offender's partner, on any one subsequent trick, to withdraw a lead or play suggested by the improper remark or gesture. There must be prior agreement as to what lead, play or line of play has been improperly suggested.

44. Card Exposed During the Auction If during the auction a player exposes a single card lower than a Jack there is no penalty. If a player exposes an Ace, King, Queen, or Jack, or a lower card prematurely led, or more than one card, such cards must be left face up on the table and become penalty cards (see paragraph 61) if the owner becomes a defender; and the partner of the offender must pass at his next turn.

45. Improper Call Overcalled If the left-hand opponent calls before the penalty for an improper call has been enforced, the auction proceeds as though it had been a proper call, except that it becomes a pass if it was a bid of more than seven, a call after the auction is closed, a double or redouble when the only proper call was a pass or bid.

46. Changing a Call A player may change a call without penalty if he does so practically in the same breath. Any other attempted change of call is void. If the first call was improper, it is subject to the appropriate "improper calls" section. If it was a proper call, the offender may either:

(a) Allow his first call to stand, whereupon his partner must pass at his next turn; or

(b) Substitute any other proper call, whereupon his partner must pass at every subsequent turn.

47. Insufficient Bid If a player makes an insufficient bid, he must substitute either a sufficient bid or a pass. If he substitutes:

(a) The lowest sufficient bid in the same denomination, there is no penalty.

(b) Any other bid, his partner must pass at every subsequent turn.

(c) A pass, his partner must pass at every subsequent turn, and if the offending side becomes the defenders, declarer may require or forbid the opening lead of a specified suit.

48. Call out of Rotation A call out of rotation is void and the auction reverts to the player whose turn it was. If the out-of-turn call was:

(a) A pass before any player has bid, or a pass when it was the turn of the offender's right-hand opponent, the offender must pass at his next turn.

(b) Any call not covered by (a), the offender's partner must pass at every subsequent turn to call.

A call is not out of rotation if made without waiting for the right-hand opponent to pass, if that opponent is legally obliged to pass; nor if it would have been in rotation had not the left-hand opponent called out of rotation. A call made simultaneously with another player's proper call is deemed to be subsequent.

49. Improper Doubles and Redoubles It is improper to state the number of tricks or the denomination in doubling and redoubling (no penalty provided for infringement). If a player does so, and names the wrong number or denomination, he is deemed to have doubled or redoubled the bid as made.

If a player doubles or redoubles a bid which his side has already doubled or redoubled, he must substitute any proper call and his partner must pass at every subsequent turn. If the offender elects to pass, either opponent may cancel all previous doubles and redoubles.

If a player doubles his partner's bid, redoubles an undoubled bid, or doubles or redoubles when there has been no bid, he must substitute any proper call, and his partner must pass at every subsequent turn.

50. Other Improper Calls If a player bids more than seven, or makes another call when legally required to pass, he is deemed to have passed and the offending side must pass at every subsequent turn; if they become the defenders, declarer may require or forbid the opening lead of a specified suit.

51. Doubly Improper Call If a player makes a call subject to penalty under two or more "improper calls" sections, either section may be applied but not both.

52. Call after the Auction Is Closed A call made after the auction is closed is canceled. If it is a pass by a defender, or any call by declarer or dummy, there is no penalty. If it is a bid, double or redouble by a defender, declarer may require or forbid the other defender to lead a specified suit at his first turn to lead.

53. Dummy's Rights Dummy may reply to a proper question regarding fact or law, ask if a play constitutes a revoke, demand that a defender correct his revoke, draw attention to an irregularity, and warn any player against infringing a law. Dummy forfeits these rights if he looks at a card in another player's hand. If dummy has forfeited his rights, and thereafter:

(a) Is the first to draw attention to a defender's irregularity, declarer may not enforce any penalty for the offense.

(b) Warns declarer not to lead from the wrong hand, either defender may choose the hand from which declarer shall lead.

(c) Is the first to draw attention to an unestablished revoke by declarer, either defender may require declarer to substitute his highest or lowest correct card.

54. Played Card A card is deemed to be played when named as one the player proposes to play, or when it touches the table after being detached from the remaining cards with apparent intent to play; a defender's card so detached is also deemed to be played as soon as his partner sees its face.

A player having named a card to be played may change his designation if he does so practically in the same breath.

A played card may not be withdrawn except as above, or as permitted after an irregularity.

55. Lead out of Turn If declarer is required to retract a lead out of turn from the wrong hand, he must lead from the correct hand, if he can, a card of the same suit; if it was a defender's turn to lead, there is no penalty.

If a defender is required to retract a lead out of turn, the card so led becomes a penalty card; or, if it is the other defender's lead, declarer may prohibit the lead of that suit.

A lead out of turn may be treated by the opponents as a correct lead. It must be so treated if the non-offending side plays a card before attention is drawn to the irregularity.

56. Premature Play If a defender leads to the next trick before his partner has played to the current trick, or plays out of rotation before his partner has played, declarer may require the offender's partner to play his highest card of the suit led, his lowest card of the suit led, or a card of another specified suit.

If declarer has played from both his hand and dummy, a defender is not subject to penalty for playing before his partner.

57. Inability to Play as Required If a player is unable to lead or play as required to comply with a penalty (for lack of a card of a required suit, or because of the prior obligation to follow suit) he may play any card. The penalty is deemed satisfied, except in the case of a penalty card.

58. Failure to Comply with a Penalty If a player is able to lead or play a penalty card or a card or suit specified by an opponent in conformity with an agreed penalty, but instead plays an incorrect card, he must correct the error on demand and the erroneous card becomes a penalty card. But if the offender's side has played another card after the erroneous card, the latter stands as played, and the offending side is penalized as for an established revoke.

59. Playing Before a Penalty Is Enforced If declarer plays from either hand before enforcing a lead or play penalty, he is deemed to waive the penalty. If a defender plays to a lead out of turn by declarer or dummy, after correction has been demanded, such lead becomes a penalty card.

60. Exposed Cards Declarer is never subject to penalty for exposure of a card. Intentional exposure of declarer's hand is treated as a claim or concession of tricks.

A defender's card is exposed if it is faced on the table or

if partner sees its face before he is entitled to in the normal course of play. Such a card must be left face up on the table and becomes a penalty card (unless another penalty is provided).

61. Penalty Cards A penalty card must be played at first legal opportunity, whether in leading, following suit, trumping or discarding. The play of a penalty card is always subject to the obligation to follow suit or to comply with a lead or play penalty.

If a defender has two or more penalty cards that he can legally play, declarer may designate which one is to be played.

62. Defender Exposing His Hand If a defender improperly exposes his remaining cards, declarer may treat all the remaining cards of either defender as penalty cards.

63. Revoke Defined A revoke is the act of playing a card of another suit, when able to follow suit to a lead.

64. Inquiry Regarding Revoke Any player, including dummy, may ask whether a play constitutes a revoke and may demand that an opponent correct a revoke. A claim or revoke does not warrant inspection of turned tricks, prior to the end of play, except by consent of both sides.

65. Correcting a Revoke A player must correct his revoke if aware of it before it becomes established. A revoke card withdrawn by a defender becomes a penalty card. The non-offending side may withdraw any cards played after the revoke but before attention was drawn to it.

66. Established Revoke A revoke becomes established when a member of the offending side leads or plays to a subsequent trick (or terminates play by a claim or concession).

When a revoke becomes established, the revoke trick stands as played (unless it is the twelfth trick as below).

67. Revoke Penalty In penalty for established revoke, two tricks (if available) are transferred at the end of play from the revoking side to the opponents. This penalty is paid from tricks won by the revoking side after its first revoke, including the revoke trick. If only one trick is available, the penalty is satisfied by transferring one trick; if no trick is available, there is no penalty.

There is no penalty for a subsequent established revoke in the same suit by the same player.

A transferred trick ranks for all scoring purposes as a trick won in play by the side receiving it.

68. Revokes Not Subject to Penalty A revoke made in the twelfth trick must be corrected, without penalty, if discovered before the cards have been mixed together. A revoke not discovered until the cards have been mixed is not subject to penalty, nor is a revoke by any faced hand (dummy, or a defender's hand faced in consequence of a claim by declarer). Failure to play a penalty card is not subject to the penalty for an established revoke.

69. Trick Appropriated in Error No matter who gathers in a trick, it is scored to the credit of the side that played the winning card.

70. Defective Trick If a hand plays too many cards to a trick or no card, the error must be corrected if attention is drawn to the irregularity before a player of each side has played to the next trick. A card withdrawn by a defender becomes a penalty card. If the irregularity is noticed too late for correction, the defective trick stands as played, and:

(a) A hand with too few cards does not play to the final trick (or tricks), and if it wins a trick with its last card, the lead passes in rotation.

(b) A hand with too many cards forthwith faces and adds to the defective trick (without changing its ownership) a card it could properly have played to it.

71. Concession of a Trick that Cannot Be Lost The concession of a trick that cannot be lost by any play of the cards is void if attention is drawn to the error before the cards have been mixed together. If a player concedes a trick he has in fact won (as by claiming nine tricks when his side has already won ten) the concession is void, and if the score has been entered it may be corrected as provided below.

72. Declarer Claiming or Conceding Tricks If declarer

intentionally exposes his hand, claims or concedes one or more of the remaining tricks, or otherwise suggests that play be curtailed, he must place his hand face up on the table and forthwith make any statement that may be necessary to indicate his intended play.

If a defender disputes declarer's claim, declarer must play on, adhering to any statement of intentions, and in any matter not covered he may not, if a defender objects:

(a) Lead a trump while either defender has a trump.

(b) Take any finesse in the suit led or in trumping. That is, unless he announced his intention to do so when he made his claim, he may not make a play that will lose a trick if a certain card lies in the hand of one defender and not the other.

Following curtailment of play by declarer, a defender may suggest a play to his partner and may expose his hand.

73. *Defender Claiming or Conceding Tricks* A defender may show any or all of his cards to declarer to establish a claim or concession. A claim made in any other manner may be liable to penalty for giving partner improper information. A concession of tricks by a defender is not valid unless his partner accedes.

74. *Correcting the Score* A proved or admitted error in any score may be corrected at any time before the rubber score is agreed, except as follows. An error made in entering or failing to enter a part score, or in omitting a game or in awarding one, may not be corrected after the last card of the second succeeding deal has been dealt (unless a majority of the players consent).

There is no redress for a call made relying on an erroneous entry or omission in the score.

75. *Effect of Incorrect Pack* Scores made as a result of hands played with an incorrect pack are not affected by the discovery of the imperfection after the cards have been mixed together.

POKER

TEN THINGS EVERY WINNING POKER PLAYER MUST KNOW

1. You will generally lose unless you have the best hand going in.

2. Treat every bet as though it were your first one—forget the money you put in the pot before.

3. Don't be ashamed to be bluffed out of a pot occasionally—all good players are.

4. Don't try to bluff a poor player, a heavy winner, or a heavy loser.

5. Drop a doubtful hand if you may later be in the middle between two strong hands.

6. Most Stud players would win instead of lose if they never tried to draw out against an open pair.

7. Raise on an early round to avoid calling a big bet later.

8. A loser will drop a close hand if raised early, a winner will stay in.

9. When you're sure you'll win a Stud pot, wait till the last round to raise.

10. The more wild cards and crazy rules, the greater the expert's advantage.

POKER

There are so many different forms of Poker that no one could even count them all. And each of them would justify a book all by itself.

Generally speaking, you can divide all the more popular forms of Poker into four main types: Draw Poker, which to most American players means the game formerly known as Jackpots; Stud Poker, which usually means Five-Card Stud; its popular variation, Seven-Card Stud; and Low Poker, or Lowball, which is a form of Draw Poker in which the lowest hand, not the highest, wins.

But all of these are played in combinations and variations. There are High-Low Poker; Blind-Opening Poker; hundreds of games that use wild cards and extra cards and special hands and odd numbers of cards. Each variation affects the proper play, and sometimes changes it completely—as in High-Low Seven-Card Stud, when you play with low combinations and drop with high ones. Almost every bit of Poker advice must depend also on the particular rules, stakes, players, and conditions.

Still, there are some principles that apply to nearly any form of Poker. I am first going to give some of those principles, and then I will take up special points that apply to the most popular variations of Poker.

GENERAL PRINCIPLES IN POKER

First I would say that a winning Poker player must have

a combination of two qualities. They are knowledge and courage.

The knowledge part is what you can read about in books. Whichever form of Poker you are playing, you have to know what constitutes a good hand in that game; you have to know the odds against having the winning hand, and compare them with the odds offered by the pot; you have to know something of betting tactics, psychology, and characteristics of the other players in the game.

The factor of courage cannot be taught; but you can't win without it. When you get into a Poker game, you aren't there to keep from losing. You're there to win. And to do that you must back your good hands to the limit, and risk your money when you think you're right.

This lack of courage is the reason so many Poker players are at a disadvantage once they start losing. Every time another player bets aggressively, their first reaction is one of fear. They check when they should bet, and drop when they should call, thus winning too little on their good hands and losing on too many of their fair hands.

I have known men who were formerly good Poker players but who lost their courage, either through a reduced financial position, or family responsibilities, or even a seemingly interminable losing streak. They promptly changed from good players to poor ones. If the amount of money at stake is frightening to you, I can only recommend that you appropriate a certain amount of money that you are able to lose and play that money as though it were an unlimited supply. If you lose it all, quit the game. While you're playing you'll have a chance to win.

The Advantage of the Top Man   Here is the first rule of Poker: Don't try to beat the other fellow; let him try to beat you.

That isn't just an introductory paragraph. It is probably more important than everything else in this section. Do yourself a favor by reading it again.

The man who has the best hand going in (in Draw Poker)

or the highest-ranking combination in the first two or three cards (in Stud Poker) will show a profit in the long run; anyone with a lower hand will show a loss. Even the man with the second-highest hand figures to *lose* unless there are at least six players in the pot altogether, in which case he will only break even.

Here's how it works out mathematically in the simplest possible case—when everyone at the table has a single pair:

WINS IN A HUNDRED POTS

Number in Pot	Number of Pots You Must Win to Break Even	Number of Pots That Will Be Won by					
		High Pair	Second Pair	Third Pair	Fourth Pair	Fifth Pair	Sixth Pair
2	50	76½	23½				
3	33½	58½	22	19½			
4	25	47	19½	17½	16		
5	20	38½	18	16½	14½	12½	
6	16⅔	31½	17	15½	14	11½	10½

The moral is not to play a single pair unless you think that no one else at the table has a better pair. The general moral is, not to stay in if you have reason to think any other player can beat your hand.

However, Poker can't be played as a sure-thing game. That is losing practice too. Your decision is based on two factors besides the strength of your hand. One is the nature of the game you are playing in. The second is the odds you are offered by the pot.

The Other Players You must make your style of play conform to the type of game you are in.

If the other players are conservative, you must be conservative. They will not play unless they have good hands; neither must you, or you will lose consistently.

If the game is a liberal one, in which most of the other players would rather play doubtful hands than be bored, you must play more liberally for two reasons. If you are too cautious, they won't like you and won't play with you. And the more liberal the game, the more players there are in the average pot, and the better odds you will get for your bets.

You can characterize the game by the average number of players in the pot, and this you will learn by observation within half an hour or less, even when the game is strange to you. (Only the game should be strange to you; you should know the players as persons even if you do not know them as Poker players. No one in his right mind makes a practice of playing Poker with utter strangers.)

The conservative player stays in only about once in four hands that he gets. In the conservative game the average pot has only two players in it, though what actually happens, of course, is that most of the pots are uncontested, and some of them have three, four, or five players.

In the liberal game slightly more than half the players are in every pot—say four players in a seven-handed game.

In a very bad or wild game nearly everyone is in nearly every pot.

Having learned the nature of the game, you don't have to wait and see every time how many will be in the pot. Even as second man, next to the opener in Draw Poker, or next to the first bettor in Stud, you can anticipate the number of players who will probably come in after you, and decide accordingly whether you should play or drop.

The Odds Offered by the Pot   Before putting any money in the pot, compare the amount needed with the money that is already there. That represents the odds you are offered. For example, if there is $5.00 in the pot, and it will cost you $1.00 to stay in, the pot is offering you 5 to 1 odds.

Now you calculate your chance of winning the pot. Occasionally this is a matter that can be decided by mathematics. More often it is a combination of mathematics and personal judgment. I will discuss both the mathematics and the judgment a little later. The point I am trying to make here is that if the pot offers you 5 to 1, and you think the odds are only 2 or 3 to 1 against your winning, you have an excellent bet at this point. If the pot offers you 5 to 1, and the odds are, for example, 11 to 1 against your winning (which are the odds against filling an inside straight), then it is a very bad bet to put your dollar in.

It is important to remember that the *pot* is offering you the odds. You must treat the pot as though it were a separate individual. Any money you put in before now belongs to the pot and not to you, and you should forget that you ever owned it.

Here you have the source of the old Poker saying, "Don't throw good money after bad." The fact that you previously put $10 in a pot doesn't justify you in spending a nickel more if your chance of winning the pot doesn't justify it.

The stakes in the game will have a great deal to do with your decision, partly because they affect the size of the pot, and partly because they can help you to anticipate future problems.

Almost all Poker games are played with a fixed limit that is fairly low. It can still be quite a stiff game. For example, a game in which you can bet $2.00 before the draw, and $5.00 after the draw (or, in a Stud game, $2.00 on the first two or three cards and $5.00 on the last one or two) is a stiff game, but it is still a relatively low-limit game. In such a game you can often stay in for $1.00 or $2.00 when there is already $10 or more in the pot. You are being given fine odds and your risk is at a minimum, because the most you can ever lose on a single bet is $5.00.

Compare it with a table-stakes game in which the average bet is the same $1.00 or $2.00 or $5.00, but in which every player has $50 or $100 in front of him and can later bet the $50 or $100 all at one time if he wants to. Suppose in such a game you toss in your $1.00 or $2.00 to draw to a straight. With $10 already in the pot you are getting good enough odds, but you are risking a situation in which you may fill your straight and then be confronted with a $100 bet. Yet, if you fill your straight, nobody is likely to call a $100 bet unless he can beat you. Therefore your potential risk is much greater than in the limit game.

In any kind of Poker it usually pays to play only when

your hand, even if it doesn't improve, has a chance to win the pot; and when your chance of improvement is as great as any other player's. For example, you have Aces and another player has Kings. If neither of you improves, you win. You have as good a chance to improve as he has, and if the two of you improve equally, you'll still win.

Whatever the game, don't play against a single opponent unless you are pretty sure you have a better hand. Don't play against two or three opponents unless there is a chance that you have the best hand. And with four or five opponents you should be pretty sure that you have at least the second-best hand going in, or that you will surely win (as with a straight or flush) if you improve.

Straights and Flushes The question of straights and flushes provides a simple illustration of Poker odds.

You are dealt five cards. Four of them are Spades and one is a card of another suit. It is Draw Poker with all cards concealed. There are forty-seven cards whose whereabouts you do not know, and when you draw, the top card of the pack may be any one of those forty-seven.

Of the forty-seven cards thirty-eight are cards of other suits, and won't give you your flush; nine are the remaining Spades, and any one of them will give you your flush. Therefore the odds are 38 to 9 against filling the flush, or a little more than 4 to 1. It makes no difference how many players are in the game, those are always the odds.

With a straight open at both ends the forty-seven cards include thirty-nine that won't fill your straight and eight that will. So the odds are almost 5 to 1 against filling the straight.

The standard theory is that you need 5 to 1 odds in either case to make it worth while to draw. The rule of thumb is that there must be at least four other players in the pot before you, because then there will usually be five times as much money already in the pot as you will have to put in.

But it is not enough to get the proper odds at the time

you stay in. The questions are: What are the odds against your winning the pot? How much will you win if you do win it? How much will you lose if you lose it?

If the betting convinces you that two or three of the players before you have two pairs, even excellent odds do not justify the risk of drawing. When two players draw to two-pair hands, it is only 5 to 1 that neither will fill. To play, you must get 6 to 1 or better from the pot.

If the players before you have one-pair hands, with not more than one having two pairs, then you may profitably stay, because you will usually win if you fill; you will lose only about once in fifty times when you fill your straight or flush and another player fills a full house at the same time. In a limit game, that will not bankrupt you.

In Stud Poker, whether Five-Card or Seven-Card, the odds are somewhat different. All the other cards that have shown up will modify them. For example, suppose the fourth card has been dealt all around and you have a four-card Spade flush. Twenty cards have shown in the hands of the other players. This leaves twenty-eight unknown cards, any one of which might be your last card. Now, if the known twenty cards included only two Spades, then of the 28 undealt cards, seven must be Spades, and the odds will be 21 to 7, or 3 to 1, against your filling your flush. The pot will almost always offer you better odds than that, and you should stay—especially since in Stud Poker you can usually know definitely from the other players' hands that no one is going to have a full house or a higher flush to beat you.

But rare are the cases in which a player in Five-Card Stud should stay in long enough to have four Spades going into the last card. For example, the round before he had only three Spades; at that point it was 23 to 1 against his eventually getting a flush.

Playing Position Generally speaking, the player who must speak first is in a bad position in Poker, the player who is late to speak has a superior position. This applies in all forms of the game.

But you cannot get a lot of action if you confine your close decisions to hands in which you have good position. You must act on the customs of the players in the game. Suppose the player at your right is first to speak and opens, or bets. If you think the pot will eventually offer you good odds, you should stay in in anticipation of that. In a conservative game, of course, you would not play any doubtful hand without waiting to see; but then, in a conservative game, you should not play a doubtful hand anyway.

In the final round of betting, position is almost everything.

The best possible position is when you are last in turn to bet, and there is only one of the other hands you are afraid of. Your turn will come after his and you will already know what he has done.

The worst possible position is between two hands that you are afraid of. If the hand before you bets, you are afraid to call even if you think you may have him beaten. The other dangerous hand comes after you and may raise.

You should always try to anticipate what your position will be on the final round of betting. Occasionally you can create a good position from a situation in which your position is naturally a bad one.

For example, in Draw Poker Player A opens early, and you know from his style that he would not do so without a fair hand, perhaps Aces, more likely two pairs. Player B at his left raises. You have two pairs, Aces up; it is a good hand, very likely the best, but you are afraid of both opponents. And you can foresee a situation after the draw in which A will check to the raiser, B will bet, and you will be caught between them.

This is a good time for you to raise again—not because you are confident of having the best hand, or because you expect to drive other players out, but because you want to put yourself in a good position after the draw.

Consider the possible effect of your previous raise. Player A checks as before. B will check to you, as the last raiser, unless he improved—and perhaps even if he did. You can now check and have a free showdown. If B does bet, in the face of your previous raise, you may assume that he has improved, and you should drop.

This type of raise is especially useful because the betting is usually lower before the draw than after. By raising at a low level you save yourself a dangerous call at a higher level.

Opportunities for this type of raise arise constantly in both Draw and Stud. Keep on the outlook for them. Here is a Stud Poker example: On the third card Player A gets a pair of Sevens showing and bets. You have a Queen in the hole and a Ten and Queen up, giving you a pair of Queens. But before your turn comes, Player B steps in, having a Nine and a King showing. You know he is too good a player to stay in against an open pair if he doesn't have a higher one; but is his pair Nines or Kings?

The only way to find out is to raise early. If no one improves, the Sevens may still check at the end, and B even with a pair of Kings may check, hoping you will bet again and he can raise. If instead they bet in the face of your earlier raise, when you could have had no better than a pair of Queens, you will know you are beaten. By your early raise you will have clarified a situation that could have been very difficult, if at the end the Sevens had checked and Player B had bet, putting you in the middle.

Concealing Your Style Every Poker player must adopt a style of his own. Some do best to sit woodenly at the table, others find it more effective to keep up a running line of chatter.

Neither type should overdo it. Every fine Poker player must be a good actor, but overacting is a heavy liability. It becomes a habit that other players can read.

The important thing is to adopt the style of play and the demeanor that best suits you, and then not stick to either one of them too thoroughly. You must vary your manners and mannerisms, and you must vary your style of play. If you ordinarily draw one card to three of a kind (mathematically it is not unsound to hold a kicker with threes, and the deceptive effect is often good), then occasionally you must draw two cards to three of a kind, and occasionally you must draw two cards to a pair and a kicker, though the latter play is usually not sound mathematically.

If you seldom stay in on a weak hand, occasionally you should do so. If it is not your style to bluff, occasionally you must bluff. Even in the ultraconservative game, where one must necessarily play conservatively or lose, you must make an occasional unsound play.

I have known dozens of superb Poker players who have only one weakness. They were observant, and analyzed—I might even say dissected—the playing habits of their opponents. It never occurred to them to draw off mentally and observe themselves in the same way. If they ever had, they could have got rid of some dead-giveaway habits of their own.

Ethics and Etiquette Poker ethics are customarily lax so long as you do not cheat. Most serious players will insist that you can use any stratagem you want to, and if it fools the opponents, so much the better. That's the principal fun of the game.

However, Poker is a social game and it would be stupid to violate the accepted ethics of the game you are playing. In games played in a club or in other serious games there is nothing wrong with checking a safe hand and then raising if a player bets into you; in some games, to do this would mark you as a boor and the other players' wives wouldn't speak to you. In a serious game you can announce that you are betting blind when in fact you have seen your hand. In most genteel games this is considered dishonorable. You have no choice but to learn the customs that prevail in the particular game and to govern yourself accordingly.

But in any game, serious or casual, there are a few matters of Poker etiquette that are necessary to the smooth operation of the game. Never throw away your hand or announce that you are dropping until your turn comes; it may help one of the preceding players at the expense of another. Don't put money in the pot without keeping it separate long enough for other players to see you are putting in the right amount.

The same applies to taking change from the pot. All experience proves that Poker games run more smoothly and are more fun if the laws of the game, as given on Page 95, are never intentionally violated.

DRAW POKER

To nearly everyone Draw Poker means a game in which you can't open without a pair of Jacks or better. On every pot each player makes some very low ante, or perhaps the dealer makes a somewhat larger ante, but generally speaking, the total ante represents about twice the average bet that is made before the draw: in other words, if the bet before the draw is $1.00, then the ante will represent about $2.00 before that bet is made.* In the usual game there are six, seven, or eight players.

Experienced Draw Poker players follow a set of rough guides that don't vary much from the following:

1. Next to the dealer, under the guns, don't open on less than Aces; second and third man should open on Kings; fourth and fifth on Queens; after that on Jacks.

2. If the pot is opened ahead of you, stay in on Kings and drop any lower pair; except, if the pot was opened late after everyone passed, stay in on Queens.

3. With two low pairs raise immediately, especially if next to the opener; with Kings up or better, don't raise if more than one player is still to speak behind you.

These, as I acknowledged before, are very rough rules similar to the "Play second hand low, third hand high" and "Cover an honor with an honor" sayings of Bridge. They are generally accurate but subject to exceptions.

Opening the Pot   You will recall my general advice: Don't

* In Blind-Opening Poker the word ante has a slightly different technical meaning: It is the first forced bet made by a player. Since he must bet it regardless of his hand, the effect is about the same as when the dealer antes in a Jackpots game.

bet unless there is at least a chance that you might be the high hand.

The following table will give you the usual hand that has an even chance to be high:

NUMBER IN GAME	EXPECTED HIGH HAND
8	Aces
7	Kings
6	Kings
5	Queens
4	Tens
3	Eights
2	Ace-King or Deuces

It will be seen that if you have a pair of Kings in an eight-handed game, there is slightly better than an even chance that someone else has Aces or better. In a six- or seven-handed game, you have about an even chance to be high with your Kings. In a five-handed game, you have a better than even chance to be high with Kings because the average high hand is a pair of Queens. Note that these are not hands that win the pot, but hands that are high before the draw.

One slight modification should be made. The side cards held with your pair affect your chance of being high. A pair of Queens with an Ace and King will be the high hand in a six-handed game as often as a pair of Kings.

These side cards do not increase the value of your hand at all; they merely limit the possibility that another player holds a higher pair going in. Once discarded, they should be remembered because they limit the chance that a player with a higher pair will get three of a kind. If you start with Queens and an Ace-King, and get three Queens, you can bet them as vigorously as you would bet three Aces.

The player who opens early is in bad position; he must bet first after the draw. For this reason I do not recommend opening anything less than Aces when under the guns in a game of seven or eight players. The only exception is when the ante is big and the bet is low; for example, in a seven-handed game in which everyone antes a quarter, starting the pot off with $1.75, and in which the opening bet is only a quarter, you can afford to open in any position on anything from Jacks up, just on the chance that you might steal the ante.

Good players recommend opening on Jacks in a five-handed game, but here again I think the odds offered by the pot should be at least 3 to 1. After all, you figure to have only the second-best pair going in, and this means that without an ante you would lose in the long run.

Aces or any two pairs are always worth opening on in any position, although occasionally it is worth passing them early for strategic purposes, expecting to come in if anyone opens later, and perhaps to raise if the pot works out that way.

The lower the cards in your hand, the more likelihood there is that the pot will be opened. A player with Fives and Deuces is strong enough to open in first or second position, but is not necessarily wise to do so. In a very conservative game he would open because of the chance that no one else would stay and he would get the ante. In a liberal game he will do better by passing and letting someone else open; his position will be much better after the draw; he may be suspected of drawing to a straight or flush, and so be called on suspicion if he bets after the draw; and if he does make a full house, he may win a big pot. It is even relatively safe to pass a low straight like 5–6–7–8–9, when there are at least five players to speak later. Another principle of the game is involved here: You do not want to steal the ante on such a good hand. If you open and everyone drops, your loss is minor when compared to the killing you might have made by passing, and then raising before the draw, especially when the pot has been raised before you.

Two pairs including a high one, or a high straight, or a pat flush including a couple of high cards had better be opened. The chance is far greater that the pot will be passed out.

Staying In With a pair of Kings you have a reasonable chance of being high in any game, and in an eight-handed game you expect to be second best, which may be profitable if enough players have already stayed or may be expected to stay after you. A lesser hand should usually be dropped.

The following table shows the hand you need to have a reasonable expectancy of being the high hand going in when the pot has been opened ahead of you:

WHAT YOU NEED TO STAY IN

Players Ahead of You Who Have Come In (Including Opener)	If Game Is Conservative	If Game Is Liberal
1	Kings	Queens
2	Two low pairs	Aces
3	Queens up	Two low pairs
4	Kings up	Tens up
5	Aces up	Queens up
6	Three Threes	Kings up

This table is not intended to advise you how to play. A high pair, such as Kings or Aces, is about as good as two low pairs in a large pot; it will take in about as much money in the long run, in the pots on which it improves, as the two low pairs will take in on the pots on which no one improves. For example, in a liberal game Aces should be played in any position if the pot has not been raised. Two low pairs, which have a better chance than Aces to be high going in, should be dropped if the pot has been raised, and no less than Tens up should be played.

When you have opened a pot, or stayed in when someone else has opened, and the pot is raised thereafter, you should usually stay in. The percentages almost always justify it if you remember that money previously put in the pot no longer belongs to you. For example, the pot was opened at your right; you stayed with a pair of Kings. The player at your left raised. The opener stayed and it is up to you. You previously put in $1.00, it was raised $1.00, and as it comes back to you there is $7.00 in the pot. Assuming that you are even

the third-best hand, and will win only about twenty times
in a hundred pots, the twenty times you win will bring you
at least $120; the eighty times you play and do not win will
cost you only $80. Although the exact figures vary with each
case, the result is usually a profit from staying.

There are many wild games in which players stay on anything and raise with little more reason. In such games you
must revise your figures because you may still be one of the
best hands going in even if there are several raises before
the draw. But in a more conservative game your policy
should be as follows:

If the pot is opened and raised before your turn comes,
don't stay without two good pairs, at least Jacks up.

If the pot is opened ahead of you, you stay, it is raised at
your left, and any player raises again, don't stay without
Aces up or three of a kind. And if there is a third raise, you
can expect to need a high three of a kind, three Tens or
better, to have the best hand going in. (And this usually
means the best hand coming out, because three of a kind is
seldom improved.)

Raising There are two purposes in raising. One is to drive
other players out. The other is merely to increase the size
of the pot.

It may seem illogical to want to drive other players out
when you think you have the best hand, because I have already shown that the best hand going in is a consistent
winner. If so, you should want to have other players in so
that the pot will be larger.

But if you consider the table on Page 80, you will see how
the net profits may vary.

Whether this is based on chips, dollars, or any other betting
unit, the maximum profit is earned on two low pairs when
you have only two others in the pot besides yourself. The
profit is least when almost everyone stays. Especially in a
game in which players make a habit of staying on any type
of pair, straight, or flush draw, you are better off to drive
them out.

PROFITS EARNED BY TWO LOW PAIRS IN A HUNDRED POTS

Number of Players in Pot	Pots You Should Expect to Win	Total Chips You Would Win	Net Profit
2	73½	147	47
3	53	159	59
4	39	156	56
5	29½	147½	47½
6	23	138	38
7	19	133	33

The reason for this is that two low pairs give you the best chance of winning when no one improves, but seldom win if anyone else improves. It is 3 to 1 that you will be high going in, but the odds are 11 to 1 against improving two low pairs; the only chance is to make a full house.

It is entirely different when you have two high pairs, such as Kings up. In this case you do not want to drive out competition, because you figure to win against players who stay and improve, but who get no better than Queens up. It is two-pair hands that are Jacks up or lower that justify the immediate raise.

With any hand that figures to be high despite the improvement of one competitor in the game, you should avoid raising if you are too close to the opener. This includes Aces up and usually Kings or Queens up; three of a kind; all straights and flushes and better hands. If the pot is opened early and you are next to the opener, you simply stay. In a liberal game you would refrain from raising, even if the pot is opened late, so long as there are players behind you, still to be heard from, who might stay on low pairs or straight and flush draws. Such hands profit most from position—you raise after nearly all players who might come in have already decided whether to come in or not. Thus you increase the size of the pot if the other players meet your raise, and do not reduce the size of the pot on hands in which others might come in if the pot were not raised.

Reraising depends on the betting limit and your appraisal of what will probably happen after the draw. Suppose you have opened on Aces up, the player at your left has stayed, a third player has raised, and everyone else has dropped. You might as well raise back. You must draw one card, and after you do so the player who raised will not bet in to you if he has two low pairs. You may drive him out with your reraise, but you won't get a call after the draw anyway.

Suppose, however, that you have opened with three Queens, the player at your left has raised, and another player after him has raised again. This time you simply call. In the first place you don't want the original raiser to be frightened out, because you expect to win the pot. Second, you can draw one card and check after the draw, with a good chance that the reraiser will bet against you, and that you can then raise when the limit is high.

In closing this section I want to return to my previous remarks about courage. It is absolutely true that three Queens are not a sure winning hand. One of the other players may have three Aces or perhaps a straight going in; either of the other players may improve and make a full house in the draw. Nevertheless, you must play your three Queens on the assumption that they are going to win, and that you must figure out how best to make the pot as big as possible when you do win it. Let yourself become fearful of the damages if you are wrong and you are not a probable winner in a Poker game.

When to Bet Another of the general Poker "rules," like the ones I cited before, is: Don't bet into a one-card draw. It is true that a hand that drew one card may turn out to be a straight, flush, or full house made by a draw to two low or moderate pairs. The theory is that it cannot pay to bet against such a hand when you have something like Aces up or three of a kind: if the hand did not improve it will not call, and if it did improve it has you beaten.

Nevertheless, if you never bet into a one-card draw, you will lose an appreciable part of the potential profits in Poker.

What you must do is decide to your own satisfaction what the one-card draw meant. Suppose there are five of you in the pot. You opened and have three Aces. The next four players stayed in; the first drew three, and the others drew one each. It would be losing practice to check. Of the first three players the one with the three-card draw probably had a pair and can hardly beat you; the other two probably had two pairs and the odds are 5 to 1 that neither made a full house; and the last player may have had a straight or flush and the odds are 5 to 1 that he did not fill. If you check, everyone else is likely to check, and you will have won nothing in this round—a sad fate to befall three Aces. There is a much better chance that someone will call a bet than that someone will have drawn out on you. Furthermore, if your bet is raised, you can be reasonably sure that your three Aces are beaten, and it will cost you no more than it would have cost to check in the first place and call a bet later, which you would have had to do unless you are clairvoyant or know your opponents awfully well.

The secret of good betting is to study the habits of the other players. Then, when you think you may have the best hand, remember how they played their current hands and what sort of hands they ordinarily play that way. You cannot tell, of course, whether or not they have improved; but you do know that the odds against improvement of any hand run from 2½ to 1 up to 11 or more to 1. If you can be fairly sure of the type of hand they started in with, then you should bet whenever the odds are against their having improved, provided your position is such that you will not run into one or more reraises and be doubtful as to whether you should call or drop.

Drawing Cards   If all your opponents were deaf, dumb, and blind, you would get the best results by consistently drawing three cards to a pair and two cards to triplets. Since they're not, you should occasionally hold kickers. The advantage of keeping the opponents guessing offsets the lessened chance of improvement. Here are comparative figures:

DRAWING THREE CARDS TO A PAIR

Result	Odds Against
Two Pairs	5.25 to 1
Triplets	7.74 to 1
Full house	97.3 to 1
Four of a kind	359 to 1
Any improvement	2.48 to 1

DRAWING TO A PAIR AND AN ACE KICKER

Result	Odds Against
Aces up	7.58 to 1
Another pair	17 to 1
Total two pair	4.81 to 1
Triplets	12 to 1
Full house	119 to 1
Four of a kind	1080 to 1
Any improvement	2.86 to 1

Compare the tables. It's a little easier to make two pairs when you hold a kicker; it's appreciably harder to get triplets.

The improved chance for two pairs suggests that it's wise to hold a high kicker (no less than Ace or King) when two pairs are needed to win, that is, when you are out to beat one opponent who almost surely has two pairs.

But holding a kicker is a good idea only in a two- or three-cornered pot. In a bigger pot draw three cards.

Holding a kicker with triplets is an even better idea. Here are the figures:

DRAWING TWO CARDS TO TRIPLETS

Result	Odds Against
Full house	15½ to 1
Four of a kind	22½ to 1
Any improvement	8⅔ to 1

DRAWING ONE CARD TO TRIPLETS

Result	Odds Against
Full house	14⅔ to 1
Four of a kind	46 to 1
Any improvement	10¾ to 1

A four of a kind is remote in either case, so it's no great loss to weaken your chance for it. Holding the kicker gives you a slightly better chance for a full house, but even that is remote. The big advantage of holding the kicker is psychological; you have a much better chance to get a little action after the draw.

As long as we're on the subject of drawing cards, let's look briefly at the question of freak draws. The most common of these odd draws are: drawing four cards to an Ace, three to an Ace-King, two to a three flush, and two to a straight-flush possibility.

ODD DRAWS

Draw	Result	Odds Against
Four to an Ace	Two pairs or better	11 to 1
Four to an Ace	Pair of Aces	3 to 1
Three to an Ace-King of same suit	Two pairs or better	12 to 1
Two to a three-card sequence in same suit*	Two pairs or better	7½ to 1
	Straight or flush	11 to 1
Two to three cards of same suit	Flush	23 to 1
One to inside straight	Straight	10¾ to 1

* Not including A-K-Q or A-2-3

And how often do you get money odds that balance such card odds?

FIVE-CARD STUD

The traditional theory of Stud Poker is not to play unless you can "beat the board." That is, if the high player has an Ace, you mustn't stay without an Ace or a pair. If he has a King, you mustn't stay without a King, Ace, or pair.

Mathematically this is sound. Let's examine a typical situation. You have a King in the hole and a Queen up, while another player has an Ace up. If just the two of you play, he'll win more than half of the pots even if his hole card happens to be a Deuce.

But if a third player enters the pot, you'll get an even break, winning about one third of the pots, provided that the newcomer can't "beat the board" either. How likely this is you must judge for yourself. You know your particular game and I don't.

In the same way a pair of Deuces is a better start than an Ace; it will win more than half the pots even if the Ace has a King along with it.

In a conservative game these facts must control your play. Other players won't be in unless they can beat the high man, and it's bad enough to buck one better hand; it's suicidal to buck more than one.

The following table shows the fate of single pairs in Five-Card Stud, *after all five cards have been dealt.*

PROFIT OR LOSS IN A HUNDRED POTS OF STUD

NUMBER IN POT

Pair	2	3	4	5	6	7	8	9
Deuces	Even	−25	−50	−70	−82	−89½	−94	−96½
Sevens	+32	+30½	+14	−15	−25	−44	−56	−68½
Tens	+54	+77	+80	+72½	+59	+43½	+24	+8
Queens	+68	+113	+140	+152½	+155	+152	+140	+129½
Aces	+83	+150½	+206	+250	+284	+309½	+328	+341

A low pair—Deuces, Threes, or Fours—must improve to win. Sevens figure to show a profit unless there are more than three opponents—raise early, if necessary, to drive out the doubtful players. With Tens or better you want other players to come in.

But any low pair is worth playing.

Suppose you start with Deuces back to back. You'll wind up with better than Deuces about twenty-eight times out of a hundred. As the number of your opponents increases, the amount of money in the pot gets steadily bigger; and although a lot of company occasionally produces a hand big enough to beat your improved Deuces, you still win often enough to make up for those losses and for the seventy-two hands that don't improve.

From these facts we can draw a few conclusions. A very small pair is played for its improvement value. If it doesn't improve, it's a calling hand at best. A middle-sized pair has natural winning chances as well as improvement value. If it doesn't improve, it's a betting hand in a small pot, but a calling hand in a big pot. A high pair is a betting hand in pots of any size.

Of course, you don't bet if you know, or have reason to fear, that there is a better hand out. In such cases the probabilities must be forgotten and you depend on card reading.

Reading the Hands   You must watch every card that shows. In a fast game it may require agile eyes to see every card that folds, but you have to try.

Your first decision to play often depends on observation of the other cards: You wouldn't play on a King in the hole if two other players show Kings, even if your upcard is a Jack or Queen. You may stay for a fourth or fifth card if none of the mates to your cards have been seen, but not if several of them have; your chance of pairing is reduced too much.

More difficult, but equally valuable, is detecting the probable hole card of each opponent.

At the beginning of the hand you can content yourself with assuming that each has either a high card or a mate to the first upcard, but as the deal progresses it becomes more and more important to get a more accurate idea.

Suppose, for example, that A's upcards (in order) are: Seven, Jack, and Queen. From his betting and your knowledge of his style you have him spotted for a pair of Sevens. B's upcards are Eight, Jack, and Queen. You have a Jack down, with Jack, Six, and Eight up. Two Queens have been folded, but you haven't seen an Ace or a King. What conclusions do you draw?

B can't have a Jack in the hole, since all four are accounted

for. For the same reason he cannot have a Queen. It's probable that he has one of the missing Aces and Kings. You
don't worry about the possibility of Eights backed, partly
because of the Eight in your own hand and partly because
your pair of Jacks is not terrified by a pair of spot-cards.
You assume, as a working basis, that B has an Ace or King
in the hole.

Ordinarily you'd avoid giving yourself away, but this time
you have to bet vigorously. You should be very anxious to
drive B out. Of the missing Aces and Kings, there should be
at least five or six still in the deck. B's chance of matching
his hole card is not at all bad—about three out of the total
number of undealt cards. If you make it expensive enough,
B won't draw his last card; if you let him in cheap he may
win the pot.

A player gets a pair back to back about once out of seven-
teen deals; an Ace or a pair, about once in seven deals; a
King, Ace, or pair, about once in five deals; a Queen, King,
Ace, or pair, about twice in seven deals; a Jack or better,
about once in three deals. You can get a fair idea of what
a player stays with by noting how often he draws a second
upcard.

When a player looks a second time at his hole card, he
seldom has much there. He'll remember a really valuable
card and will avoid looking again for fear that another player
may catch a glimpse of it.

Betting Your Open Pairs When you make an open pair, a
skillful opponent will drop unless he has you beaten. Nevertheless you must bet the maximum every time (in a limit
game, that is), or you won't win the maximum when occasionally your hole card gives you three of a kind or two
pairs.

If you get only one call, think back to find out whether
your opponent is a good player or just a die-hard. If he's
good, check to him after you get your next card. It's a grand
feeling when he bets into your cinch hand; and if you haven't
happened to improve, you've saved yourself a raise. If he's

a die-hard, you have to bet to him; you can't let him try to outdraw you without paying for the privilege.

When an open pair is held against you, drop unless you have it beaten. The only exception to this rule occurs when the pot is big and you have a one-card draw to a straight or flush; or when he can't possibly have three of a kind (because the two other cards of the rank are dead) and you have several chances to beat him with three of a kind or two pairs that he can't beat. Even in that case, however, it doesn't pay to call a large bet or to stay in if there is more than one card to go. You're interested only in drawing your last card when the bet is small in comparison to the size of the pot.

Sucker Draws and Bets   Most experienced players know the sort of thing to avoid, but it can do you no harm to glance at a few of them.

It doesn't pay to draw to two-card or three-card flushes and straights. The odds against completing them are terrific. Your decision to stay for two or three more cards should be based on high cards or pairs.

The worst sucker bet in Stud is to a hand that will either raise or drop. A perfect example is an exposed pair of Aces against a possible straight or flush. If your opponent has it, you'll be sorry; if he doesn't, he won't call.

Incidentally there's a saying among Poker players: "Never bet into a possible cinch hand." Take it with two or three grains of salt. It's true that you can't get into much trouble playing so cautiously, but it's no less true that you'll lose a lot of juicy calls. You can afford to get hooked once if you collect five or six other times. The only thing to make sure of is that you're not betting to a hand that must either raise or drop.

SEVEN-CARD STUD

In this game Aces up or low triplets win the average pot, but straights, flushes and full houses are so common that you can't bet on anything less if the exposed cards of the other

players (plus their previous betting) would justify any idea
that higher hands are out. It is both possible and quite common for a player to have a full house without a single pair
showing—as, for example, when he has two Nines and a Six
as his three down cards, and a Nine and a Six among his four
upcards. There is no very good protection against such a case
except when the player has previously bet so boldly that he
must have had a pair or more all the way.

Most of the money losses in Seven-Card Stud can be
blamed on the seductive nature of a game in which you start
with three cards and have four more cards to go. Almost
anything might happen. Nevertheless, the following should
guide your play except in the most liberal games:

Stay in originally only on a concealed pair; a medium split
pair; three cards of the same suit; three cards in sequence
no less than J-10-9; and occasionally an Ace and a King if
the show cards around the table are quite low.

A concealed pair is one with both cards down—for example, two Threes in the hole and a Seven up. A split pair would
be a Three and a Seven in the hole and a Seven up.

Many of the best players hold that a split pair of Fives or
under is not worth an original play. My observation would
lead me to believe that the important decision in Seven-Card
Stud is not made on your first upcard but on your second.
If you play on a low pair and do not improve materially; if
you play on a three-card sequence and do not get a card to
fit it, or at most one removed (as the King or Seven to the
J-10-9); if you play on three low cards of the same suit and
do not get a fourth card or a pairing card or an Ace; drop
fast on the second round of betting.

The general rules of betting apply in Seven-Card Stud as
in Five-Card Stud, except that in Seven-Card Stud you must
be prepared for an occasional freak outcome, like the totally
concealed full house referred to above. This occasional occurrence should not deter you from betting your Aces
up and three of a kind when they seem to be the best hand
out.

LOWBALL

This game is especially popular west of the Rocky Mountains. High hands count for nothing; the lowest hand wins. However, straights and flushes don't count at all, so 7–5–4–3–2 all of one suit, or 8–7–6–5–4, is still a low hand. The Ace is nearly always ranked low, so that the lowest possible hand is 5–4–3–2–A (called a bicycle). A pair of Aces ranks lower than a pair of Deuces.

The average winning hand is Nine high, but in a conservative game no combination containing a Nine or higher card is worth drawing to. The draw by each hand is almost invariably one card, unless the hand is pat, and no draw should be made to four cards headed by more than 8–5 or 7–6. No three-card draw is ever worth while.

The lowest betting hand after the draw is Eight high; the lowest raising hand is Seven high; and to reraise you should have 7–4–3–2–A or a 6–5 hand.

HIGH-LOW DRAW POKER

As usually played, this is simply Draw Poker in which the highest hand and the lowest hand split the pot. In playing for high, play any hand that you would play in regular Draw Poker, and in addition any straight or flush draw, like 8–7–6–5, that might turn out to be low. In this game the Ace is not usually ranked as the low card, and straights and flushes do count, so the lowest possible hand is 7–5–4–3–2 not all of one suit. Any four-card combination headed by Eight or less is worth drawing to; a Ten-high hand is usually low.

The nature of the game is that more players usually draw for low than for high, so that the low hands are only slightly worse than in Lowball (see above); the high hands may run slightly above those in regular Draw Poker because of the additional straights and flushes. Nevertheless, it is usually superior to draw to a good high possibility than to a good low one.

HIGH-LOW SEVEN-CARD STUD

This is regular Seven-Card Stud in which the high and low hands split the pot. However, the same hand may win both ways, using different five-card combinations from the full seven cards. In most games, no declarations are required as to whether the player is trying for high or for low.

Of all the high-low games this is the most appealing and the most exciting. There are two-card, five-card and six-card High-Low Stud games, and a new kind of six-card High-Low Stud called Symington, that are all quite popular; but none of them offers the over-all excitement that the seven-card game does.

One of the great thrills in Poker is to win a pot both ways in a high-low game. This happens more often in the seven-card game than in any other, simply because you have more cards dealt to you from which to pick out both a winning high hand and a winning low hand.

Every High-Low Poker player's dream is to hold something like this:

Down cards: ♠ 6   ♠ 4   ♠ 2
Upcards: ♠ 5   ◇ K   ♡ 7   ♠ 3

The upcards make it appear that you might have a good low, but the hand looks quite harmless for high. Actually you have a straight flush for high and a "perfect low" (7–5–4–3–2) for low. In this game the Ace counts high only.

This hand leads me to the subject of the winning strategy in this game: Generally play for low. Sometimes your low combinations will turn into straights and flushes and you will win high instead, or may win both ways.

The aim of all Poker players is to have a sure thing on the last round of betting. This can often happen to a player going for low—almost never to a player going for high.

Let's say you have an A-K flush made and no pairs are showing on the board at the end of the hand. This fine hand can easily lose to a completely concealed full house, as I mentioned in the section on regular Seven-Card Stud.

I differ with most experts on the type of hand that is worth playing at the start. Many experts advise playing only with three low cards or three of a kind. I believe in playing on quite a few different combinations. The time to drop is after you receive your next card, when you have two up and two down.

However, if you are the kind of player who once you start in a pot can't stop, the advice I am going to give you may get you into some trouble.

Playing for High Any high pair or better is worth playing once, but drop immediately if you don't get three of a kind or two pair on the next card. Here is a very important word of warning: I just wish I had the money I have seen lost on two pair in Seven-Card High-Low Stud. So be prepared to drop even your two pair if you don't improve to a full house in the next card or so, or if the betting gets too high.

Almost any three-card flush or straight should be given one chance, but drop immediately if there is no improvement on the next card.

Playing for Low All authorities say any three cards headed by an Eight are worth playing. I say play any three cards headed by a Nine, but drop if you get a pair or draw a Ten or higher on the next card.

Play once on a low pair and a low card. (This is quite contrary to all other authorities.) If you draw another low card or three of a kind, stay in for another card. Otherwise, drop.

I would even play on this three-card holding: ♡Q ♡5 ♡2. But I drop next time unless I draw a fourth heart or a card below a Nine that does not pair me. In a liberal game I would play once more even if I drew a Nine.

I might even play on ♡10 ♡5 ♣2; but any card

above the Eight, except the ♡9, would cause me to drop on the next round.

The determining factor on borderline hands is: What do I have to gain?

If a questionable hand might turn into a two-way winner, it is worth while taking some risk. Another time to take a chance is when the element of surprise might give you a big pot. An example is when you hold what looks like a low hand and you actually have a concealed full house.

Here is the kind of hand on which you might call even a large bet and stay in for the last card, because you have so much to gain:

Down cards: ◇ 5   ◇ 7
Upcards: ◇ A   ♣ 4   ◇ Q   ♠ 2

If you draw the right low card, you will get low. If you draw any Diamond you will probably win high. And if you draw a very low Diamond you might easily win both ways. Change just one card—make either the five or the seven of Diamonds in the hole some other suit—and I wouldn't dream of calling a big bet, in spite of my chance for low.

DEUCES WILD

The average winning hand is three Aces, but not three natural Aces. The fewer Deuces you have in your hand, the stronger you can expect the other hands to be. Two pairs never win, and if you play on them they should be split. Two Deuces always justify a play, and it is better to draw two cards to two Deuces and an Ace or King than to draw three cards to the two Deuces. A natural three of a kind, except Aces, is not even worth opening the betting. Three cards in sequence and a Deuce, or three cards of a suit and a Deuce, should be played.

AVERAGE WINNING HANDS IN VARIOUS FORMS OF POKER
With Seven in the Game

Draw Poker	Jacks up
Five-Card Stud	Aces or Kings
Seven-Card Stud	Three Eights
Lowball	9–6 high
Deuces Wild	Three Aces
High-Low Draw Poker	{ Jacks up / 9 or 10 high
Spit in the Ocean	Four Tens
Poker with the Bug	Aces up
Poker with a Joker	Three Eights

POSSIBLE POKER HANDS IN A FIFTY-TWO-CARD PACK

Straight flush	40
Four of a kind	624
Full house	3744
Flush	5108
Straight	10,200
Three of a kind	54,912
Two pairs	123,552
One pair	1,098,240
No pair, less than above	1,302,540
Total	2,598,960

CHANCES OF BEING DEALT POKER COMBINATIONS
IN THE ORIGINAL FIVE CARDS

Royal flush	1 in	649,740
Straight flush	1 in	64,974
Four of a kind	1 in	4165
Full house	1 in	694
Flush	1 in	509
Straight	1 in	255
Three of a kind	1 in	47
Two pairs	1 in	21
One pair	1 in	2½
No pair	1 in	2

LAWS OF POKER

The following laws apply to all forms of Poker:

1. Players Two to eight or (in Five-Card Stud) nine. Each plays for himself.

2. The Pack The standard pack of fifty-two cards.

3. Bank of Cards A (high), K, Q, J, 10, 9, 8, 7, 6, 5, 4, 3, 2, A (low only in the sequence 5-4-3-2-A, or in certain forms of Low Poker).

4. Wild Cards A wild card may be designated by its holder to represent any card in the pack he does not actually hold. (The rules of some games permit a wild card to be designated as a duplicate of another card in the hand, so that, for example, a wild card, ♡A, and three other Hearts could be called a "double-Ace-high Heart flush.") In all cases, a wild card may be designated as a card of a fifth suit for making "five of a kind."

5. Rank of Suits The suits have no relative rank in Poker. See Section 13, *Ties*.

6. Seats at the Table Players take seats as they please.

7. First Dealer Any player shuffles the pack and deals the cards, face up, one at a time to each player in turn, and the person to whom the first Jack falls becomes the dealer for the first deal. After this the deal passes around to the left in clockwise rotation, each player dealing in turn. A player may not voluntarily forego his turn to deal.

8. The Shuffle Any player has the right to shuffle the cards, the dealer last. The dealer should shuffle at least once.

9. The Cut After the shuffle the dealer must present the pack to the player on his right to be cut. This player may cut the cards, or he may refuse to do so. At least five cards must be left in each packet when the cards are cut. If there is any confusion in the cut or if a card is exposed in the process, the pack must be reshuffled and cut again.

10. The Deal The cards are dealt one at a time to each player in clockwise rotation, commencing with the player on the dealer's left. Dealing procedure varies with the form of Poker being played. See "Draw Poker" and "Stud Poker."

11. The Pot All the chips bet on the outcome of a deal go into the center of the table and form a pool called the pot. The pot is composed of (a) an ante, or opening contribution of one or more players, as required by the rules of the game, and (b) voluntary bets of the players, each bet representing a player's assertion that he holds the winning hand.

12. Rank of Hands Poker hands rank, from highest to lowest:

a. FIVE OF A KIND Possible only when there are one or more wild cards. As between two hands, each containing five of a kind, the higher-ranking cards win: Five Sixes beat five Threes, etc.

b. STRAIGHT FLUSH Five cards of the same suit in sequence. The Ace is high in the straight flush A-K-Q-J-10 and low in the straight flush 5-4-3-2-A. The highest straight flush is A-K-Q-J-10 of the same suit, called a royal flush. The lowest straight flush is 5-4-3-2-A of the same suit. As between two straight flushes, the one containing the highest card wins.

c. FOUR OF A KIND Four cards of the same rank. As between two hands each containing four of a kind, the four higher-ranking cards win. When there are several wild cards, it is possible for two players to hold four of a kind of the same rank. In this case the winning hand is the one with the higher-ranking fifth card.

d. FULL HOUSE Three cards of one rank and two cards of another rank. As between two full houses, the one with the higher-ranking three-of-a-kind holding is the winner. When there are several wild cards, two players may have full houses in which the three-of-a-kind holdings are of the same rank. In such cases the higher of the two pairs determines the winning hand.

e. FLUSH Five cards of the same suit. As between two flushes, the one containing the highest card wins. If the highest cards are of the same rank, the higher of the two next-highest cards determines the winning hand, and so on.

f. STRAIGHT Five cards in two or more suits, ranking consecutively: as 8-7-6-5-4. The Ace is high in the straight A-K-Q-J-10 and low in the straight 5-4-3-2-A. As between two straights, the one containing the highest card wins, so that 6-5-4-3-2 beats 5-4-3-2-A.

g. THREE OF A KIND Three cards of the same rank. As between two hands, each containing three of a kind, the one with the higher-ranking three of a kind wins. When there are several wild cards, there may be two hands containing identical threes of a kind. In such cases the highest-ranking unmatched card determines the winner. If these cards are of the same rank, the higher-ranking of the fifth cards determines the winner.

h. TWO PAIRS Two cards of one rank and two cards of another rank, with an unmatched fifth card. As between two hands each containing two pairs, the one with the highest pair wins. If the higher pairs are of the same rank, the one with the higher-ranking second pair wins. If these too are of the same rank, the hand containing the higher of the unmatched cards is the winner.

i. ONE PAIR Two cards of the same rank, with three unmatched cards. As between two hands containing pairs of the same rank, the highest unmatched card determines the winner; if these are the same, the higher of the second-highest unmatched cards, and if these are the same, the higher of the third unmatched cards.

j. NO PAIR As between two such hands, the one containing the highest card wins; if these two cards are tied, the next-highest card decides, and so on.

13. *Ties* If the two highest hands are in all respects the same except for suits, they divide the pot. Wild cards rank in all respects as equivalent to the "natural" cards they represent, but an odd chip in the pot when it is divided should go to the hand containing fewer wild cards.

14. *Rotation* The turn to bet begins with the assigned first

bettor, according to the rules of the game, and passes from player to player to the left, skipping over players who have dropped.

15. Betting　Each player in turn, in each betting interval, must either bet that his hand is the best, or must drop; however, in most forms of Poker a player is permitted to check, which is a bet of nothing, provided always that no bet of one or more chips has been made by another player in that betting interval. (In theory a player who checks is making a bet so small that it is not worth while putting that amount in the pot.) In every case, to stay in the pot, a player must put in enough chips to make the total he has bet at least equal to any other player's.

Therefore a player has these options when his turn comes:

a. He may drop, discard his hand, and forego any further interest in that pot. Once a player has discarded his hand, or in turn has announced that he drops, he may not change his mind and remain in the pot.

b. He may check, or may bet any number of chips up to the limit, if no other player has bet during that betting interval.

c. He may call the bet of any player before him, by putting into the pot exactly enough chips to equalize that player's bet. For example, A bets two; B bets four, representing a two-chip raise; A may call by putting in two more chips, for then his total contribution will be four chips, the same as B's.

d. He may raise by putting in more chips than he needs to call, up to the limit. The excess over the number of chips needed to call constitutes the amount of his raise. (See the example in the preceding paragraph.)

16. Betting Interval　A betting interval begins when the assigned first bettor checks or bets; it ends when all bets have been equalized (including a case in which all players have checked), or when all players but one have dropped.

A player may not raise his own bet, or reraise his own raise, if no other player has raised after him; for in such case the bets must have been equalized and the betting interval is ended. For example, A is the first bettor and bets two; B, C, and D each call, putting in two each; all other players drop. A may not increase his two-chip bet. But: A bets two; B raises, making it four; C and D call for four each; the others drop. A may raise again, putting in two chips to call B's raise plus as many more chips as the limit allows.

At the end of the betting interval, if all players but one have dropped, the surviving player takes the pot; if two or more players remain, the dealing is resumed in accordance with the rules of the game; or, if it was the final betting interval, there is a showdown.

17. The Showdown Whenever two or more players remain after the final betting interval, each must show his full hand face up on the table. The player with the highest-ranking Poker hand then takes the pot. It is not necessary for a player to announce what hand he has; and if he does so announce, and makes the wrong announcement, it does not affect the result of the pot: "The cards speak for themselves." But if a player discards his hand after another player's announcement, he may not later claim the pot even if the announcement is proved to have been incorrect, for a hand once discarded may not be reclaimed and a player without a legal hand cannot win a pot.

In the showdown a player who concedes victory to another player may not discard his hand without showing it. The right to see every hand at the showdown belongs to all players at the table, including those who have previously dropped. But if a player makes a bet that no one else calls, he takes the pot without showing his hand; and a player who drops at any previous time need not show his hand.

IRREGULARITIES

The following rules govern irregularities that are common to all forms of Poker:

18. Misdeal, Redeal A distinction is drawn between a misdeal, which is deemed to be the dealer's fault; and a redeal, in which the error necessitating another deal is not necessarily chargeable to the dealer.

A misdeal loses the deal (the deal being an advantage in Poker); the next dealer in turn deals. Any ante made by the dealer or antes made by all players, if all ante equally, remain in the pot. A misdeal may be called only by a player who has not intentionally seen any face-down card dealt to him, and only if:

a. The pack was not shuffled, or was not offered for cutting, provided the dealer has not begun dealing the second round of cards.

b. The dealer gives two face-up cards to the same player in Draw Poker (or any other form of closed Poker), provided the misdeal is immediately called by the player in question.

c. The dealer gives too many cards to more than one player. However, the dealer may withdraw surplus cards and restore them to the pack unless a player objects.

A redeal requires a new shuffle and cut and a new deal by the same dealer. It too may be called only by a player who has not intentionally seen a face-down card dealt to him, and only before the dealing of the second round of cards begins, if:

d. A card was exposed in cutting, or the cut left fewer than five cards in each packet.

e. Two or more cards are faced in the pack.

f. The pack is incorrect or imperfect in any way.

g. A player is dealing out of turn (in this case the deal reverts to the proper dealer).

If no misdeal or redeal is called within the time limits above, the deal stands as a regular deal in turn.

19. Irregularities in Betting

a. BETTING OUT OF TURN Any player who bets out of turn, whether it is to bet, raise, or call, must leave in the pot any chips already contributed. Play is resumed at the proper place and the player in error may make the same bet and meet any raises, or else contribute the amount that he put in, and drop; and he may not add chips to raise.

b. PASSING OUT OF TURN   A player who passes out of turn is out of play for that hand.

c. IMPROPER BETTING   Chips once placed in the pot even by mistake, may not be taken out again.

d. LOOKING AT DISCARDS   No one may look at another player's discards.

e. FOUL HAND   Any hand with more or less than the correct number of cards, or the hand of a player who opened without openers, is foul whenever discovered, and cannot win a pot. If a player has a foul hand on the call and there is another player with a fair hand with which to contend it, the player with the fair hand gets the pot, regardless of the value of his hand. If there are two players in the call in this case, the one with the higher hand gets the pot. If there are no players with legal hands in the call, the pot remains on the table and is added to the next pot.

f. INCORRECT PACK   When an incorrect pack is discovered (wrong number or duplication of cards), play is abandoned immediately and all bets in that pot returned to the players. This rule does not apply to previous deals, played before the incorrect pack was discovered.

g. CARDS EXPOSED BY PLAYERS   There is no penalty when a player exposes his own card, nor any redress. The player may continue in the play.

h. DEALING THE LAST CARD   Under no circumstances may the last card be dealt to a player. If, because of the large number of players or the type of game played, the dealer finds that all cards but one have been dealt, this card must be placed among the discards. The discards are then shuffled and cut for further dealing.

LAWS OF DRAW POKER

Five cards are dealt, one at a time, face down, to each player in rotation. There is then a betting interval, after which each active player in turn may discard one or more cards, and the dealer serves him that number of cards from the top of the pack, to restore his hand to five cards. After the draw there is another betting interval, and if two or more players remain after this betting interval, there is a showdown.

The Draw

1. Method of the Deal   All players who have stayed in may draw cards to improve their hands. A player may discard any or all of his original five cards, or he may "stand pat" by keeping his original hand. Each player in turn must state distinctly the number of cards that he wishes, which are at once given to him off the top of the pack. When serving himself, the dealer must state aloud the number of cards that he takes.

If the opener in a game of Jackpots remains in the game for the draw, he may place his discard under the chips in front of him, regardless of what he holds or what he is drawing to. This discard must remain there throughout the game, even if other discards are gathered up and redealt. He may split his opening qualifications if he wishes to do so, and he is not obliged to state this fact. He need not put his discards in the pot.

Dealing cards for the draw begins with the active player on the dealer's left and proceeds as usual from one active player to another around the table. No player should discard until it is his turn to draw cards.

2. Incorrect Dealing in the Draw

a. EXPOSED CARD   If a card is found faced in the pack, exposed by the dealer in dealing, turned over by the wind in the deal, or otherwise shown so that it can be identified by name by any player: A player must accept such exposed card if it is the first card drawn or to be drawn by him; any subsequent exposed card which would have fallen to the same player must be placed face down among the discards. It cannot be replaced until all other players, including the dealer, have been served their required number of cards.

b. INCORRECT NUMBER OF CARDS   If a player asks for the correct number of cards and the dealer fails to give them to him, the error must be corrected the moment the dealer's attention is called to it, provided that the player has not lifted or looked at any of the drawn cards, in which case his hand is foul. If he has not looked at them and has a surplus card, this card should be placed on the top of the pack and dealt in the usual order. If he has too few cards, additional cards should be supplied immediately, without waiting for others to be served; but if any card has been served to a player after him, he may only increase his discard to make room for the excess draw, or drop.

c. DRAW OUT OF TURN If a player allows a person on his left to be served out of his proper turn, he must play the hand without drawing, or abandon it. If he has discarded, his hand is foul. (Some permit such a player to play with an insufficient number of cards.)

d. CARD KNOWN TO PLAYER DRAWING IT Whether or not the player to be served can see a card about to be dealt to him, unless it is exposed on the table, he must take that card.

e. IRREGULAR DRAW BY DEALER If the dealer deals too many cards for himself, he must take them. If he looks at any of them before discarding enough cards to accept them, his hand is foul. If he has not looked at any of the cards drawn, he must discard enough cards from his original hand to make a correct number with the draw.

If the dealer takes too few cards, his hand is foul. (Some players allow the dealer to play with an insufficient number of cards.)

f. IRREGULAR DRAW CORRECTED If a player asks for too few cards before discarding and before the next player has been served, the error may be corrected. If he has looked at any of his new cards, his hand is foul.

If a player asks for too many cards before discarding and before the next player has been served, the error may be corrected. If he has looked at any of the cards to be drawn, his hand is foul. If he has not discarded and the next player has been served, he may correct the error by discarding enough cards from his original hand to make a correct number with the draw.

g. SHUFFLING AND CUTTING   Not allowed, except when the cards are exhausted and discards must be used for further draws.

h. A player must have five cards, including his discard and the cards held in his hand, in order to draw.

i. A card taken from a player's hand and discarded face down on the table may not be taken back under any circumstances.

j. No player is allowed to give any information concerning the number of cards drawn by a player, except in the case of the dealer. A player who is still in the game and has not yet bet may ask how many cards the dealer drew, and the dealer must give the required information.

k. If a player, before discarding, intentionally sees the face of any card dealt to him in the draw, his hand is foul.

3. *Final Betting Interval*   After the draw has been completed, the final betting interval starts. The duty of starting the betting falls to the player who opened the pot before the draw. If the opener is not still in the game, the privilege passes to the next active player to his left.

If the opener drops, he must show his opening qualifications face up, and the rest of his hand face down, in order to prove a fair hand of five cards.

4. *False Openers*   If a player has opened without the necessary qualifications, or has a foul hand, the following rules apply:

a. If it is discovered after the draw that the pot was opened falsely, the opener's hand is foul and he loses all claim to the pot. In addition he forfeits any of his chips already bet. Those players still in the game are allowed to remain and play, regardless of the false opening.

b. If the opener announces before the draw that he does not have openers, any player who has openers and wishes to open may announce the fact. This player takes the place of the original opener, and the game proceeds. If there is no opener, all players except the false opener withdraw their bets and the deal passes. The antes and the bets of the false opener remain in the pot for the next deal.

c. If no one calls the false opener before the draw, all chips remain in the pot for the next deal. If no one calls the false opener after the draw, all other players may withdraw from the pot any chips they put in, except antes; but the opener's chips and the antes remain in the pot for the next deal.

d. If the false opening is not discovered before the showdown, the opener's hand is foul and the pot goes to the highest fair hand; if all hands have been abandoned, the pot remains upon the table for the next deal.

LAWS OF STUD POKER

In Stud Poker each player receives one or more cards, face down—his hole cards—and his remaining cards face up. There is a betting interval after each round of face-up cards is dealt, and—in Seven-Card Stud—an additional betting interval after the deal of the last cards, which are dealt face down.

1. Five-Card Stud There is no ante (except by special house rule). The dealer gives each player in rotation a face-down card, then each player in rotation a face-up card. The deal is then interrupted for the first betting interval.

In each betting interval the player with the highest Poker combination showing in his face-up cards has the first right to bet. In the first betting interval this person must make a bet of at least the minimum established for the game; in any later betting interval the player may check.

If two players tie for high card, or for the highest Poker combination showing, the one nearest the dealer's left (that is, the one dealt first) outranks the other for purposes of betting first. In the showdown this factor is not considered and identical hands tie.

Following the first betting interval the dealer gives another face-up card to each active player in rotation; there is another betting interval, another round of face-up cards to the remaining active players, another betting interval, then a final round of face-up cards and a final betting interval. If two or more players remain after the final betting interval, there is a showdown in which each player turns up his hole card. If a bet or raise goes uncalled in any betting interval, the pot is taken and the deal passes in rotation.

A player who drops must immediately turn down all his face-up cards.

It is the dealer's duty, after each round of cards is dealt, to designate the first bettor (as by saying, "First King bets," "Pair of Sixes bets," etc.); and, after the third and fourth face-up cards are dealt, also to indicate holdings that may become straights or flushes ("Possible straight," "Possible flush"). A possible straight or flush has no effect on the determination of the first bettor.

2. *Seven-Card Stud* (also called Down the River, Peek Poker, or Seven-Toed Pete)   In the initial deal each player receives two cards face down and then one card face up, all dealt one at a time in rotation. There is then a betting interval. Each active player then receives three more face-up cards and one more face-down card in that order, with the deal interrupted for a betting interval after each round of cards is dealt. In the showdown, each player turns up all his hole cards and selects five of his seven cards as his hand; he must separate these five cards from the other two, which he discards. The cards then speak for themselves, as in any other form of Poker, and the player may not reclaim his two discards if he finds he could have made a better five-card combination.

3. *Irregularities in Stud Poker*

   a. BOTTOM CARD EXPOSED   If a player can correctly name the bottom card of the pack, before any voluntary bet has been made, there must be a new shuffle and cut before the deal is resumed. (It is wise to keep a blank card on the bottom of the pack.)

   b. CARD FACED IN PACK   If a card is found faced in the pack before the dealer has completed dealing the first round of face-up cards, or before he has completed dealing any later round of cards, the player to whom that card falls must take it. If a faced card appears at the end of any round of cards except the first, Section e, below, applies.

c. EXPOSING A HOLE CARD If a player exposes his own hole card, he should turn it down immediately and continue play without penalty or redress. If the dealer exposes a card in dealing a hole card, this card should remain exposed and the next card dealt to the player face down. If the dealer, by mistake, continues to deal face-up cards to that player, the player has no redress until he has received four cards (in Seven-Card Stud, five cards) all face up; at this point he may withdraw from the pot any chips that he has contributed up to this time. The dealer must not intentionally serve any such card face up. If the player chooses to stay in and receives his last card face up, he may withdraw from the pot, withdrawing all chips he has put in, and the dealer must supply chips to replace them.

d. INCORRECT DEALING OF EXPOSED CARDS If a dealer omits a player in dealing the exposed cards, the cards already dealt must be shifted backward until the player has his proper card, and the deal proceeds.

e. (i) OPTIONAL If during any betting interval a card of the pack is illegally exposed (either faced in the pack or prematurely dealt), such card is placed on the bottom of the pack but the deal continues and every player receives the card he would have received in regular rotation. For example: Five are still in the pot—A, B, C, D, E. Dealer mistakenly deals six cards. The sixth card is placed on the bottom of the pack. On the next round of dealing, the dealer gives the first card to B, and so on in order, giving A his card last.

(ii) OPTIONAL Before dealing the next round, the dealer must burn (discard) from the top of the deck as many cards as there are active players in the pot, this number of cards to include any card prematurely dealt.

LOW AND HIGH-LOW POKER

1. High-Low Poker Any form of Poker may be played high-low; most games in which there are many wild cards, and most Seven-Card Stud games are now played high-low. In a high-low game there are usually two winners of the pot, the player with the highest hand taking one half the pot and the player with the lowest hand taking the other half, the high hand taking the odd chip if the pot will not divide evenly. But in some cases there may be a single winner, thus:

2. *Seven-Card High-Low Stud*   Each player in the show-down may select any five of his cards as his high hand and any five as his low hand; he may win both ways and take the entire pot.

3. *Declarations*   Some play that after the final betting interval, but before the showdown, each player must declare whether he is trying for high, or for low, or for both. There are three methods of declaring, and the players should agree in advance which will be used. The methods are:

   a. Each player in turn, beginning with the player on the dealer's left, states whether he is playing for high or low, before any hands are shown to the table.

   b. Before any hands are shown, each player decides whether he is playing for high or low. If he decides upon low, he takes a white chip in his hand without letting other players see it; a red chip if he decides upon high. When all have decided, the players expose the colors of their chips. If all players in the call decide the same way, the best hand that way takes the whole pot.

   c. Playing for both high and low. In addition to taking a white or red chip, as explained in the preceding paragraph, the player may take a blue chip to signify that he is contending for both high and low. The player selects mentally two hands of five cards each from among the cards that he holds; this is possible when playing with wild cards or in Seven-Card Stud. If a player claims both high and low, and is tied or beaten on either, he loses any title to the pot. If no one wins in full accordance with his declaration, all declarations are disregarded and the active players divide the pot equally.

4. *Rank of Low Hands*   The usual rank of Poker hands is observed: therefore, the lowest possible hand is 7–5–4–3–2, not all of one suit. Players are apt to become confused in

ranking the low hands; the easiest way to avoid confusion is to determine which is the higher of two hands, according to the usual Poker standards, whereupon the other must be the lower. For example, 8–7–4–3–2 and 8–6–5–4–3; the 8–6 hand is the lower, because in regular Poker it would lose to the 8–7 hand in the showdown; the Deuce in the 8–7 hand has nothing to do with it because Poker hands are ranked from the top down.

5. *Lowball* Every pot is won by the lowest hand. Straights and flushes do not count, and the Ace is always low. The lowest hand is 5–4–3–2–A, called a bicycle or wheel. There are no minimum requirements for opening a pot.

GIN

1. Minimize mechanical errors by orderly arrangement of your hand.

2. Get on score before playing for big hands.

3. Expect opponent's early discard to be a "fish."

4. It is more important to make safe discards from poor hands than from good hands.

5. With poor hands pick up a card that gives you a double combination—don't with good hands.

6. Don't break up your hand to hold a doubtful player for your opponent.

7. It usually pays to knock as soon as possible.

8. Late in the game, risk adding to opponent's meld rather than throw a live card.

9. Don't lose your composure, no matter how bad your cards—it only helps your opponent.

10. Don't play hunches—play percentages.

GIN RUMMY

As much money changes hands at Gin Rummy as at any other card game. It is one of the finest two-handed games, and is also an excellent game for four, six, or eight players.

I believe its popularity is due to three reasons: (a) it is easy to learn; (b) in two-handed, as generally played, you don't have a partner to find fault with you; (c) everyone thinks he is good at the game. Contract Bridge is a difficult game, and you have a partner to point out your errors. One is seldom convinced that he is the local champ, without some foundation. Gin being a game of far less skill, even poor players win occasionally, so that everyone becomes convinced that he plays well. In no other game do you find so many self-elected local authorities.

Before I try to convert you from a run-of-the-mill player to a consistent winner, let me dispel at once a popular misconception—that "Gin is all luck." Nothing could be further from the truth. Gin involves a certain amount of psychology, like Poker, the laws of probability, like Bridge, and knowledge of the opponents, like Canasta. Don't misunderstand me: I am not saying that Gin is one of the highly scientific games. It is not. But there is a great deal of skill in it. If you lose, it is because you are not as good as the other fellow, not because of the "awful cards" you hold.

PLAN YOUR STRATEGY

Arranging the Hand On picking up your hand arrange the cards so that all combinations are evident at a glance. This

advice may seem superfluous, yet I have been amazed at how
many experienced Gin players occasionally throw a useful
card because they failed to notice its connection with another:

Usually all combinations will show up well enough if you
arrange your hand by rank. But sometimes a card is better
placed out of order of rank, to show a sequence connection.
Suppose you pick up:

♠	♡	◊	♡	♡	♠	♣	♠	♣	◊	(Ex. 1)
3	Q	8	10	2	K	6	Q	8	7

A natural arrangement is as follows:

♠	♠	♡	♡	♣	♣	◊	◊	♠	♡
K	Q	Q	10	6	8	8	7	3	2

However, if you invariably put all your high cards at the
left, and low cards at the right, you will often present your
opponent with valuable information. I do not say that it is
ethical to watch where a player pulls his discards from, or
where he puts the cards he keeps, but I do say that the most
ethical player in the world cannot blind himself to information thrust upon him by thoughtless opponents. We have
all seen the player who, when he draws a card from the stock
that gives him a meld, elaborately reassorts his hand. Such
mannerisms thrust themselves on the attention and tell a
story even if you try not to see them.

Telltale habits to be avoided are:

1. Always sorting the hand in the same way, as high to
low from left to right. Mix up the order occasionally—high
cards in the middle, or on the other end.

2. Reassorting the hand at any time. Put a card in the
right place the first time, and let it stay there until you discard
it or until you knock.

3. Making breaks in your fan of cards so as to separate
melds from unmatched cards.

4. Betraying that you want the upcard, before opponent,
having first choice, has refused it. In this connection I wish
to tell a story on a good friend, one of the foremost card

players of the country. After a long series of Gin battles between us he remarked to me:

"Johnny, I wish I could guess right as often as you do. I know that I hold my cards close, and you don't get a peek, but every time I deal and I want the upcard, you take it. I know that you know I want it, because many times it is no use to you."

I replied, "You know I never guess when I have a sure thing."

"What do you mean?"

"I suppose I shouldn't tell you, because it will cut off a lucrative source of revenue. But here it is: you never leave me in doubt when you want the upcard. You pick out your discard, put it at the end of your hand, and look at me expectantly. When you don't want the upcard, you sit back and wait your turn without a move."

Estimating the Hand   Your hand usually falls into one of the following categories:

(a) Excellent—needing one or two perfect picks to knock. (The kind of hand my opponent always holds!) For example:

♠ ♡ ◇ ♠ ♡ ♡ ♠ ◇ ♣ ◇   (Ex. 2)
K K K 10 10 9 3 2 A A

You already have one meld, four low cards, and a three-card combination toward a second meld. You could not ask for more.

With a fine hand like this plan to discard any odd card you draw for several rounds, and to knock the moment you fill the second set.

(b) Fair—two potential melds and several low cards. The great preponderance of hands dealt fall in this category—neither very good nor very bad. For example:

♣ ♣ ◇ ◇ ♠ ♠ ♡ ♡ ♣ ◇   (Ex. 3)
J Q Q J 7 6 6 5 2 A

With such a wealth of combinations this hand has excellent chance to fill two melds quickly. It is not in the first category, however, since you will have to get at least three right cards before you can knock.

Another typical example:

$$\diamond \; \spadesuit \; \diamond \; \clubsuit \; \heartsuit \; \spadesuit \; \spadesuit \; \clubsuit \; \diamond \; \heartsuit \quad \text{(Ex. 4)}$$
$$\text{K} \; 10 \; 10 \; 8 \; 7 \; 7 \; 6 \; 3 \; 2 \; \text{A}$$

This is not so strong in combinations as the previous example, but is about an average hand. Three perfect draws would put you down.

With hands of this category plan to play offensively for several rounds, keeping all the combinations. After that your course will depend on whether you have improved.

(c) Poor—requiring four or more perfect cards to be able to knock. For example:

$$\heartsuit \; \diamond \; \clubsuit \; \heartsuit \; \spadesuit \; \clubsuit \; \diamond \; \spadesuit \; \diamond \; \clubsuit \quad \text{(Ex. 5)}$$
$$\text{K} \; \text{J} \; 10 \; 10 \; 8 \; 6 \; 5 \; 4 \; 3 \; 2$$

With such hands you should begin thinking of safety at once. This doesn't mean to give up your chance of winning the hand, but you choose your discards carefully.

Offense vs. Defense   On 90% of the hands you pick up you should play an offensive game for at least the first two rounds. This means that you should discard what is useless to you, keeping all your combinations intact.

Even with a poor hand you commence by looking to improvement of the hand, rather than balking your opponent. Until he has made a couple of discards, you have no idea anyhow what he can use and what he can't.

With a good hand you of course save all your live combinations and let go what you must to do this.

As the play progresses you may be compelled to change gradually to defensive strategy. You will have a basis for it in the inferences to be drawn from your opponent's discards, from the cards (if any) that he has taken, from the table and from the discards he has failed to take.

EARLY PLAY

The Upcard   If you are the first player, and the upcard is an Ace, you should always take it unless you have such an excellent hand that it is absolutely no use to you. With most hands you will need to collect low cards as well as fillers, and the Ace is ideal. Furthermore, if you let the Ace go, your opponent may take it, to his great benefit. For example:

♡ ♣ ◇ ◇ ♣ ♠ ♡ ♡ ♠ ♡   (Ex. 6)
K Q Q J 10 10 10 9 2 2

Holding this hand, take the Ace automatically. Discard the King, and hope to get another low card to replace the Nine, besides a filler for the three-card combination.

♡ ◇ ♣ ♠ ◇ ♣ ♠ ◇ ♠ ◇   (Ex. 7)
K Q J J 10 8 8 6 3 2

This is a poor hand. You take the Ace automatically lest your opponent get it and knock before your hand has materially improved.

♡ ♣ ♣ ♠ ◇ ♡ ♡ ♠ ◇ ♡   (Ex. 8)
J J 10 8 8 8 3 2 2 A

Here is one of the rare cases where you should refuse the Ace. It would not help your hand appreciably. You already have all the low cards you need. Taking it just to keep it away from your opponent seems useless, because your discard would have to be a low card (the ♡3). Better to pass, and so keep the advantage of the first draw from the stock.

Speculation Normally you take the discard only if it completes a new spread. The only exception I have so far discussed is the taking of a low card, when you need low cards for a two-meld knock.

But it sometimes pays to take the discard on sheer speculation. If you pick your "angle" for this play, a speculation not only helps your hand, but often has a demoralizing effect on your opponent.

There are good and bad speculations. To take the discard merely to make a two-card combination is a poor investment. If the improvement of your hand is the sole object, speculate only for a three-card combination. Thus, take the ◇10 when you hold the ♡10 and ◇9, or even the ♠10 and ◇Q.

I do not mean to imply that speculating to make a three-card combination is always good. On the contrary, it is good only in certain circumstances.

Speculate only with a poor hand. If you have a good hand, draw from the stock. You may get a filler. Even with a poor hand, take the discard only if it is almost as good as you might get from the stock.

$$\spadesuit \quad \clubsuit \quad \heartsuit \quad \diamondsuit \quad \heartsuit \quad \diamondsuit \quad \diamondsuit \quad \heartsuit \quad \heartsuit \quad \clubsuit \quad \text{(Ex. 9)}$$
$$\text{K} \quad \text{Q} \quad 10 \quad 9 \quad 7 \quad 5 \quad 5 \quad 4 \quad 2 \quad \text{A}$$

Upcard: the $\diamondsuit$ 10

You may well take the $\diamondsuit$ 10. This turns a very poor hand into a fairly good hand with two playable combinations. This purpose is at the moment more important than filling a spread among your low cards.

Let's change just one card in Example 9, thus:

$$\spadesuit \quad \spadesuit \quad \clubsuit \quad \heartsuit \quad \diamondsuit \quad \diamondsuit \quad \heartsuit \quad \heartsuit \quad \heartsuit \quad \clubsuit \quad \text{(Ex. 10)}$$
$$\text{K} \quad \text{Q} \quad \text{Q} \quad 10 \quad 9 \quad 5 \quad 5 \quad 4 \quad 2 \quad \text{A}$$

Now you should not take the $\diamondsuit$ 10. Enough of your high cards are already connected. You have two three-card combinations—you don't want another.

Always bear in mind the factors against speculating:

1. You lose a draw from the stock, which might give you a spread.

2. You warn your opponent what not to discard.

3. You lose the opportunity to assure yourself of some fairly safe discards by refusing the discard. Thus, if you refuse it in Example 10, you can then discard the $\heartsuit$ 10 and $\diamondsuit$ 9 with fair safety.

Warning your opponent what not to discard is a weapon that cuts both ways. You may compel him to keep in hand several odd cards, only one of which would help you but all of which embarrass him. Used deliberately for this purpose, the speculation is one of the subtlest weapons at your disposal. It is most effective as to the original upcard. Your opponent's early discards are likely to be odd cards: taking one of them has much less chance to tie up other cards in his hand.

There are even occasions to speculate in the upcard, not to improve your hand, but to mislead your opponent. Gin experts sometimes indulge in this sort of bluff:

♡ ◇ ♣ ♣ ♡ ◇ ♣ ♣ ♡ ♡ (Ex. 11)
K Q Q J 6 5 4 2 2 A
Upcard: the ♠8

Take the ♠8 and throw the ♡K. The potential gains by this play are:

1. He might easily have used the ♠8.

2. The ♡K is safer to give him. It also advertises for you, encouraging a discard of the ♣K or ♡Q.

3. Your opponent may be forced to hold some useless odd cards—Eights, and Spades near in rank to the Eight. In consequence he is more likely to let go cards that you actually want.

Contrast the above hand with:

♡ ◇ ♡ ♡ ♠ ◇ ♣ ♠ ♡ ♣ (Ex. 12)
K 10 10 9 5 5 4 2 2 A
Upcard: the ♠8

Here it would be folly to take the ♠8. The last thing in the world you want to do is discourage your opponent from discarding the ♡8 or ♠10.

Offensive Position As I said before, your first couple of plays should be chiefly offensive. At this early stage your only object is to win the hand. After two or three rounds, unless your hand is unusually good, you must consider defense as well as offense.

Here is an example. The upcard is the ♣10, which you both refuse. Your opponent draws, then discards the ♡Q. You draw, and your hand then is:

♡ ♡ ◇ ♣ ♠ ♡ ♠ ♠ ♡ ◇ ♣ (Ex. 13)
10 8 6 6 6 K 7 4 3 2 A

The question is what to discard. The ♡10 is almost 100% safe. But to give it up now would be unthinkable. Should you next get the ♡9, you could actually knock at once. So the choice rests between your two odd cards. Let the ♡K go, as the safer of the two—it could be used only for Kings.

Your opponent draws from the stock, then discards another

King. You draw the ♢9. Now you should discard the ♠7, which has an element of safety, as you have the ♠6. It would be poor play at this point to advertise with the completely dangerous ♢9.

Your next draw is the ♡4. Now, unless your opponent has just thrown a Nine, you had better give up hope for the ♡9 and throw the safe ♡10.

Calling One Card   After several turns you hold:

$$\spadesuit \quad \heartsuit \quad \heartsuit \quad \heartsuit \quad \diamondsuit \quad \clubsuit \quad \spadesuit \quad \diamondsuit \quad \clubsuit \quad \spadesuit \quad \text{(Ex. 14)}$$
$$\text{J} \quad \text{J} \quad 10 \quad 7 \quad 7 \quad 7 \quad 3 \quad 3 \quad 2 \quad \text{A}$$

Now you draw the ♣Q. No Queens or high Clubs have shown. However, two Nines (but not the ♡9) have been discarded.

You should gamble by discarding the ♣Q. If it gets by, you are almost sure to win. To break up such a pat hand at an early stage is unthinkable.

A fine point of percentage play in choosing between wild discards is shown by the next example. After a couple of turns you have been so fortunate as to collect this lovely hand:

$$\spadesuit \quad \clubsuit \quad \diamondsuit \quad \heartsuit \quad \clubsuit \quad \spadesuit \quad \diamondsuit \quad \clubsuit \quad \spadesuit \quad \heartsuit \quad \diamondsuit \quad \text{(Ex. 15)}$$
$$\text{K} \quad \text{K} \quad \text{K} \quad \text{Q} \quad \text{Q} \quad \text{Q} \quad 9 \quad 5 \quad 3 \quad 2 \quad \text{A}$$

You will of course discard either the ♢9 or ♣5; any of fifteen cards will then allow you to knock. Both of these cards are wild—either may fill a set for your opponent. The correct choice then is the ♣5. If he fills, he reduces his count less than if he filled with the ♢9.

DISCARDING

Proper discarding can turn a losing Gin player into a winner overnight. As in Canasta, Samba, and a great many other games, throwing the proper card at the proper time can make a tremendous difference. Whatever your general play may be, in throwing away your odd cards at the beginning of each hand, you must *vary your strategy*.

Advertising   Advertising (also called baiting, fishing, or booting) is the discard of a card in the hope that your opponent will discard another card of the same ranks which you want.

This is a delightful plan—when it works. The best time to advertise is on your first or second discard. Your ad card is nearly always a wide-open card which the opponent might use for either a sequence or a group. The early stage is the only time to figure that you might get away with throwing such a complete "stranger." Any time after your first couple of plays, an advertising card may be very dangerous, as by that time your opponent will have had several plays in which to match up his hand.

Here is an excellent principle to guide your advertising campaign:

If you have a card safer than your "advertiser," throw it; if you have two or three equally wild cards, throw the "fish."

♠	♡	◇	♠	♠	♡	♣	◇	♠	◇	♡	(Ex. 16)
K	K	K	J	10	10	9	5	2	A	A	

If this is your hand after drawing on your first or second play, you automatically discard the ♣9, hoping to bait your opponent into throwing you the ♠9 or ♣10. At your third or fourth turn the ♣9 should be viewed with considerable suspicion as to its safety, although with such a well-set-up hand, you would have to risk it. After five or six plays, if no Nines, or Clubs in the neighborhood, have shown up, you should break up your Jack-Ten-Ten combination, and salt away the ♣9.

Spotting an Ad Your opponent will always advertise, if able, on his first or second discard. If you have a card that offers any safety whatsoever, throw it rather than answer a "fish." For example:

♠	♣	◇	♡	♣	♡	◇	◇	♣	♡	♠	(Ex. 17)
K	Q	10	8	5	5	5	3	3	2	A	

This is your hand after your first draw. Your opponent drew first, and discarded the ♣10.

The natural inclination is to discard the ◇10. But either the King or Queen is preferable. Withhold the ◇10 until the situation is clarified, or until you have to let it go to avoid discarding the completely wild ♡8.

Study your opponent's game and learn his habits. Many players cannot throw a "fish" casually. They squirm or twist or in some way give away their anxiety about the fate of the card. Apart from such mannerisms, a player will occasionally betray himself by an unnatural sequence of discards. I know of one player so stereotyped that he will even make this giveaway play:

Part of his hand: ♡K ♠J ♠10 ♡10 ♣9   (Ex. 18)
                    Upcard: the ◇K

He is so anxious to fish with his Nine that he will throw it first, and then on his next play, will throw the safe King. If you are a shrewd player you will notice this and be wary of throwing him a Nine.

Discarding Habits Many Gin players develop little habits which, if you catch on to them, will stand you in good stead. Some players are "King holders." They always hang on to an odd King until it is safe to throw. Others always throw from the top, that is, they start out automatically throwing their highest odd card, starting with the King and going right on down the line.

Many players are apt to follow the trend that is started at the beginning of each hand. Have you ever noticed how many hands of Gin start out with the first eight or ten discards all falling in a group? Either all the Kings, Queens, and Jacks show up, or a large number of Nines, Eights and Sevens, or occasionally every Ace, Deuce, and Three will be thrown away in the first few plays. For want of a recognized name, I call this "zone discarding."

Zone Trapping Zone discarding develops so often that you should make every effort to start the trend in the direction that suits you best. Go in for "zone trapping."

♡ ◇ ♣ ♡ ♠ ◇ ◇ ♣ ♡ ♠ ♣   (Ex. 19)
Q 9 9 7 6 6 4 3 2 A A
          Upcard: the ◇8

Throw the ♡7. Your opponent, seeing an Eight and a Seven, may easily throw either a Six or Nine, just to stay in the zone that has been started. If you throw the ♡Q, he may stay in the high zone, and not throw you a useful card for some time.

♠	♡	◇	♣	♣	◇	♡	♠	◇	◇	♣	(Ex. 20)
J	9	9	9	5	4	4	3	2	A	A	

Upcard: the ♣7

Throw the ♣5. It has certain safety (the ♣7 turned up) and may encourage your opponent to throw some fairly low card like a Four. If you start the Jack, you may play several rounds before you are fortunate enough to draw your own Four.

♠	♡	◇	♣	♡	♠	◇	♣	◇	♠	♡	(Ex. 21)
K	K	J	9	9	9	5	4	2	A	A	

Upcard: the ◇7

Here, even though you have the ◇5, which has certain safety because of the turned-up ◇7, start your own trend by throwing the ◇J. This may start a picture-card pattern and give you a King very quickly.

Breaking Combinations The switch to defensive-offense, after the opening rounds of purely offensive play, often entails breaking up some of your combinations. Make every effort to choose the safest discards, while leaving yourself in a playable position.

Suppose that the question is which of these two pairs to split:

◇	♣	♡	◇	(Ex. 22)
Q	Q	9	9	

If any Queen or Nine has already been discarded, you will of course pick that rank to split. With no such guide break the pair that offers the two safest discards. If the ♣J or ◇J is dead, break the Queens—being careful to throw first the Queen of the same suit as the dead Jack, for if it is then taken you know that your opponent has a group, not a sequence. Of course, if the Nines can be used only for Nines, while the Queens are open for either Queens or a sequence, throw the Nines first.

Here is a tip: If you have two pairs equally safe, it often pays to break the lower pair first. Most Gin players in this situation throw the higher first. For instance, having pairs of Kings and Jacks, equally safe (or unsafe), break the Jacks first. Your opponent, seeing two Jacks go, is not apt to read you for a pair of Kings.

Let's look at a typical situation arising after two or three rounds. You have just drawn a Three, and your hand is:

$$\heartsuit \quad \spadesuit \quad \spadesuit \quad \spadesuit \quad \heartsuit \quad \clubsuit \quad \heartsuit \quad \diamondsuit \quad \clubsuit \quad \diamondsuit \quad \clubsuit \quad \text{(Ex. 23)}$$
$$Q \quad Q \quad J \quad 8 \quad 8 \quad 8 \quad 3 \quad 3 \quad 3 \quad 2 \quad A$$

Having filled a second meld, you now want to exchange your high cards for low in order to knock. You have got to break up the three-card combination. The correct discard is the ♡Q, for (a) it is fairly safe (you have another Queen); (b) you are left with a good combination (♠Q ♠J); (c) if the ♡Q is not taken, you are sure of a second absolutely safe discard (the ♠Q).

If no high Hearts have shown, some very conservative players will discard the ♠Q first. But such cowardly tactics abandon the offense too soon. This is a discard for ultrasafety, which might be advisable at a much later stage, but certainly is not in the early play.

If a Jack has been thrown, you will naturally discard the ♠J, and play for a Queen. However, the moment you draw a low card, you will throw the ♠Q (whether your first discard was the ♡Q or ♠J), and will then need only another low card for a knock.

If the ♠K or ♠10 has been discarded, or if your opponent has picked up a King for Kings, or a Ten for Tens, the prospect of your Spade sequence is impaired. In this case you should make the riskier discard of the ♠J and play for either of two Queens rather than hope to fill the one-ended Spade sequence.

Finally, if your opponent has picked up a King, Jack, or Ten, which you know is for a sequence, your play is clear. Throw away the ♡Q.

Gain vs. Loss In Example 23 I showed a situation where you break up a three-card combination because you have already filled two melds and need only some more low cards to knock.

The question of what to discard is not always so clear-cut. More frequently after a few rounds you are faced with the problem of whether to let go a dangerous odd card or to break up a combination as a measure of safety.

The answer is to be sought in the potential gain or loss by either course. Let's look at a couple of examples.

♠ ♠ ♠ ♡ ♠ ♡ ♣ ♣ ♢ ♡ ♡ (Ex. 24)
Q Q J J 8 8 8 4 2 2 A

This hand differs from Example 23, despite many resemblances, in the presence of only one completed meld. The temptation is strong to keep the whole picture-card combination intact, in the effort to fill a second spread. But to discard the wild ♣4 is too dangerous. If your opponent needs only a low card to knock, and this is it, he will catch you with a staggering count. The time has come to play safe and commence unloading. Let go the ♣Q or ♡J, whichever is less likely to be wanted in a sequence.

♠ ♡ ♣ ♢ ♠ ♠ ♡ ♣ ♢ ♡ ♡ (Ex. 25)
10 10 10 10 7 6 6 4 2 2 A

This is a horse of another color. Though it might be safer to throw the ♠7 or ♡6, you ought to risk the ♣4 instead. If your opponent knocks, you don't get caught with so much as in Example 24. By saving the three-card combination you are calling any of four cards for an immediate knock. (In Example 24, if you save both pairs and fill one of them, you are still unable to knock.) Finally, if you are lucky enough to get a Deuce, or the ♡3 you have an excellent prospect for a gin hand, should you wish to try for it.

Late Blocking When you are dealt a very poor hand, you resort to defensive tactics to avoid losing a large number of points. Suppose that you have succeeded in playing safe down to a late stage of the deal. Then you finish off by "blocking" in an effort to reach the end of the stock without a knock.

This is all-out defensive discarding, in which safety overtops all other considerations.

♠ ♠ ♡ ◇ ♡ ♠ ♣ ♡ ◇ ♠ ◇   (Ex. 26)
8 7 7 5 4 4 3 2 2 A A

This is your hand at a late stage. Most of the Kings, Queens, Jacks, Tens, Nines, and Eights have been accounted for. Your opponent's last discard was the ♣5. You have drawn, and you discard the safe ♠8.

Your opponent draws, then discards the ♣4. You do not take it! Although you could fill a spread by taking it, you would thereby leave yourself without a safe discard. Any card in your hand might allow him to knock or even go gin. Yet, if you can keep all your dangerous cards, it is virtually impossible for him to gin and very difficult for him to knock.

By continuing this policy of throwing only perfectly safe cards, regardless of any melds of your own, you may well transform an almost sure losing hand into a stand-off.

Discarding a Meld   The urgency of keeping your opponent at bay, while holding your own chance to fill an indifferent hand or to run out the stock in a stand-off, may dictate a discard from a meld. For example:

You and your opponent have started zone discarding in the low bracket. After five rounds of play only Twos, Threes, Fours, and Fives have been discarded. Your hand after the draw is:

♠ ♣ ♡ ◇ ◇ ♣ ♣ ♡ ♠ ◇ ♣   (Ex. 27)
K Q J J 10 8 7 7 A A A

Your best discard now is an Ace. This is not truly a blocking play, in that you plan to try to win the hand. However, at this stage, you dare not throw the ♠K or ♣Q, holding so many points. Abandoning the Aces gives you three safe discards and time to build up your hand.

With the same hand, by the way, if you had three Jacks or three Sevens, you would risk the King, holding two spreads and hoping to match up your third spread.

LATE PLAY

The expert enjoys his greatest advantage at gin after the first four or five rounds. With well over half the pack in play the element of luck is reduced considerably, and skill pays dividends.

When to Knock   A decision you are frequently called upon to make is whether to knock or to play on for gin. Here I want to give you a piece of advice that will save you thousands of points. *When in doubt—knock.* Play for gin only if you have an excellent chance or if you strongly suspect that you will lose if you knock. In the early play of any hand, unless your hand is exceptional, knock at once.

After the draw you hold:

◇ ♣ ♣ ◇ ♠ ♡ ♠ ♡ ◇ ♣ ♡   (Ex. 28)

K K 10 10 10 10 6 6 6 2 A

Don't play for gin by throwing the Ace or Deuce, hoping to get a King. Instead, throw one King this time, and then knock if you draw any one of twenty-three cards that put you under 10 next time.

♠ ♡ ♣ ◇ ◇ ♡ ♡ ♡ ♣ ♡ ◇ ◇   (Ex. 29)

K K K K J 10 9 7 3 3 2

Discard the Seven and knock with 8 at once. Though any of four cards would give you gin, your opponent is not likely to throw you the right low card at this stage, and your chance of drawing the perfect card is remote. Take a nice profit by knocking now. You might easily play a little while with this and let your opponent reduce by 30 or 40 points, and even eventually beat you.

♠ ◇ ♣ ♡ ♡ ♡ ♠ ♣ ◇ ♡ ♠   (Ex. 30)

K K K Q J 10 8 8 8 3 A

This, I admit, is tempting at an early stage, but even here you should knock. Only three cards give you gin. It is true that by playing on you would be in a position to undercut your opponent if he knocks, but even that would not compensate you for what you can get by an early knock.

When to Gin The only time to consider playing for gin is when you have either seven or nine cards matched (except when you don't dare knock because you may be undercut). The ideal hand, of course, is one in which you have nine matched cards with a great many chances to gin and a probable undercut if the enemy should knock. I am sure everyone knows the perfect gin hand:

♠	♠	♠	♡	♡	♡	◇	◇	◇	♣	(Ex. 31)
9	8	7	9	8	7	9	8	7	A	

Nine chances for gin, and a sure undercut if your opponent knocks—nice to dream, isn't it? However, you needn't wait for this ideal hand. Any hand typified by the four following examples is worth a gin try.

♠	♡	◇	♡	♡	♡	♣	♣	♣	♣	(Ex. 32)
Q	Q	Q	10	9	8	9	8	7	A	

A very good gin hand—five chances (the ♣Q, ♡J, ♡7, ♣10, ♣6) and a sure undercut.

♠	◇	♣	◇	◇	♠	♡	♡	♡	♡	(Ex. 33)
K	K	K	10	9	9	9	9	8	7	6

A very good gin hand—five chances (the ♡K, ◇J, ◇8, ♣9, ♡5). However, your opponent might knock and beat you, as you have 10 points in hand. Of course you could throw away the Ten and keep a low card for undercutting purposes. However, that would reduce your gin chances from five to three.

♡	♡	♡	♣	◇	♡	♠	♠	♠	◇	(Ex. 34)
J	10	9	4	4	4	6	5	4	5	

An excellent hand—six gin chances (the ♡Q, ♡8, ♠7, ♠3, either of two Fives), and a very probable undercut.

♣	♣	♣	♠	♡	◇	♠	♡	◇	♣	(Ex. 35)
Q	J	10	8	8	8	6	6	6	2	

A fair gin hand—four chances. If all alive and unknown to your opponent, definitely play. On the other hand, if your opponent is known to have three Kings and knows you have either Eights or Sixes, you probably should knock.

As a general rule, with four or more gin chances and nine cards matched, play for gin. With only two chances, knock. With three chances, use your judgment; but if playing extra boxes or bonuses for gin, it generally pays to play a good three-chance hand.

A typical three-chance hand that should not be played for gin is the following:

♠ ◇ ♡ ♠ ♡ ◇ ♠ ♡ ◇ ♣   (Ex. 36)
Q Q Q 8 8 8 6 6 6 A

If your opponent knows any of your cards, knock. Notice also that the Eight and Six you lack are both in the Club suit. If your opponent happens to have the fourth Queen and a Club run including the Eight and Six, you have exactly zero chance to gin.

Judge your gin chances by asking yourself the following questions:

1. What spreads of mine does my opponent know about?
2. What spreads do I know my opponent has that use cards that are important for me?
3. What spreads *might* he have that would hurt my hand badly?

Question 1 speaks for itself. If you have picked from the table a Queen for Queens and an Eight for Eights, the chance of getting another of either is very remote.

To illustrate Questions 2 and 3, suppose you hold the following excellent five-chance gin hand:

♣ ◇ ♡ ♠ ♠ ♠ ◇ ◇ ◇ ♠   (Ex. 37)
Q Q Q 9 8 7 9 8 7 A

You suddenly remember that your opponent picked up the ♠K for a Spade run. Well, too bad, but it is still a wonderful four-chance gin hand. Now your opponent picks up a Six that you discard, for three Sixes. Well, that's really poor luck, because now you are reduced to a rather poor two-chance gin hand. However, you're stubborn and continue to play for gin. After a few draws you realize that no Tens have shown up. My goodness, the chances are at this late stage that your opponent has three Tens. Look what's hap-

pened—my beautiful five-chance gin hand has become practically a zero-chance gin hand.

Now, let's look at the rosier side of the picture. After
several plays you hold:

      ♣ ♣ ♣ ♣ ◊ ♡ ♠ ♡ ◊ ◊   (Ex. 38)
      Q J 10 8 8 8 2 2 2 A

The upcard was the ♣2, which your opponent took. Each
of you has thrown Kings and Nines, but none in Clubs. You
have now only a three-chance gin hand, but your cards are
"live"—a good gamble to play.

Hands like this are usually played until complications set
in. A typical complication is the discovery that you have
two cards, both of which are too dangerous to throw. Suppose
you know that your opponent has three Sevens, and now you
draw a Seven. Well, you decide to gamble and pitch the Ace,
holding the Seven to play off. A round or so later you draw
the ♣4. There are no Fours or low Clubs showing; your
opponent picked up ♣2 upcard. Now you are in a spot.
You've been very unlucky, but don't be stubborn—knock
with the Four.

Gin Position The previous section dealt with playing for
gin with nine matched cards. The other accepted time to play
for gin is when you have seven matched cards, comprising a
four-card spread, a three-card spread, and a group of three
set up in combination. A typical hand is the following:

      ♡ ♠ ♠ ♠ ◊ ♡ ♠ ◊ ♣ ♡   (Ex. 39)
      Q Q J 8 8 8 5 5 5 5

This is a good gin position with four chances. However, a
seven-matched-card hand must be handled very delicately.
It is wonderful to have and should be given a good try for
gin, but beware of being too stubborn. Many points are lost
by the average player's just playing blindly for gin.

With this hand, after five or six draws, if you suddenly
pick up the ♣10, and no Tens or near Clubs have shown up,
you just cannot let that card go. If you do, don't be surprised
to have your opponent knock or gin immediately. Your correct play is to break up your combination and throw the ♡Q

(see Example 23). Very late in the hand the correct play would be a safe Five.

If you hold:

$$♡ ♡ ♡ ♡ ♠ ♡ ◇ ♡ ◇ ◇ \quad \text{(Ex. 40)}$$
$$Q \quad J \quad 10 \quad 9 \quad 7 \quad 7 \quad 7 \quad 6 \quad 6 \quad 5$$

you have very little to lose and six chances for gin (the ♣7, ♣6, ♠6, ♡8, ♡5, ◇4). I would gamble more on this hand than on the preceding example. But even here caution must be exercised, if, near the end of the hand, you draw a complete "live card."

$$♠ ♡ ♣ ◇ ♠ ♡ ♣ ♡ ◇ ◇ \quad \text{(Ex. 41)}$$
$$10 \quad 10 \quad 10 \quad 8 \quad 8 \quad 8 \quad 8 \quad 3 \quad 3 \quad 2$$

This hand should simply be treated as a regular knock hand, even though you have several chances for gin. It generally doesn't pay to play hands that require a perfect low card for gin.

$$♡ ♣ ◇ ♠ ♡ ♠ ♠ ♠ ♡ ◇ \quad \text{(Ex. 42)}$$
$$K \quad K \quad K \quad Q \quad 10 \quad 10 \quad 9 \quad 6 \quad 6 \quad 6$$

This type of hand is difficult to hold very long. In addition it needs the exact card, the ♠J, for gin. If after a few draws you pick a card that is too dangerous to throw, then discard whichever is safer between the ♠Q or ♠9, naturally preferring to throw the ♠Q.

Forced Gin I remarked earlier that you play for gin only if you have a very good chance, or if you are afraid to knock. In hands where you know you are apt to lose if you knock you are sometimes forced into playing for gin.

How do you know you can't win if you knock? One obvious instance is if your opponent has taken two or three cards and doesn't knock for several rounds. Another and not so obvious instance is when you know your opponent. No good gin player, after many rounds of play, will discard very wild cards or very low cards, unless he is in gin position, or is able to undercut you if you pick up his low discard and knock.

$$♠ ♡ ◇ ♣ ♠ ♡ ◇ ◇ ♣ ◇ ◇ \quad \text{(Ex. 43)}$$
$$Q \quad Q \quad Q \quad 10 \quad 8 \quad 8 \quad 8 \quad 4 \quad 2 \quad 2 \quad A$$

Under normal circumstances you would of course throw away the odd Ten and knock. However, in the late stage of this hand, knowing your opponent has picked up a Ten for three Tens and the ◇ 7 for a Diamond run, and realizing that no Kings have yet shown up, you see that your opponent is in gin position. In confirmation of this reading his last couple of discards have been Threes and Aces. In fact, you can be practically sure your opponent's hand is the following:

♠ ♣ ♡ ♠ ♡ ♣ ◇ ◇ ◇   (Ex. 44)
K K K 10 10 10 7 6 5

He also has an odd card, probably a Queen or Eight, to play on you.

In this situation, you just can't knock, because you must lose. You are forced into a drastic play for gin, even though only one card, the ◇ 3, will make it. Your proper discard, therefore, is the ♣ 2. You have a fair chance of coming out on top. The only card that would give him gin is the last King. If you draw it, you are assured of a stand-off by playing safe. Of course, he might draw the King and gin you—but you have an equal chance of drawing the ◇ 3 and ginning him.

TIPS ON PLAYING FOR GIN

1. Try for sequences rather than groups.
2. One four-card spread is enough.
3. Don't hold a five-card sequence, as a rule.

If you happen to have the following hand:

♠ ♠ ♠ ♠ ♠ ♠ ♠ ♡ ♠ ◇ ♡   (Ex. 45)
K Q J 10 9 7 6 6 2 2 2

you should throw the ♠ K or ♠ 9, whichever is safer. A five-card spread is never a help when playing for gin. The perfect discard is the ♠ 9 if it is safe, encouraging your opponent to think the ♠ 8 will not help you.

Here is a fine bluff play used by some experts. Your hand is:

♠ ♡ ♣ ◇ ♣ ♡ ♠ ♠ ♡ ◇   (Ex. 46)
K K K K 10 10 10 5 5 A

Your opponent knows that you have Kings and Tens, as you picked up each previously. A round or two ago he threw the ♣6, which you refused, and now he throws the ♠6.

The bluff consists in picking up the ♠6. You discard the Ace (a couple of Aces have already been discarded). Believing that you now have three spreads, Kings, Tens, and a Spade run including the Six, your opponent will concentrate on defending against that holding, and will throw the ◇5 or ♣5 without a thought. In addition you improve your own chance of gin at no expense.

Late Play Technique The longer a hand progresses, the more clearly defined your correct play becomes. The basic principle of discarding in a late stage is:

Contribute a fourth card to your opponent's known meld, rather than throw a wild card that will probably give him a new meld. This is your hand at a late stage:

♡	◇	♣	♠	♠	♠	◇	◇	◇	♣	♡	(Ex. 47)
Q	Q	Q	10	9	8	6	5	4	7	K	

Your opponent has picked up a King for Kings and the ♡5 for a run. He is evidently playing for gin. No Hearts between the ranks Nine and Three have appeared. Your Seven is wide open for Sevens and Clubs. What can you discard?

Throw the King! Though a sure player for the enemy, this card stands to help him less than the ♣7, for:

1. The chances are strong that he has a four-card Heart sequence; a second four-card spread will not help him.

2. The ♣7 will surely help him, probably gin him.

3. If the King gins him, the Seven probably would have, anyway.

♡	♠	◇	♣	♡	♠	◇	♣	♡	◇	◇	(Ex. 48)
J	9	9	9	7	7	7	6	4	2	A	

Here is another hand after your draw. What should you discard?

At an early stage you would let go the ♣6 on the principle exemplified by Example 15.

But this is a late stage. No Jacks have shown up, and no Sixes and no Clubs of near rank. It is unlikely that at this late stage your opponent is clinging to a pair of Jacks. He might have *three* Jacks, but then your ♡ J will help him less than would the ♣ 6 if he has only a pair of Sixes or it fills a Club run. So discard the ♡ J.

Refusing a Player   To refuse to take a card that helps you goes against the grain, but it is often the right play. For example, after several plays your opponent throws the ♡ K; you hold:

♠	◇	♣	♡	♣	♣	♣	◇	♡	♠	(Ex. 49)
K	K	K	8	8	7	4	2	A	A	

Why take it? You give up a chance to draw a card that might put you right down. If you take it, you either must break your combination, which cuts in half your chance of a quick knock, or you must throw a low card which might permit your opponent to knock. With the same hand, even if you should draw a King, it is often a good play to throw it away, keeping your best combination for a quick knock and avoid giving a helpful card to the enemy.

Play for Stand-Off   The worst blunder you can commit is to discard a card that gins your opponent near the end of a hand.

♠	♡	◇	♣	♣	♣	♣	◇	♡	♣	♠	(Ex. 50)
10	10	10	7	6	5	2	2	2	9	4	

This is your hand with only two or three draws left. You have been playing for gin for several rounds. Your opponent has K-Q-J of Spades and three Nines. You block off the Spade run and have his fourth Nine, but now you have just drawn the ♠ 4, and no Fours have appeared. What do you throw? A safe Deuce. Too bad to give up such a beautiful gin hand, but the Four might easily gin him. You are practically assured of a stand-off by playing safe. You might knock, but you would probably be undercut.

Watch the Score   In the play of any hand the state of the score should always be taken into consideration. The prime object in any game of Gin is to *get on score*. That may seem obvious, but it is amazing how many players overlook its importance. Once you are on, playing hands wide open or gambling for gin is in order; but until you have first scratched, your every effort should be exerted just toward winning the hand. One of America's finest Gin players, Jack J. Dreyfus of New York City, has often made the following proposition:

Playing three 100-point games at a time, with a shut-out doubling the entire score, Mr. Dreyfus, if he wins the first hand by a big score, around 50 to 60 points, offers to take just one point for that hand, provided his opponent will concede him victory by one point for the second deal.

WE	THEY	WE	THEY	WE	THEY
1		1			
2					

This may seem like a generous concession, but in reality Mr. Dreyfus has the best of it. His next score counts on all three games and he is assured of not being blitzed on the second game.

In the late stage of any game watch the score very carefully. If your opponent is playing for gin, be sure to keep yourself "under," that is, try not to have enough points left in your hand to lose the game if he gins. The corollary to the above is: Play for gin if it would give you the game and a mere knock would not. Suppose you have 78 points on a 100-point game, and after several draws you are able to knock. But your opponent has picked a card or two, and you feel sure that you would not win the required 22 points. It might easily pay you to play for gin, even though your hand is not particularly suited. First of all, your opponent might try to knock, in which case you undercut him. Secondly, you may be fortunate enough to draw gin. In either case you would win the game.

CARD READING

This is the most important factor in Gin and will repay study, even though it is quite complex.

Every discard that is made by your opponent, every discard you make that is not taken, and every card that either player takes from the table, has a subtle meaning to the Gin expert. Gin players all over the world continually give away their holdings. Fortunately for them, their opponents, not being fine card players, do not know how to take advantage of this information.

The Gin expert spends most of his time analyzing what his opponent has or has not, and at the same time makes every effort to conceal the nature of his own hand.

In this chapter I am going to reveal some hitherto undisclosed secrets, which only a handful of Gin players know—and are keeping to themselves.

Identify a Meld   I will first discuss the more or less obvious clues that every good Gin player should know, before going into postgraduate work.

Every Gin enthusiast realizes the importance of remembering any card picked up by an opponent, and of course tries to identify as soon as possible whether it is being used for a group or a sequence meld. And I will pause here to give you a couple of pieces of advice.

1. Don't keep repeating aloud the card or cards your opponent has picked up. It may often be to his benefit.

2. Don't let on, as by a knowing look, when some card you draw or some card he plays permits you to identify how opponent is using a card he picked up earlier.

As a rule the cards taken by your opponent can be identified fairly quickly with either a group or a sequence. For example, if the ♠J has been discarded, or you have it in your hand, and your opponent takes the ♠K or ♠Q, you know he is using either card for a group meld. If your opponent picks up the ♡10 when a couple of other Tens have been thrown, then of course he has a Heart run. (Even if only one other Ten has been thrown, the odds are overwhelmingly in favor of his having a sequence.)

Unfortunately, detecting how your opponent is using certain cards is not always so easy. Very often you must take into consideration what card he did *not* take previously, plus the card that he throws after taking your discard. For example, the upcard is the ♠Q, refused by both of you. You draw and discard the ♣K, your opponent draws and discards the ♣10. You draw from the stock and you then discard the ◊J, upon which your opponent pounces and discards the ♡Q. A couple of draws later your hand is:

♣   ◊   ♠   ♡   ♣   ♣   ♡   ◊   ♡   ♠   ♣   (Ex. 51)
J   10   7   7   7   5   5   5   3   2   A

You must of course decide right now to throw one of your odd cards, the ♣J or ◊10. In this situation there is no such play as throwing the ♡3 and holding both cards. You must throw one and play for a quick knock. This may look like a complete guess, but it is anything but.

Your most important clue is this: Your opponent's first discard was the ♣10, when he obviously had a much safer ♡Q to throw. Since he held the ♡Q, it must be because he was holding it for a combination. Remember, however, that he was not dealt a pair of Queens, or he would have taken the turned Queen. So therefore he held the ♡Q to match either a pair of Kings, Jacks, or Tens.

He didn't have Kings—you threw him one. He didn't have Tens—his first discard was the ♣10. So he must have had Jacks. You can now bet your bottom dollar that his holding before picking up the ◊J was:

♡   ♡   ♠   (Ex. 52)
Q   J   J

Now your problem is solved. You throw the ◊10, and hold the ♣J as a player.

This play might lose on one very remote possibility that is hardly worth considering. We know your opponent did not have two Queens dealt to him, or he would have taken the ♠Q, the original upcard. If his first draw was exactly a Queen, he might have held a combination of cards that would allow him to use the ◊J in a run.

Conceal Your Melds Every Gin player knows how important it is to remember a card the opponent has picked up

and to classify it as soon as possible. But many players don't
realize that it is also important to remember the card you
pick up and to conceal your holding from your opponent.

If on the first play you pick up the ♡10 to go with the
♣10 and ♠10 for three Tens, and you have an odd ♣K,
♡Q, and ♠J, throw the ♣K and ♠J first, rather than the
♡Q. As soon as you release the ♡Q, if your opponent has
either the ♡8 or ♡9, you tell him that you have three Tens,
which may be of great importance to him in the play of
his hand.

Holding Players   One of the most common failures of even
the best Gin player is to hold doubtful players. The best
policy is this: Never hold a doubtful player at the cost of
breaking up your hand.

Suppose your opponent has picked up the ♡10, which
you have failed to identify, and your hand is:

♠ ♡ ♣ ♠ ◇ ◇ ♣ ♠ ♣ ♡   (Ex. 53)
K K K 6 6 4 3 2 A A

If you now draw the ♡8, which is safe against Eights,
throw it and keep your hand intact. It is 4 to 1 against your
opponent's having exactly J-10-9 of Hearts. Even if you draw
the ♡9 you should risk playing it to keep your position.
Your opponent is a 3-to-1 favorite to have three Tens. It is
worth this risk to keep the maximum number of combinations in your hand.

The next situation is one in which you must make an
immediate decision. Your opponent has picked up the ♣10,
which you haven't been able to classify. You hold after the
draw:

♠ ♡ ◇ ♣ ♡ ◇ ♡ ♡ ◇ ♡ ♣   (Ex. 54)
K K K J 10 6 6 5 2 A A

In this situation you should not hold both cards, the ♣J,
♡10, but should try to guess which to throw and keep
your hand in a playable condition. If no Jacks have appeared,
you would throw the ♡10 rather than the Jack, which might
give the opponent a second brand-new meld. If the Jack is

safe against Jacks, your guess is as good as mine—but you must guess, and then throw one or the other.

POSTGRADUATE GIN

In the next few sections I will reveal some inside information known to only a handful of experts. As I mentioned in the beginning of this chapter, there is a great deal more skill and science applied to Gin than people realize. And, as in every Rummy-type game, good discarding is 99% of good play.

Problem Hand Here is a problem to test your knowledge of discarding—I will discuss this hand in full at the end of this chapter. I don't believe there are a hundred people in the country who would discard this hand correctly.

You dealt. The upcard was an Ace, which your opponent took, and he discarded the ♣8. Your hand after the draw was:

♠	♡	◇	♣	♡	♠	♡	◇	♣	◇	♡	(Ex. 55)
K	Q	J	9	7	3	3	3	2	2	2	

You obviously have five possible discards. Name their order of safety. I'll gladly take half your game in the future if you answer this correctly. (See Page 140.)

Here is the most important theory utilized by experts. For lack of a better name I will call it:

BASIC THEORY OF EARLY DISCARDING

Your safest discard is a card of adjacent rank to that thrown by your opponent, but in a different suit.

This theory applies to early discarding. The basis is that your opponent, if he is any good at all, on the first couple of plays will not break up a combination. Let's look at a specific example:

♣	◇	♠	♡	♣	♠	♡	♡	◇	♣	♣	(Ex. 56)
J	9	7	7	7	5	5	4	3	2	A	

Upcard: the ♣6

Each player refused the ♣6 and your opponent's first discard is the ♣10. You have drawn and now must discard.

Having a completely matched hand, you of course would discard either the ♣J or the ◇9. I'm sure you would pick the ♣J. That's a mistake—it's 2 to 1 in favor of the ◇9.

The ◇9 can be used in the following six ways:

(a)	◇J	◇10	◇9
(b)	◇10	◇9	◇8
(c)	◇9	◇8	◇7
(d)	♠9	♣9	◇9
(e)	♣9	♡9	◇9
(f)	♠9	♡9	◇9

But remember, we assume that the opponent is not breaking a combination. Therefore, he does not have another Ten, or the ♣9. Since he does not have another Ten, you can cross out (a) and (b). Since he does not have the ♣9, you can cross out (d) and (e). So now there are only two ways he can use the ◇9—(c) and (f)—provided he is not breaking a combination.

The ♣J, however, may be used in four ways:

(a)	♠J	♡J	♣J
(b)	◇J	♡J	♣J
(c)	♠J	◇J	♣J
(d)	♣K	♣Q	♣J

Don't tell your friends—just remember my "Basic Theory of Early Discarding" and watch the points roll in.

The Fish Problem Here is one of the few situations in Gin (or in any other game for that matter) in which the correct play is against percentage. Remember this: Any Gin player, good, bad, or indifferent, will throw an advertising card the first or second play if he happens to have one. Here is an example:

You each refused the turned card—the ♣J—and your opponent's first discard was the ◇8. After drawing your hand is:

♠	♣	♡	◇	♣	♠	♠	♠	◇	◇	♣	(Ex. 57)
K	Q	8	6	6	6	4	3	2	A	A	

You obviously have three possible discards—the ♠K, ♣Q, ♡8. Most people would pick the ♡8, which can be used only three ways, with the ♡10-9, ♡9-7, or ♡7-6. But actually this should be your last choice. You should first discard the ♣Q, which also can be used only three ways for Queens. Your next discard should be the ♠K, even though that card can be used four ways as compared to the ♡8, which can be used three ways. The likelihood that the ♢8, thrown by your opponent, is an ad more than overcomes the consideration that the ♡8 can be used only three ways and the ♠K four ways.

Gin Mathematics

1. A wild King (or Ace) can be used four ways.

2. A wild Queen (or Deuce) can be used in five ways.

3. Any other live card can be used six ways.

4. If you split a pair (open to all sequences), the card can be used four ways (exception: Queens three ways, Kings only two ways).

5. If you split a pair (not open to sequences), the card can be used only one way.

The above general information will help show up a few common mistakes made by players who like to play safe.

This is your hand after several draws, when some thought must be given to safety:

♡ ♢ ♣ ♠ ♣ ♢ ♠ ♢ ♢ ♠ ♣   (Ex. 58)

K 10 10 7 7 7 5 5 4 2 A

Here many players would throw the Tens, even though open to sequences, figuring them to be safer than the completely live King. Actually the mathematics of the situation proves that either Ten is just as dangerous as the King. Such being the case, of course you should throw the King and hold the pair of Tens as a combination. Even if your odd card was a Queen instead of the ♡K, you should still throw the Queen, in spite of the fact that it would be a fraction safer in this instance to throw one of the Tens. The difference in safety is so little that you should lean toward holding your pair.

Special Tips for Experts

1. Your safest "blind" odd-card discard is a King. Your next safest is a Queen.

2. The odds are only 3½ to 1 against your opponent's taking a completely live card below a Queen or above a Two on your first play, and become considerably less as the hand progresses.

3. If you split a pair of completely live Jacks, Tens, Nines, Eights, Sevens, Sixes, Fives, or Fours, it is 3 to 1, if your opponent takes it, that he has a sequence. If you split a pair of completely live Queens or Deuces, it is 2 to 1 that your opponent has a sequence. If you split a pair of live Kings or Aces, it is exactly even whether your opponent is using it for a group or sequence.

Problem Hand I hope the solving of the problem I gave you on Page 137 is a little easier now that you have read the contents of the last few pages. I'll repeat the hand:

You dealt, the upcard was an Ace, which your opponent took, and discarded the ♣8. Your hand after the draw was:

♠	♡	◇	♣	♡	♠	♡	◇	♣	◇	♡	(Repeat of Ex. 55)
K	Q	J	9	7	3	3	3	2	2	2	

You obviously have five possible discards. Here they are in order of safety:

1. ♡7, only a two-way player. (See "Basic Theory of Early Discarding," Page 137.)

2. ♣9, a four-way player. (See Page 137.)

3. ♠K. Any live King is a four-way player.

4. ♡Q. Any odd Queen is a five-way player.

5. ◇J. Any completely live card below a Queen is a six-way player. The odds are only 3½ to 1 against this card's being taken by the opponent.

LAWS OF GIN RUMMY

1. Players Two play. Three may participate in the same game, usually with one sitting out while the other two play. Four or more, in pairs up to almost any number, may play a partnership game, but this is done by playing separate two-hand games and combining scores.

2. The Pack   A regular pack of fifty-two cards. Two packs should be used, so that while one player deals the other shuffles for the next deal.

3. Rank of Cards   K (high), Q, J, 10, 9, 8, 7, 6, 5, 4, 3, 2, A.

4. Value of Cards   Face cards count 10 each; Aces, 1; other cards their pip value.

5. The Shuffle and Cut   One pack is shuffled and spread, and each player draws a card; if he draws one of the four cards at either end, he must draw again.

a. The player drawing the high card has choice of cards and seats, and whether or not he will deal first. If the cards drawn are otherwise of the same rank, the suits rank; Spades (high), Hearts, Diamonds, Clubs.

b. Either player may shuffle, the dealer having the right to shuffle last. The nondealer must cut the pack.

6. The Deal   The dealer distributes the cards one at a time face down, alternately to his opponent and to himself until each has ten cards.

a. The undealt remainder of the pack is placed face down in the center of the table, becoming the stock. The top card of the stock is turned face up and placed beside it; this upcard starts the discard pile. (Some play with no upcard; instead the twenty-first card goes to the nondealer, face down, and he begins play with a discard.)

b. The winner of a hand deals the next hand. The winner of a game deals the first hand of the next game. (Some follow the rule that loser deals.)

7. Object of Play   To reduce one's count of deadwood to less than the count of the opponent, by forming matched sets consisting of three or four cards of the same rank or three or more cards of the same suit in sequence.

8. The Play   The nondealer plays first, and the turn to play alternates thereafter.

a. In each turn a player must draw either the upcard (top

card of the discard pile) or the top card of the stock, and then must discard face up on the discard pile. He may not discard a card taken from the discard pile in that turn. It is optional with the players whether previous discards are open to inspection (see paragraph 43).

b. On the first play, if the nondealer does not wish to take the upcard, he must so announce and dealer may have the first turn by taking the upcard; if the dealer does not wish the upcard, nondealer draws the top card of the stock and play proceeds. (When the nondealer is dealt eleven cards, play begins by his discard.)

9. *Knocking* Each hand begins when a legal deal is completed, and ends when either player knocks.

a. A player may knock in any turn, after drawing and before discarding, if the value of the unmatched cards in his hand (after he discards) will be 10 points or less. He need not knock when able to do so. Having knocked, he discards one card face down and spreads his hand, arranged into matched sets and unmatched cards. The opponent then spreads his hand, removes from it any unmatched sets, and lays off whatever cards he has that match the knocker's matched sets (but see Section 11).

b. The point values of the two players' unmatched cards are then compared, and the result of the hand is scored (see *11, Scoring,* below).

10. *Drawn Game* None of the last three cards (or two, in some circles) may be drawn; if the player who draws the forty-ninth card discards without knocking, his opponent may not take the discard and the hand is a draw. The same dealer deals again.

11. *Scoring* If the knocker's count is less than his opponent's, the knocker wins the hand; the difference in counts is scored to his credit.

a. If the opponent ties or beats the knocker, he has undercut him; he wins the hand, and scores 25 points plus the difference in counts, if any, subject to Section 11. (Many make the undercut bonus less—10, 15, or 20.)

b. If the knocker has a count of zero (has all ten of his cards matched in sets) he is gin; his opponent may not lay off and the knocker wins the hand even if the opponent also has a count of zero; and the knocker receives 25 points plus the difference in counts, if any. (Many allow laying off on a gin hand, but the knocker gets the gin bonus even if opponent reduces his deadwood to zero. Many give extra box scores; the most popular scale is one for undercut, two for gin.)

c. A running total of each player's score is kept, with a line drawn under his score every time he wins a hand. (Example: A player wins the first hand by 11 points; he scores 11 and draws a line under it. The same player wins the next hand by 14 points, he writes down 25 and draws another line.)

12. *Game* The player first scoring 100 points or more wins the game. He adds to his score a 100-point game bonus. (Many different game requirements and bonuses are adopted, the commonest being 125, 150, and 200 points.)

a. If the loser has not won a hand during that game, the winner adds an additional 100 points shutout bonus. (A popular variant is that winner's entire score is doubled.)

b. Each player then adds to his score 25 points for each hand he has won (called a line or box bonus).

c. The two players' total scores are then determined and the player with the higher score wins the difference between the two scores.

IRREGULARITIES

(Condensed, by permission, from the *Laws of Gin Rummy,* by Walter L. Richard, C. E. Van Vleck, and Lee Hazen.)

13. *New Deal* A deal out of turn may be stopped at any time before the upcard is dealt; thereafter it stands as a correct deal.

a. There must be a new deal by the same dealer if it is found, before the completion of the deal, that the pack is imperfect or that a card is faced in the pack; or if a card is exposed in dealing, or if a player has looked at the face of a card.

b. Other occasions for a new deal are covered in laws governing other irregularities.

14. Irregular Hands If either player's hand is discovered to have an incorrect number of cards before that player has made his first draw, there must be a new deal.

a. After the first draw, if it is discovered that both players have incorrect hands, there must be a new deal. If one player's hand is incorrect and the other player's hand is correct, the player with the correct hand may decide either to have a new deal or to continue play. If play continues, the player with the incorrect hand must correct his hand by drawing without discarding, or by discarding without drawing, and may not knock until his next turn to play.

b. After a knock a player with too few cards is charged 10 points for each card missing, and may not claim the undercut bonus; if the knocker's opponent has more than ten cards, the hand may not be corrected, the offender may not claim an undercut bonus, and can lose or tie, but may not win the hand.

c. If the player who knocks has an incorrect number of cards, the penalty for an illegal knock applies.

15. Imperfect Pack When two packs are being used, a card from the other pack found in the stock is eliminated and play continues. If it is discovered, after the knock, that the pack is incomplete, the deal stands. Discovery that the pack is imperfect in any way has no bearing on any score that has been entered on the score sheet.

16. Premature Play If nondealer draws from the stock before dealer has refused the upcard, the draw stands without penalty as his first play. If a player draws from the stock before his opponent has discarded, the draw stands as his proper play.

17. Illegally Seeing a Card If a player drawing in turn sees any card to which he is not entitled, every such card must be placed face up next to the discard pile. The offender may not knock until his next turn to play, unless he is gin. The nonoffender has the sole right to take any of the exposed cards until first thereafter he draws from the stock; then the offender has the same right until first thereafter he draws from the stock; when each player has drawn from the stock, the exposed cards are placed in the discard pile.

a. If a player drawing out of turn sees a card to which he is not entitled, the rule given in the preceding paragraph applies, except that the offender may never take such cards, but may draw only his opponent's discard or the top card of the stock in each turn.

18. Exposed Card A card found exposed in the stock, or in the other pack or away from the table, is shuffled into the stock and play continues. Accidental exposure of a card in a player's hand is not subject to penalty. An exposed card becomes a discard when the holder indicates intent to discard it; when his opponent has seen and can name such a card, the holder may not thereafter knock in that turn.

19. Illegal Knock If a player knocks with a count higher than 10, but his opponent has not exposed any cards before the error is discovered, the offender must leave his hand face up on the table until his opponent has completed his next play.

a. If the knocker has more than 10 points, and the error is discovered after the opponent has exposed any of his own cards, but before he has laid off any cards, the opponent may choose which of the following penalties to apply: To make the knocker play the rest of the hand with all his cards exposed; or to permit the offender to pick up his hand, in which event the offender may not score for any undercut or gin bonus in that hand.

b. If the knocker has an incorrect number of cards, his opponent may demand a new deal; or may require the offender to play with his hand exposed and to correct his hand on his next play or plays, either by drawing without discarding or by discarding without drawing.

c. If a player, after knocking, inadvertently discards a card which makes his knock illegal, he may replace that discard with a discard which makes his knock legal.

20. Looking Back at Discards Players may agree in advance that looking back at discards will be permitted. In the absence of such agreement a player who looks back at a covered discard loses his right to his next draw.

21. Picking up Wrong Discards If a player inadvertently picks up the wrong discard, he may correct or he may be made to correct the error, if attention is called to it prior to his opponent's next discard.

GIN VARIATIONS

In addition to those mentioned parenthetically in the foregoing laws, there are many other variant rules followed in various localities.

A feature I have met with increasing frequency is the proposal to toss in the cards, void the current deal, and have a new deal. Either player may make such a proposal at any time. The opponent may accept before continuing play; any further move by him constitutes a refusal.

Simultaneous Games Another idea that spread from Hollywood and now is quite generally played is to score in three games simultaneously. The method is as follows:

The score sheet is laid out with three double columns, one for each game. The first hand won by a player is entered only in Game 1; the second hand he wins is entered in Games 1 and 2; the third hand he wins, and all subsequent wins, are credited to him in Games 1, 2, and 3.

When either player reaches 100 or more points in any game, that game is ended and no more scores are applied to it, but scoring goes on in the other two games. So, if one player wins a shutout game, meaning that in Game 1 he reaches 100 before his opponent has scored, then the opponent's first score will apply to Game 2, since Game 1 is now closed.

Bonuses for undercut, gin, game, and shutout are awarded

in the usual manner. Play continues until all three games have been completed.

Gin for Four Players Four players may compete at Gin in two partnerships, by either the alternating method (described in this section) or the team method (described in the next section).

The players draw cards, and the two high are partners against the two low. All four may sit at one table, with partners opposite each other. A game is played as a series of deals of two-hand Gin, between two opposed couples using separate packs. Each partner of a side plays alternately (that is, in alternate deals) against his left and his right opponent. The scores resulting from each deal in the two matches are combined as a single score for one side or the other. A draw deal is not replayed, but is treated as a score of zero. If both matches are drawn, they are replayed. The side winning a deal deals next.

A player may advise his partner of his legal rights in case of an irregularity, but may not give him technical advice until after his partner's opponent has knocked.

Team Gin In a match between two teams, each of two or more players, the teams sit on opposite sides of a long table (or row of tables). Each player engages the opponent opposite him in a two-hand game. These oppositions remain unchanged until the game is finished, after which they can be changed as the teams agree. (Some allow the team losing a deal to rearrange the oppositions for the next deal.) All scores from the first deal are combined as a single score for a team; likewise with the second deal, and so on, so that the deals in all the matches must be synchronized. The game requirement is usually set at 200 or 250 with six players, and 250 or 300 with eight. (Some give an extra bonus to a team when all of its members win their matches in any one deal.)

OKLAHOMA GIN

TEN THINGS EVERY WINNING OKLAHOMA GIN PLAYER MUST KNOW

1. Always remember the knock number; if you have to ask, you give away your hand.

2. The first object is to get on score.

3. With a high knock card (Ten, Nine, or Eight), play for two spreads and a quick knock.

4. With a medium-size knock card (Seven or Six), play for at least seven matched cards, very often nine matched cards.

5. With low knock cards (Five to Deuce), aim for three spreads.

6. Most very low knock hands (Three and Two) are won by ginning.

7. With a low knock card discard a great deal more freely than with a high knock card.

8. On a must gin hand, remember Kings and Aces are the least valuable cards in your hand.

9. Watch the score carefully on Spade hands.

10. With a low knock card it often pays to block your opponent by breaking up your hand.

OKLAHOMA GIN

INTRODUCTION

Oklahoma Gin first became popular about 1945. This new game contains all the skill and science of Gin, and is a great deal more exciting. Its popularity has increased tremendously in the past eight years, and today it is one of the most popular two-handed games played in the big cities.

Because of the difference in scoring, it is not at all unusual for a player to win a game in two or three hands. In fact, to "skunk" your opponent in one hand is not impossible.

Rules for Oklahoma Gin There is really only one great difference between Oklahoma Gin and regular Gin. The twenty-first card dealt is turned face up on the table, and as in Gin it is called the original upcard. However, *the face value of this card determines the maximum amount on which either player may knock on that particular hand*. If the upcard is a picture card or a Ten, then ten is the knock number as in regular Gin. If the upcard is a Nine, neither person may knock with more than a Nine; if it is an Eight, neither person may knock with more than eight; and so on, down to an Ace, in which case both players must go for gin.

In addition, if the turned card is a Spade, the score of that hand is doubled.

Upcard Since the conditions of play of each hand are determined by the original upcard, it is very important to keep careful track of that card throughout the hand. As in regular Gin, however, either player may take it if he so desires.

If it is not taken, it is customary to place the card at the side of the table in clear view of both players, and in such a way that there is no chance of its becoming mixed with the discard pile.

If the first upcard is taken by either player, then the score-keeper writes the knock number for that hand very clearly on his score sheet, so that it is plainly visible to all players. If he simply writes 4, 6, 10, or whatever the value of the card was, then it is considered a "plain" knock number—in other words, it was a Heart, Diamond, or Club. If the original upcard was a Spade, then the value of the card is written down in the same way, except the number is circled, meaning that the entire score for that hand is doubled.

Scoring   The accepted method of scoring for this game is as follows:

200 points is game (some play 150, some 250).

200-point bonus for winning the game (or 150 if playing 150 for game, etc.).

25-point bonus for going gin.

25-point bonus for undercutting your opponent (some play only 15 or 20 for undercut).

25-point bonus for each box.

If one side wins the game before the other side has scored, called blitz, skunk, shutout, schneider, etc., the entire score of that game is doubled. (Because of the frequency of schneiders, many players give only an extra game bonus, that is, an extra 200 if playing 200 for game, 250 if playing 250 for game, etc.)

Just to make the game more exciting, many players give two extra boxes for gin and one extra box for undercut.

A Spade hand doubles *everything*—points won, gin and undercut bonuses, and any extra box bonus that you are playing. In other words, if you gin your opponent, who has 32 points, you receive 32 + 25 for gin: 57, doubled: 114, and four boxes (if you are playing that additional bonus) will later count 100 more.

Pays to go gin in Spades, doesn't it?

Over-all Strategy Your strategy in play in general, so far as percentage, mathematics, and over-all play of the hand are concerned, is identical with that of regular Gin. If you are a good Gin player, you will automatically be a good Oklahoma Gin player.

However, your entire course of action in this game is guided by just one thing—the size of the original upcard. If the knock card is high, a Ten, Nine, or Eight, you play one way. If it is an in-between card, such as a Seven or Six, you change your play slightly. If it is a low card, a Five, Four, Three, or Two, you must change your strategy completely. I will cover each of these categories separately.

Here is a word of caution, if you have never played Oklahoma Gin before: the size of the average game is about twice as big as in Gin. An average game of Gin is about 300 points; at Hollywood (three games at a time), the average game is about 800. An average Oklahoma Gin game is about 500 points, or, playing Hollywood, about 1600 points.

Knock Card 10, 9, or 8 In approximately half of all Oklahoma Gin hands the knock card will be 8 or higher.

With a high knock number, 10, 9, or 8, your strategy should be to play your regular game of Gin. Try for the regular two three-card melds and a group of four low cards totaling your knock requirement or less. There are a great many combinations of four low cards that total 10. There are almost as many that total 9, and quite a few that total 8. Even though there are not as many combinations of low cards that make 8 as there are 10, it is still worth while to play for two melds and the required group of low cards.

Suppose that 8 is the number, and after the draw you hold:

$$\spadesuit \quad \clubsuit \quad \diamondsuit \quad \heartsuit \quad \diamondsuit \quad \diamondsuit \quad \heartsuit \quad \spadesuit \quad \spadesuit \quad \heartsuit \quad \heartsuit \quad \text{(Ex. 1)}$$
$$\text{K} \quad \text{K} \quad \text{K} \quad \text{Q} \quad \text{Q} \quad 8 \quad 8 \quad 8 \quad 3 \quad 2 \quad \text{A}$$

Your correct play with this hand, as in regular Gin, is to split your pair of Queens and play for a Deuce or an Ace, or a fourth King or fourth Eight. There are eight chances here, as compared to only two chances to fill the Queens.

If your knock were 9, you would be even surer of a quick knock, as, in addition, any three you draw would also put you down, thereby increasing your chances to eleven possible cards, as against the two Queen possibilities.

In addition, throwing the ♠3 might be just the card that would permit your opponent to knock and catch you with two Queens.

Knock Card 7 or 6   When you must knock in the 7–6 zone, your plan of campaign must change. Here six matched cards (two three-card melds) probably will not be sufficient for you to be able to knock. If the knock card is 6, and you have only six matched cards in your hand, your four odd cards must be exactly 2-2-A-A. If the knock card is 7, your four odd cards must be exactly 2-2-A-A or 3-2-A-A. So unless you start with three of these key cards in your hand, it is wiser to play for seven matched cards (a four-card spread and a three-card spread), or three three-card spreads.

You will find that as the knock goes lower the number of gin hands increases. This is only logical, as the more cards you must match up in order to knock, the closer you are to gin.

Let's suppose you have the following hand, after a few draws, with 6 the knock number:

♠	♡	◇	♡	♡	♡	◇	♣	♣	♣	◇	(Ex. 2)
K	K	K	10	9	6	6	6	4	2	A	

You have just drawn the third King and now must discard. Your correct play is the ♣4, hoping for the ♡J or ♡8. If you throw either the ♡10 or ♡9, then you must have two perfect draws to be able to knock. If your knock were a high one, such as a 9 or 10, then you would throw whichever was safer, either the ♡10 or ♡9, and play for a low card to knock.

To follow through on this example, on the next couple

of draws you pick the fourth King or fourth Six. Now you would break up your 10–9 of Hearts and play for any Ace, Deuce, or Three with which to knock.

Another possibility is that you might draw an Ace or Deuce, which would give you three very low cards and an excellent chance to get down to 6. If this should happen, once again you would break up your Heart combination.

On the other hand, if you managed to get the ♡J or ♡8, you would be able to knock with three spreads. Of course, in this situation the temptation would be great to play for gin. In fact, if you were on score, and most of your cards were "live," you should gamble to go gin.

Remember, this is a wild and woolly game, with big scores being the rule rather than the exception. With the extra box bonus and the possibility of a schneider being so much greater because of the frequency of Spade hands, a fairly good gin hand should be given a good play. But don't be stubborn. If you draw a dangerous card, don't just blindly close your eyes and say, "I've got to gin this hand." Knock instead, and take a small profit.

Knock Card 5, 4, 3, or 2   With a low knock card you always plan your campaign toward a nine-matched-card, three-meld-type hand. At a requirement of 5 or 4 you are sometimes able to knock with seven matched cards, but at 3 or 2 three melds are a must.

♠	♡	♣	◇	◇	♡	♡	◇	♣	♣	♣	(Ex. 3)
Q	Q	Q	9	8	8	6	6	6	3	A	

This is your hand after the draw, with six or seven rounds of play having gone by. If the knock requirement is very low, you should throw the ♣3 or ♣A, whichever seems safer, and keep your maximum combination for the third spread. With a high knock requirement such a play at this late stage would be unthinkable, as the chances are that your opponent would simply pick up your discard and knock.

With a low-card knock you can discard a great deal more freely than with a high-card knock.

Here is an example where the knock card is a 5:

♠ ♡ ◇ ♡ ♡ ♣ ♣ ♣ ◇ ♣   (Ex. 4)
K K K J 10 8 7 6 2 A

You've been playing for some time for your third meld, as both the ♡Q and ♡9 are live, when you suddenly draw the fourth King. Since you now have seven matched cards and two very low cards, the percentage is to give up your Heart combination and play for any Ace or Deuce or the ♣9 or ♣5 and then knock. There are eight possible cards to put you down, as against holding your ♡J, ♡10 for one of two possibilities. Of course, either the ♡Q or ♡9 would gin you, but to maintain your gin position you must throw an Ace or Deuce, which might easily put your opponent down and leave you holding the bag with the ♡J, ♡10.

Experience will show that when the knock is 3 or less, well over half the time someone goes gin. Let's review the last example with a knock requirement of 2 instead of 5. Now, after drawing the fourth King, you should throw whichever is safer, either the Ace or Deuce, hold your ♡J, ♡10, and play for gin.

Here is a fine play used by experts on this type of hand. I'll repeat the hand for you, with a different set of facts. After the draw you hold:

♠ ♡ ◇ ♣ ♡ ♡ ♣ ♣ ♣ ◇ ♣   (Ex. 5)
K K K K J 10 8 7 6 2 A

The knock is 2, and your opponent took the upcard, the Deuce of Clubs. The game has progressed to a late stage. No Aces or Deuces have shown up. What should you do?

To throw either low card looks too dangerous. Such discard might gin your opponent, or at least put him down. On the other hand, to throw your Heart combination away would be a give-up play. Your correct play therefore is to throw the ♡K. True, you are giving up your gin position, but you are still able to knock if you get either the ♡Q or ♡9. By making this play you avoid the risk of a big loss and at the same time give yourself a reasonable chance to show a profit.

Knock Card Ace Here is real excitement. Both players must go for gin. If the Ace happens to be Spades, well, the tension can be felt in the next room. Even the most hardened Gin veteran is bound to let out a sigh any time the Ace of Spades is turned up. By the way, I'd better mention here that in some parts of the country an Ace turned up permits a player to knock with 1—not, however, in my games or in my books!

To play for gin properly in the early part of the hand, you play what would be called bad Gin—you simply throw everything you don't want and keep every possible combination in your hand. In a must gin hand you can't win if you start busting up your chances right away.

Don't get the idea that you play all the way through the deck, blindly throwing what you don't want—you certainly don't. But as a rule, think only of your own hand the first five or six rounds, then start worrying about your opponent's hand.

The most important thing to remember in playing for gin is that you must have a four-card spread. Since a sequence meld is easier to extend than a group meld, whenever you have a chance to play for sequence rather than a group, do so. If you have this combination:

$$\heartsuit \quad \spadesuit \quad \diamondsuit \quad \diamondsuit \quad \diamondsuit \quad \text{(Ex. 6)}$$
$$10 \quad 10 \quad 10 \quad 9 \quad 8$$

hold the Diamond run and throw the Tens, even though they may be more dangerous discards than the $\diamondsuit 9$, $\diamondsuit 8$. Holding the Diamond run serves two purposes: (a) most important, you have two chances to garner the all-important four-card spread, as against the one chance of drawing the fourth Ten; (b) it is very easy for your opponent, if you keep Tens, to hold up the fourth Ten, but it is difficult, without ruining his hand, for him to try to hold two cards guarding a sequence, particularly when he can seldom be sure exactly how the sequence runs.

Here are two tips for playing for gin:

1. In the early part of the hand, in choosing among your odd cards to throw, get rid of end cards—Kings and Aces first, then Queens and Deuces. They are the hardest cards around which to build good combinations.

2. If you know or suspect that your opponent has a four-card meld, add to that meld or some other established meld rather than throw him a live card.

Knock Card Be sure always to keep track of the knock number. Don't be like Mrs. Jones of Philadelphia, who, every time she reduces her hand close to 10, carefully looks to see what the knock requirement is. Such a mannerism informs your opponent that you have a hand close to knocking.

Discarding You discard as you would in regular Gin when the knock is 8 or higher. You play offensively the first few rounds, then you must consider defense as well as offense in your discarding.

If the knock card is a middle card, 7 or 6, you can take more liberty in discarding, in that your opponent may not be able to knock even if you should give him two spreads in the early part of the game.

With a very low knock card, 5 or less, you play a strictly offensive game until you suspect your opponent is close to knocking or ginning. I have already pointed out that with a low knock one player or the other goes gin well over half the time. In such circumstances low cards are not necessarily more important than high cards, and it is not unusual to see many Aces, Deuces, and Threes discarded early.

Blocking In the section on regular Gin I mentioned that occasionally you play to block your opponent. In regular or in Oklahoma Gin, with a high knock, a block is hard to maintain except near the end of the hand. The lower the knock, the easier blocking play becomes. A stand-off is not at all unusual in Oklahoma Gin.

Look at this example. Your opponent has not taken a card, and the knock is 2. You have:

| ♡ | ◇ | ◇ | ♠ | ♣ | ♡ | ♠ | ◇ | ♠ | ♡ | ♣ | (Ex. 7) |
| K | K | Q | J | 10 | 10 | 8 | 8 | 7 | 7 | 7 | |

Seven or eight rounds have passed. The discard pile is full of Aces, Deuces, Threes, Fours, Fives, and Sixes, and a couple of Nines. If you wish, you can assure yourself of a stand-off by just breaking your three Sevens and playing safe for the balance of the hand. With the diversified high cards that you have, if you just sit tight and hang on to them, your opponent simply cannot get three spreads together and knock. As a matter of fact, it is extremely likely that your opponent has very much the same type hand that you have. If you offer him a new deal (which is a common practice in many Gin games), he will probably accept with pleasure.

Watch the Score No single piece of advice in Oklahoma Gin is more important than this: *Be sure to get on the score.* This may seem like "old stuff" to most Gin players, but in the Oklahoma variation it is particularly important. Remember that in this game to score 120 points in one hand is not impossible. To schneider your opponent in two hands is not uncommon. The winning of the first hand of a game of Oklahoma is very important. If you win, you immediately have your opponent under pressure, and then if a Spade turns up, you are in a position to gamble for a big score. Such being the case, play the first hand all out to win. The advantage of winning it is even greater, of course, in playing Hollywood (three games at a time). For additional excitement many players have started to play as many as six games at a time.

It is also important to keep track of the score at all times. Remember, a Spade hand will be played on the average of every four hands. With the huge number of points that stand to be won or lost when a Spade is turned up, you must know exactly how you and your opponent stand with respect to the game. I have heard many Gin players say, when they lost 60 or 90 points, "My goodness, that exactly puts you out . . . isn't that a shame." It is a shame, yes, but it's their own fault.

If you watch the score carefully, you should be able to pace yourself so as to avoid losing a game on any particular hand; and of course the corollary of this is to gamble to win the game by a possible play for gin or undercut if you are almost out.

LAWS OF OKLAHOMA GIN

The laws of Oklahoma Gin are identical with the laws of regular Gin, with the following exceptions:

(a) The twenty-first card dealt is turned face up on the table. The face value of this card (except the Ace) determines the maximum count of unmatched cards with which you may knock in that deal. Thus, if the upcard counts 10, the game is the same as regular Gin. If the upcard is 9, 8, etc., this lesser number is the maximum count for a knock.

If the upcard is an Ace, a gin hand (no unmatched card) is required for a knock.

(b) If the upcard is a Spade, all scores of that deal are doubled, including gin and undercut bonuses, and any extra box bonus allowed by agreement.

(c) Game is 200 points (some players prefer 150 or 250).

For the reader's convenience the Gin laws on knocking with an incorrect count are here summarized:

Illegal Knock If a player knocks with a count higher than the required knock number, but his opponent has not exposed any cards before the error is discovered, the offender must leave his hand face up on the table until his opponent has completed his next play.

If the knocker has more points than the required knock number, and the error is discovered after the opponent has exposed any of his own cards, but before he has laid off any cards, the opponent may choose which of the following penalties to apply: To make the knocker play the rest of the hand with all his cards exposed; or to permit the offender to pick up his hand, in which event the offender may not score for any undercut or gin bonus in that hand.

CANASTA

1. Seldom meld from your hand until the pack is taken.

2. If the pack is big and an opponent makes the initial meld without taking it—*freeze the pack*.

3. Make your dangerous discards while the pack is small.

4. Safest late discards match your left-hand opponent's earliest discards.

5. When you take the pack, try to help your partner get the next pack.

6. Don't meld just to score the value of the cards; always have some other reason.

7. Try to keep at least one wild card in your hand.

8. Forget about the extra bonuses for natural canastas and concealed hand.

9. Think twice before saying "No" to "May I go out?"

10. It's worth *at least* 200 points to keep your score under 1500, and 350 points to keep your score under 3000.

CANASTA

The first Canasta players were Rummy fans. They were used to "small profits and quick returns." In Gin and many other of the Rummy variants, the winning play is to go out as quickly as possible, taking even a small profit rather than prolonging the play for a possible gin bonus or suchlike extras. The early books, it is true, cautioned that Canasta is a game of scoring by melds rather than by going out, and preached the virtues of deliberately prolonging the play. But even they did not realize how very different Canasta to win is from Gin to win.

The Big Game Today experts realize that winning at Canasta is a matter of holding back for a *big* score in each deal. The effort to go out fast is relegated to a defensive measure, adopted by a side that has been licked in the battle for big profits. The battle centers around the effort to get *control* by taking the first big discard pile. The side that wins this battle has every prospect of keeping control to the bitter end and of increasing its margin of victory at every draw.

The lines of battle have become more finely drawn. The tactics have been systematized, and have been welded into an overall strategical plan. Each play, meld, or discard must be weighed in the light not only of the immediate situation, but also of this indicated plan. A natural consequence has been the development of conventional meanings whereby partners communicate their holdings and intentions to each other.

Stages of Play The play of a deal in the *big game* usually
follows a well-marked chronology. Not all the stages may
develop—the play may be curtailed by a quick out. But it
is convenient to discuss principles as they must vary in the
following stages:

FIRST—appraisal of the hand.
SECOND—the play for the pack.
THIRD—after the pack is first taken.
FOURTH—freezing the pack.
FIFTH—dealing with the frozen pack.

In addition I will discuss some general principles applicable
to all stages.

APPRAISAL OF THE HAND

The last card is dealt; you pick up your hand and look it
over. Maybe you consider it "good" or "bad," but that kind
of appraisal is not very helpful in deciding what to do about
it. For guidance in the early play make up your mind as
soon as possible to which of three categories your hand
belongs. These I will call briefly:

Pack taker, early meld, and quick out.

In the paragraphs below I will describe each of these
types of hands, and in so doing will foreshadow the line of
play it naturally calls for.

Pack-Taker Hand The pack taker is a hand that:
   (a) is able to make an initial meld;
   (b) holds several pairs.

The dream hand for a pack taker is something like this
(requirement 50):

$$A A A 7 7 6 6 5 5 4 4 \quad (Ex. 1)$$

But you can't expect to get, much less keep, five pairs.
For practical purposes a good pack taker has three pairs,
or possibly two low pairs.

Joker A Q Q 10 10 8 8 7 4 3	(Ex. 2)
2 A A K J 10 7 7 4 4 3	(Ex. 3)
Joker A K 10 8 6 6 5 5 4 3	(Ex. 4)

Examples 2 and 3 are obviously good prospects, having three pairs. Example 4, though it has only two pairs, is every bit as good because both pairs are low.

It is not too much to say that the pack taker is the *normal* type, since at least 75% of the hands dealt are properly classed as such. Also any other type may develop into a pack taker after a few draws.

Early-Meld Hand The early-meld type is a hand that:

(a) is able to make an *economical* initial bid;

(b) has some good reason for doing so.

Examples of hands that can make an economical early meld:

2 (A A A) K J 9 8 6 5 4
          (requirement 50)   (Ex. 5)

2 (Joker A A) Q 10 10 7 6 5 4
          (requirement 90)   (Ex. 6)

(Joker Joker K K) J J 9 7 7 5 4
          (requirement 120)   (Ex. 7)

The immediate meld of the bracketed cards is recommended when circumstances are right. A good rule, however, is: When in doubt—don't meld.

Quick-Out Hand The quick-out type is a hand that either:

(a) is already largely matched up, but mainly in two ranks; or

(b) holds an excess of wild cards (three or more).

Here are some examples:

2 2 2 A A A 7 7 7 5   (Ex. 8)
2 2 2 2 Q 9 8 8 8 8 4   (Ex. 9)
2 2 K 8 8 8 8 8 5 5 5   (Ex. 10)

The poverty of ranks makes such hands initially poor pack takers, and to develop into pack takers, by saving additional pairs drawn, they would have to dip into the sets or the wild cards for discards. Manifestly such waste is unthinkable. To capitalize on their riches, such hands should head for a quick initial meld and an effort to go out fast. Example 10 might also be played for a concealed hand, since any Five, Eight or wild card puts you out.

I will return to this subject under "Initial Meld."

Occasionally you are dealt a hand that looks two ways—one draw may make it a typical pack taker, while a different draw may steer it into a quick out.

Joker 2 2 K K 8 8 8 6 4 4   (Ex. 11)

As it stands this is a good pack taker. The draw of a Six would certainly encourage you to treat it as such. But the draw of an Eight, King, or wild card would convert into a good out prospect.

Nondescript Hand   Not all hands can be instantly clapped into one of these categories. The hand that every Canasta player claims that he invariably is dealt, the "dog," is a nondescript having few pairs, wild cards, etc.

A K J J 10 8 7 6 6 5 4   (Ex. 12)
Joker 2 2 A J 10 9 9 7 4 3   (Ex. 13)

Despite the reputed high incidence of such hands, most of them develop quickly into one type or another. Example 12 is "blah," yet it is typical of many that quickly develop into pack takers through quick pairing and the draw of a wild card.

Example 13 at the moment has *"embarras de richesse"*— too many wild cards—but of course could quickly develop into an out hand if it fills a couple of sets. At the same time it must not be overlooked that this hand, in common with most nondescript hands, has an excellent chance to become a pack taker through the very diversity of its ranks.

THE INITIAL MELD

Early books on Canasta stressed the advantage to be gained by making an initial meld as early as possible, "thus unfreezing the pack for self and partner." Later experience has shown, however, that their recommendations for early melds (made without taking the pack) are much too broad.

The Quick Meld   By a quick meld I mean one made within the first two rounds and without taking the discard pile. The reason for making an early meld can only be one of three:

(a) to relieve partner of having to meet the count; (b) to unfreeze the pack for your side; (c) to launch a quick-out campaign. The last reason is not a true early-meld proposition, for it is a reason for melding at any stage, early or late. I will discuss this matter later.

Rule of 0-4-6 To avoid any misunderstanding, let me repeat that the "quick meld" is fit and proper—if at all— only within the first two rounds of play. Thereafter the importance of defending the pack outweighs any possible gain to be had by unfreezing the pack (since the opponents will freeze it again).

The present practice of most players as regards the quick meld (merely to "take the strain off") is expressed by the rule of 0-4-6:

To make an initial, expend: at 50, zero cards, at 90 no more than four cards; at 120, no more than six cards. The typical economical melds are:

   (90) Joker 2 K K   (120) Joker A A K K K   (Ex. 14)

However, top experts when competing against each other require the perfect type of meld before coming down. You might call theirs the rule of 0-3-4. Examples are:

   (90) Joker A A   (120) Joker Joker K K   (Ex. 15)
                            Joker 2 A A A

The foregoing does *not* mean you should make an economical initial meld every time you are able to. It means you should not consider for a moment making an early meld unless you can make it economically and on the first or second round (or, with a perfect meld as in Example 15, the third round). Whether you should do so still depends on your judgment of other factors. The ranks you meld are probably dead for your side as regards pack getting. Putting down Aces is probably no loss, since you don't ever expect an early discard of an Ace. Putting down one rank of high cards is some impairment of the hand, but may be worth while. Exposing two ranks of high cards is less good, and melding any rank of low cards is a serious impairment.

Also, after one to three rounds you may be able to judge

whether your partner does or does not need help in preserving his hand.

The predominant factor, however, in deciding whether to meld is the character of your own hand—how good it is as a pack taker.

Joker A A K K K 10 10 8 7 5 4   (Ex. 16)

Almost devoid of pairs outside the 120 meld, this hand might meld at once, giving partner maximum chance to take the pack without having to meet the count.

Joker Joker J J Q 9 7 7 5 4 4 3   (Ex. 17)

Although able to make a perfect meld of 120 with four cards, this hand should not do so. Because of the low pairs it is already as good a pack taker as you can expect to get at that high count. On this type of hand you are best advised to play a solo game, concentrating on getting the pack yourself and letting your partner suffer what pangs he must.

Quick Meld at 50   The rule of 0-4-6 says that you should expend zero cards to meet the minimum requirement of 50, in other words, that you should not meld at all. This is sound advice as a general rule. Assume, as is almost always the case, that your partner can scrape together 50, if need be, to take the pack. Don't "take the strain off him" to the detriment of your own hand.

There is, however, an occasional case in which you stand to better your own prospects by a first- or second-turn meld at 50. This is a hand able to meld economically, but almost bereft of other pairs, as:

2 2 A A A J 9 8 7 5 4 3   (Ex. 18)

Here the diversity of ranks promises an early opportunity to take the pack with one natural and one wild card—if it is unfrozen. You would be interested in taking a pack of only five or six cards if you could thereby add several pairs to your hand. Finally, the Aces are scarcely better in your hand than out. The natural play is therefore to put down the Aces immediately and discard the black Three.

Showing the Quick-Out Hand   At an early stage the only

sound motive for trying to go out quickly is to capitalize a hand fine for that purpose and therefore poor for pack taking. At a later stage the motive may be to cut the loss, the opponents having taken the first pack and obtained control.

In either case there is no sense in halfway measures. Go all-out or not at all. That means that when one partner declares quick-out intentions, the other must meld and lay off every card he can.

In declaring a quick-out hand by an early meld, therefore, make your intention unmistakable by putting down *more* than the required count. This means a whole set more than is necessary. Suppose that your hand (at requirement 50) is:

2 2 2 A A A Q 6 6 6 4 3   (Ex. 19)

If you meld only A, A, A, your partner is bound to assume that you are making the self-help "quick meld at 50" (Example 18). Meld the three Sixes also.

When the initial melder puts down an extra meld beyond what is necessary to meet the count, his partner is bound to interpret the act as a desire to go out.

The Small First Pack   As a general principle, a first pack of four or less cards is not worth taking, while a pack of nine or more *must* be taken, if possible. In the latter case keeping the pack out of your opponent's hands is vital, no matter what you get for yourself.

There remains an area of option, when the pack contains about five to eight cards. The question whether to take it depends on the precise situation. Having a good pack taker, usually wait for a bigger pack, unless the small one is rich with just the cards you need. If you have already made an initial meld, usually take the small pack if you thereby will have a larger hand after melding. With a depleted hand any substantial increase is welcome.

EARLY DISCARDING

The question of what is and what is not a safe discard is most acute at the very beginning of a deal, before any meld has been made. Here is some advice based on experience.

Matching Discards On rounds one and two any discard you make may be wild as regards your left opponent. But you should not worry about giving the pack at this time, since it is so small. Concentrate, rather, on keeping your right opponent in the dark about your own hand. For this purpose you cannot do better than to match his discards. If he throws a Seven, discard a Seven if you have one and can spare it. All you tell him is that you don't want Sevens—which he already knows. Also, you avoid showing him a second safe rank.

On rounds three and four, it becomes important to protect the pack, now of respectable size. For this purpose your safest course is to match the discards made by your left opponent on the first two rounds. The presumption is that he does not have a pair left in a rank that he has discarded so early. Sometimes you will be wrong, but more often you will be right.

Blind Discards Now suppose that you are unable to match the adverse discards. What should you do? Well, in general, you will have to let go odd cards of no immediate use to you. Sometimes you will be able to "trap," of which more anon. But let us first take the situation where you have to guess what to let go from several odd cards. To take a concrete example:

2 2 K Q Q 10 10 10 6 4 4 3   (Ex. 20)

This is your hand on a very early round. You have to choose from the King, Six, and Three. Your left opponent has discarded no King or Six. What should you choose?

Here the mediocre player exactly reverses the proper procedure. He starts with the safe Three, then the Six, and finally the King (if forced). In all common sense the right order is to discard in order: King, Six, Three. Let go the most dangerous card first, when the pack is small, saving the safest for the time when the pack is larger.

Trap Discard A trap discard, also called "advertising," is one from a set of three or more. Many players make a fetish of beginning with a trap discard. For example:

2 2 A A J 9 8 7 5 5 5 4   (Ex. 21)

With this hand—as too many "authorities" recommend—the tyro will gleefully discard a Five at his first turn.

The idea of inducing your right opponent to discard a Five is seductive, but is it worth while? If the opponents get the pack, this hand will be left with an embarrassing pair of Fives. If the early draws turn this nondescript hand into a quick-out proposition, as well may be, the sacrifice of the Five will be bitterly regretted.

The impulse to discard from the trio in such hands often comes from fear that the odd cards are dangerous. True, they may be, but the danger only waxes as time passes. Deferring it one round is short-sighted policy.

Still worse is the trap discard from a set that may be needed to make the count in taking the pack:

A A Q J J 9 8 7 5 5 5 4   (Ex. 22)

To make even 50, this hand will have to draw a useful card. If that card happens to be a Jack, it is still short unless the three Fives are kept intact. To trap-discard a Five would be criminal folly.

The natural hand for a trap discard is the powerful pack taker:

Joker A A Q Q 6 6 6 6 4 4 3   (Ex. 23)

Let go a Six here, since it can be spared in all respects. It is not needed to make the count (50 or 90), and should the opponents get it by taking the pack the hand is not embarrassed—it is still an excellent hand with a convenient meld.

Hands of the following type offer a choice:

A A A J J 8 7 5 5 5 3 3   (Ex. 24)

At 50, you can afford to discard a Five. An important point is that with two black Threes you can look ahead to at least two later safe discards, during which time the pack grows and your right opponent gets opportunity to discard a Five. The trouble with many would-be traps is that the hand has no safe discards anyhow, and that after the trap the hand has to begin to shed odd cards. As explained previously, unmatched high cards are better discarded immediately.

When option of a trap discard offers, be guided by the

common-sense principle of varying your style from deal to deal, so as to keep your right-hand opponent guessing.

Spotting the Trap Spotting the trap discard in every early round is sheer guesswork—unless your left opponent is a "wooden" player who traps at every opportunity. But from the fifth round on clues may show up the trap.

When the pack is very large—twenty cards or more—suspect the breaking of a new rank by your left opponent to be a trap. True, he may have been compelled to part with a residual odd card. But from his point of view this is wildly dangerous: he is much more likely to have dipped into a trio or quartet as being the rank of which your partner is less likely to have a pair.

When Not to Play Safe The foregoing advice on discarding is intended to apply in any situation where the two sides are on equal or near-equal terms. It must not be overlooked that safety in discarding becomes secondary when the situation is markedly unbalanced. Specifically, a side needing 120 for the initial meld cannot hope to defend the first pack against a side needing only 50, and is at a considerable disadvantage against opponents needing 90. The disparity is not so great when one side needs 50 and the other 90, but the latter must nevertheless recognize that it is at a disadvantage, and comport itself accordingly.

The side needing the higher count is bound to treat the pack as a boon that might come its way but is more likely to go to the opponents. Discarding here is motivated primarily by preserving one's own prospects, building toward the count—defending the pack, trap discarding, etc., must go by the board.

The side enjoying the lower requirement should press its advantage home by defending the first pack to the last ditch, until it has grown to size worth taking. This may involve discarding wild cards, either for safety or to keep active pairs in hand. It may involve remodeling an ideal quick-out hand to make it a pack taker, by discards from a set of four or five. A quick out is the last thing to strive for when you have a distinct edge in meld requirement: building up a pack taker even from a measly start figures to net you thousands of points more than you could make by going out quickly, even though you thereby set the opponents back.

AFTER THE FIRST PACK IS TAKEN

The side that first takes the discard pile thereby gains a great advantage, which is sure to be decisive if the pack is large, and may be crushing even if the pack is moderate.

The strategy you should now follow depends of course on whether you are the victor or the vanquished.

YOUR SIDE TAKES THE PACK

Keep Control Your long-range objective is to exhaust the stock before going out. Your opponents—the dogs!—will probably try to curtail the play, for the longer it continues, the farther you are likely to pull ahead of them in canasta bonuses.

Having gained control, you and your partner should co-operate to keep it. This means cinching all future packs for your side, preventing the opponents from taking any worthwhile pack, and forestalling their defense of their going out.

Cinching Future Packs A big pack provides you pairs of so many different ranks that the opponents will be hard put for safe discards. However, to retain this advantage against a possible freeze, you have got to keep the pairs in hand. Therefore, meld only what you must to take the pack, plus whatever you can spare without giving up valuable pairs.

Suppose that you take a pack of twenty cards with a Seven, holding:

2 A J J 10 10 10 7 7 6 6   (Ex. 25)

To meet the requirement of 50, you meld 7-7-7-2 and 10-10-10. The rest of the pack contains:

A K K Q 10 10 9 7 7 6 6 6 6 5 5 5 5 5 3 3

Do not add the Tens and Sevens to your initial meld. Keep these pairs in hand. Meld three Fives or three Sixes, keeping the remaining pair in hand. But don't meld both of these sets. Keep all five of one rank in hand—the one known to be safe from your left opponent. These will furnish pack-saving discards if need be.

Having taken a big pack, keep most of it in hand to retain control. Be ultrasafe in discarding. In the above situation you have two black Threes that offer safety. But that is a slim margin. By keeping back one set of five, you have a run of seven safe discards while the pack builds up for your aggrandizement.

After the recommended melding here is the situation:

MELDED

10 10 10   2 7 7 7   6 6 6

IN HAND

A A K K Q J J 10 10 9 7 7 6 6 5 5 5 5 5 3 3

The only ranks with which you now could not take a frozen pack are Queen, Nine, Eight, Four. You may develop pairs even here, and in any case the opponents cannot discard these ranks exclusively without wrecking their hands.

Don't Be a Pack Hog   Having taken a big pack, don't be in a hurry to take the next pack. In the first place you want to let it build up; you want to get something worth while. In the second place—and more important—you want to throw the next pack to your partner, if you can.

The big killings are brought about by two partnership hands, both of which have more than their original eleven cards. A large hand on only one side of the table is not nearly so powerful. So—don't be a pack hog. Let your partner in the game.

Watch for Danger   Holding back as advised above does run a certain risk—that the opponents may go out suddenly and leave you with a big hand and few or no canastas.

An opponent may defend by melding all he can, trying for a quick out. If his partner's hand happens to match well, they may go out in short order. Your course is to estimate this danger and play accordingly.

To continue the preceding example, suppose that after you have taken the pack and melded as described, your left opponent melds from his hand:

Joker 10 10   5 5 5   (Ex. 26)

(Not likely, but it illustrates the point.) Obviously you have no cause for alarm. Neither of these sets can become a canasta, since you have five of each rank.

At the other extreme suppose that your left opponent melds:

Q Q Q Q   8 8 8   (Ex. 27)

Surely, your right opponent can complete a canasta at his next turn. Quite possibly he can go out. Your partner should unload everything he can, making what canastas he can.

Suppose that your right opponent in turn does complete a canasta but does not go out. Now it is up to you to unload everything. Your left opponent may have a completely matched hand that needed only the completion of a canasta to go out.

To summarize, you must usually unload everything immediately after the opponents, trying for quick out, have completed a canasta. When one opponent melds a base or a set that probably can be built quickly into a canasta, the next player of your side had better cash in at least to the extent of completing what canastas he can. If the opponents meld nothing, you string along with your big hand, trying to reach the end of the stock before going out.

OTHER SIDE TAKES THE PACK

The test of the expert is not how well he plays the good cards but how well he plays the bad. Many people play good cards well, and poor cards badly. Whether you go in for Canasta, Blackjack, dice, horses, or the stock market, you cannot win without the steel nerve to cut your losses when the run of luck is against you.

If the opponents get the first big pack, make up your mind that *you are licked!* Don't launch a head-on fight for the next pack—the odds are overwhelmingly against you. Don't freeze

—that's a wild card gone, probably without effect. Concentrate on the fact that your only real hope is to go out as soon as possible, limiting your losses.

To launch the campaign for a quick out, begin with an initial meld that has real prospects of producing a quick canasta. Meld ranks not already melded by the opponents or known to be held in abundance by the pack taker. Example 26, which I gave previously, an initial meld of Joker-10-10, 5-5-5, when the pack taker is known to have five Tens and five Fives, is really insane. Better not to meld at all than to put down these useless sets.

As in any quick-out drive the partner of the initial melder should at next turn lay off all natural cards he can on the initial meld, plus all other sets he can spare.

Discarding At any time that your side chooses or is forced to adopt a quick-out effort you should co-operate to the utmost in discarding. This means that you should discard what your partner discards, and save what ranks you infer he is saving. The purpose is to form the two hands so far as possible into identical ranks, so that each new set melded gives the other hand layoffs.

Begin this co-operation as soon as the big pack has gone to an opponent. Don't wait for an initial meld by your side to signal the quick-out campaign—you should both know that that policy has been forced on you. Good partnership discarding here often brings about a situation where the initial meld, when finally made, lets the other hand go out at his next turn.

As a consequence of partnership discarding you will find that you will have to discard cards useful to the opponents. So what? Let such cards go without a qualm. You are better off giving the opponents an extra canasta or two now, if that helps to get you out quickly, than to prolong the game and let the opponents pile up a half-dozen extra canastas. Also bear in mind that many of the cards you might shrink from giving the opponents are not actually needed by them. In the foregoing example, where you were stuck with some Tens and Fives, the pack taker being known to have five of each rank, what matter if you feed your cards to him? You could not, by withholding these cards, prevent him from completing the canastas. At worst you might give him an extra 200 points, the difference between a mixed and a natural canasta.

The golden rule of the all-out campaign is to save only those cards that you can meld yourself sooner or later. Get rid of the off-cards no matter how useful they may be to the opponents.

Safety Discarding Exception arises even to the foregoing rule. There comes a time in every man's life when he has to give up. If the pack is nearly exhausted, you have not succeeded in going out, and the opponents still have the whip hand, there is no use in contributing further to their riches. You do whatever you can to play safe—you either freeze the pack, or you avoid discarding cards of any value to them.

FREEZING THE PACK

The question whether or when to discard a wild card is one of the most perplexing in the game. All that can be said in a general way is that before freezing the pack you should have clearly in mind what you expect to gain, and should weigh the chance of success against the chance of losing the wild card as well as the objective.

I distinguish six situations in which freezing the pack may be advisable. These are described in the following sections.

Freeze Before Any Meld The discard of a wild card before any meld has been made has the effect of freezing the pack, but that is not its primary purpose. The discard does not affect the terms on which the pack can be first taken, but simply deprives a quick-melding hand of incentive. The reason for a wild discard at this time must be to show an excellent pack taker, and to save room in the hand for more useful cards.

For example:

Joker 2 2 A Q Q 9 9 7 7 4 4   (Ex. 28)

The pack has built up and the Ace is unsafe. Rather than break a pair, let go a Deuce.

If your partner makes such a discard, assume:

1. that he can spare the Deuce and still make the count for initial meld;
2. that he has a fine pack taker.

You should therefore bend your energies toward protecting the pack for him, even at the cost of impairing your own hand.

Sometimes the wild discard is precipitated by a particular situation. For example, your right opponent discards a Six, and you have one Six. You draw, and get another Six. Having no other safe discard, you may well let go a wild card at this juncture, hoping that your right opponent was splitting Sixes and will favor you with another Six shortly.

Freeze After Adverse Initial Meld When an opponent makes an initial meld without taking the pack, and the pack is worth defending, you are practically forced to defend by freezing the pack. The next player of your side should discard a wild card if he has one to spare. This play is so much a matter of routine that it is rarely omitted. The only good reason for failing to make it is that you positively cannot spare a wild card (or have none). You can always spare a wild card at count of 50. At 90 or 120 perhaps you cannot spare one if you have a fair pack taker and need all your wild cards to make the count:

2 2 A A K J J 10 6 6 5 3   (Ex. 29)

Both sides need 50. This is your hand after your third draw. Your right opponent has just melded A-A-A. You should discard a Two automatically. You could temporize with the Three, but why do so? You can afford to part with a Two, and maybe your partner cannot.

2 A K K K 9 8 7 7 5 5 3   (Ex. 30)

In the same situation as above this is your hand. Here you should discard the Three. To discard your only wild card would leave you unable to take the pack. Temporize to see whether your partner can afford to freeze. If he does not do so at once, you should part with the Two at your next turn.

Joker 2 Q Q Q 10 10 8 8 4 4 3   (Ex. 31)

Both sides need 90. This is your hand after your fourth draw. Your right opponent has just melded Joker-A-A. You should discard the Two. You can spare it and still make 90 in taking the pack.

2 A K K J J 10 7 7 7 6 6   (Ex. 32)

In the same situation as above, this is your hand. If the Ace or Ten is surely safe, discard it, hoping your partner can freeze. But if neither is safe, discard the Two. It will then be harder for you to collect 90, but you are already so far away that you had better concentrate on defense and leave it to partner to make the initial meld.

Joker A A K 10 10 9 9 8 5 5 5   (Ex. 33)

This is your hand after your third draw. Both sides need 120. Left opponent has melded Joker-A-A, Q-Q-Q. Your partner has failed to freeze, but his discard got by your right opponent. Now it is up to you. Should you part with your Joker? No, you cannot afford to do so. You can make the count in taking the pack, and presumably your partner cannot. To leave both hands destitute of the count would be just as dangerous as giving away the pack. Discard a Five. Very probably this is safe, since your left opponent has just stripped himself to five cards. Your partner will probably realize your predicament, since you twice failed to freeze, and will make every effort himself to freeze, in which event your hand will become an excellent pack taker.

Mid-Game Freeze for Defense   If the opponents have taken a big pack and obtained control, freezing the next pack as a defense is useless. As I have said, your only salvation is in going out fast.

But situations do arise in which both sides take packs, with neither side having gained the whip hand. In such balanced situations freezing the pack may be an effective method of defense.

Since your wild card will freeze the pack for you as well as for the opponents, be sure before playing it that you will be hurt less than they. The typical situation for this freeze is that the opponents have melded several more ranks than your side. Another is that with equal melding your side has retained pairs matching the melds, while the opposing side has not. The point is that the freeze (if correct) establishes more ranks for you as safe discards than for the opponents.

Offensive Freeze If both opponents have depleted their hands and your side has not, you have a strong offensive position. Your chances of getting future packs are much better than theirs. Generally, in such a situation, an unfrozen pack is advantageous to the strong side.

But don't overlook that even here you may stand to gain by freezing. If you have melded little or nothing, or if you have retained pairs matching your melds, the freeze hurts you not at all. But it may hurt the opponents by letting you discard cards matching their melds. The fewer the cards left in their hands, the less likely they are to have matching pairs.

Temporary Freeze This is a freeze made to tide you over a temporary situation. You are striving to go out, you have a couple of dangerous cards that you must get rid of, and you hope to draw out soon. For example, you have completed a canasta of Queens, and have several minor melds, and are down to:

$$2\ 2\ A\ K\ 7\ 7 \quad \text{(Ex. 34)}$$

Among the adverse melds are five Aces and six Kings. You can spare a Deuce to freeze the pack, so as to be able to discard your Ace and King on the way out.

Terminal Defensive Freeze I have mentioned that even though you are the victim of a squeeze, occasion may arise for defending the pack. This is usually at the last stage of a game, where you can but hope to deprive the opponents of another canasta or two that they might have by taking the last pack.

Such terminal safety play, especially by freezing, is common at the last stage of any deal that reaches the bottom of the stock. Even when the positions are balanced, one side or the other will usually find that it must freeze.

DEALING WITH THE FROZEN PACK

Pack Born Frozen The pack born frozen—through turning a wild card or red Three as the first upcard—intensifies the struggle for the first pack. The quick-meld type of hand vanishes. To meld without taking the pack and also without unfreezing it for your side would be pointless. In consequence your appraisal of your hand is practically limited to two types: pack taker or quick out (with the pack taker representing at least 90% of cases).

The fact that even a small pack is worth taking, in order to get the wild card or red Three, impels you to defend earlier than usual—starting your traps and safe discards even before the pack has grown to any size.

A point to be remembered, however, is that you should not embark on this intensified fight if you start the deal with a marked disadvantage—as through needing 120 while opponents need only 50.

Pack Frozen Later This is the usual situation where the pack has been deliberately frozen by the discard of a wild card. In the previous section I have described the common situations calling for such a freeze.

The deliberate freeze is in effect an assertion by that side that it has achieved an advantage. The terms in which such advantage can be stated are as follows:

1. Number of cards A side holding more cards than the opponents has an advantage roughly proportional to the ratio between the two holdings. Obviously the bigger the hand, the better its chance of taking the pack.

2. Number of melds A side having melded fewer ranks than the opponents has an advantage. The more ranks a side melds, the greater the efficacy of defensive freezing. This is not to say that when you meld three Sevens, keeping two Sevens in your hand, the opponents are any better off. But taking it in large, the more cards you meld, the greater the chance of pointing out to the opponents exactly those ranks in which you do not have reserve pairs.

3. Positional disparity A player having to discard from a depleted hand to an enlarged left opponent suffers a disadvantage in defending the pack. Such advantage may accrue even when the totals of cards on both sides are equal. For example, suppose that North and East each has fifteen cards, South and West each has six. The latter two, having depleted hands, are at relative disadvantage in discarding, while North and East enjoy greater option. But South discards to West— a small hand—while West discards to North—a big hand. West will find it harder to defend than will South, so that the East-West partnership suffers a marked disadvantage.

When faced by an adverse freeze, you should at once evaluate for yourself the factors on which it was evidently based. If you reach the same conclusion as the opponents— that they have a marked advantage—your course is clear. You steer out of the battle for the pack, more or less conceding it, and concentrate on going out as soon as possible.

If, on the other hand, you decide the opponents have misjudged the situation, and that you can fight on equal terms, you proceed to do so.

When feasible, respond to the freeze immediately with a discard that indicates to your partner your appraisal of the situation. If you concede defeat, throw a couple of dangerous odd cards. If you decide to fight, throw a wild card, or cards valuable to the adverse melds that you would not otherwise risk placing in the pack.

Many Canasta players are inclined to be unduly optimistic in the face of a freeze. While it is true that there are balanced situations, they are far fewer than the optimist realizes. Nine times out of ten the deliberate freeze is based on sound and clinching considerations, and to refuse to face the fact merely contributes to the upkeep of your opponents.

PARTNERSHIP CONVENTIONS

The logical interpretation of certain plays—if made with sound reason—is so unmistakable that they have given rise to "conventions." A convention is a prior agreement between partners, known to the opponents, as to the meaning of a play. The only prior agreement involved in most Canasta conventions is to refrain from making certain crucial plays unless the logical meaning is actually intended.

Overmelding I have already noted that putting down more cards than are necessary to meet an initial meld signals a desire to go out as soon as possible.

Gratuitous Melding Melding anything at all "out of the clear sky"—that is, when you are not making an initial meld, and when you are not taking the pack—abandons some chance for the pack. It becomes a clear signal for out in certain situations:

1. when you lay off on completed canastas and meld new ranks;
2. when the pack is large.

Canasta Request This is a common-sense way of asking your partner to complete a canasta, even at the cost of his only wild card. It consists in:

1. adding two wild cards to a base of four;
2. adding one wild card to a base of five and reducing your hand to three or less cards.

Asking Permission Asking your partner, "May I go out?" at a time when he holds so many cards that he must obviously say, "No," really says, "Partner, unload everything you can. I could go out now [else the question would be illegal], but I want you to cash in first."

Discard of an Ace at 120 To meet an initial count of 120 usually requires Aces as well as Jokers. At all events Aces are hoarded in the early play at this level. Hence, if you discard an Ace at this time you fairly scream that you have 120 (or close to it) already in hand. You tell your partner that he can abandon the effort to amass the count and can concentrate on defending the pack.

Wild Discard to a Frozen Pack   Discarding a wild card to a pack already frozen obviously says that the wild card can be spared. It shows determination to fight for the pack, and so asks your partner to co-operate in defending it. There is some implication that he can afford to give up some of his own pack-getting prospects, the better to defend, since your own prospects are excellent.

Red and Black Convention   This was a purely artificial convention devised and used by Oswald Jacoby and me in our challenge matches. (We challenged all comers to a fifty-game match, and posted a bond of five thousand dollars, which was to go to charity upon our defeat. As yet we have not been defeated.)

The convention is intended for use only at a player's first discard when his side needs 120 or 90 for an initial meld. The discard of a red card announces here that the hand will have great difficulty in meeting the count. A black discard, conversely, shows good prospect of reaching the count soon.

The value of the signal is of course that it avoids duplication of effort to make the initial meld. One partner is left free to form his hand as a pack taker with low pairs, while the other saves high cards toward the initial meld.

GENERAL PRINCIPLES

Concealed Hand   The bonus of 100 points for going out concealed is a trifle. The enormous labor of collecting a wholly matched hand is not recompensed by this paltry amount. Why should you ever try for a concealed hand?

The answer is: because it does offer two other advantages, slight though they be, and the course may be forced on you in a desperate situation.

Suppose that at a mature stage of a deal you hold:

2 2 Q Q Q Q 7 7 7 7 K 10   (Ex. 35)

The opponents have melded four or five each of Kings and Tens. Your side, needing 120, has yet to break the ice.

What can you discard? If you defend by letting go a wild card or breaking up a set, you are farther than ever from amassing an initial meld. The only course with any prospects is to hang on for a concealed hand. To do so, you will have to feed the opponents a King or Ten or both. So what? You stand to minimize your loss if you draw a wild card, Queen, or Seven.

This example typifies the two advantages of going out concealed: (a) you do not need to meet initial count; (b) you may catch the opponents flat-footed, with hundreds of points still uncashed.

Economizing in Wild Cards   The most common mistake of mediocre players is to expend wild cards too freely, particularly to complete canastas when no great urgency presses.

Wild cards seem cheap at times, but the supply is not unlimited. The time to use your wild cards to good advantage is when one side or the other is on the point of going out. Until then, be parsimonious. You will find plenty of occasions when a hoarded wild card is a lifesaver—in a tight fight for a big pack, or in matching up the odd pairs of your hand to go out.

A part of the story is, of course, that your minor melds are more embarrassing to the opponents than your completed canastas. Suppose that you have laid four Jacks on the table. Your opponents now will hesitate to discard a Jack, even on a small pack. The Jack alone may be worth taking, since it saves a wild card. But once you complete the canasta of Jacks, the opponents can discard Jacks freely, so long as they do not thereby give you worth-while packs. The Jacks themselves have become worthless to you.

Waiting Hand   When your side is striving to go out, your partner's decision what or how much to meld often depends on whether you have a "waiting hand"—one that can be laid down if (a) you can draw a right card, or (b) he can complete the first canasta. You should therefore try to inform him whether your hand is waiting or not.

In many cases the situation is obvious. Let us say that you hold:

2 2 K K Q   (Ex. 36)

and your side has melded 6-6-6-6-6. You lay off one Deuce (not two) on the Sixes, and discard the Queen. Obviously you are asking him to close the Sixes if possible, and your expenditure of a wild card for this purpose tells him that you have a waiter. Leaving yourself with only three cards implies that you have a completed set.

The clearest indication you can give, outside of laying off a wild card, is to strip down to exactly one, three, or six cards. Any sudden melding so as to reduce to one of these exact numbers asks partner to complete the first canasta at all costs, or complete others as he can, or in general to unload everything worth cashing. If you do not actually have a waiting hand, try to strip to a different number of cards. In effect you tell your partner to try to complete his own hand, since your prospects are poor. For example, having six cards including no pair, but including a wild card, lay off the wild card where it will do the most good.

Percentage Play   With a choice of two canastas to complete by a wild card pick the one having less chance to be completed naturally.

For example, suppose your side has melded:

2 2 9 9 9 9   7 7 7 7 7 7   (Ex. 37)

The deal is well advanced; and you have a wild card available to use.

The temptation is strong to keep the Sevens open in the hope of making a natural canasta. But with fewer Sevens than Nines outstanding you have less chance of drawing a Seven than a Nine. The percentage play is to put your Deuce on the Sevens, preserving the best chance to complete the second canasta by the draw of a natural card.

Play to the Score   To have a lower initial-meld requirement than the opponents is an evident tactical advantage in pack getting, with all its consequences on discarding. To put yourself into a higher bracket—even though you have to do so in order eventually to win—incurs a handicap.

A refinement of expert play is to keep track of the score meticulously and to avoid going over the crucial points of 1500 and 3000 except by a big margin. I must give credit for this refinement to the English players, Terence Reese and Colin Harding, whose brilliant maneuvers to stay "just under" I have found a pleasure to watch.

The English experts estimate that it is worth about 300 points to stay under 1500, and 500 to stay under 3000. This means that you should shoot for a score of 1495 or 1800, of 2995 or 3500, rather than for a score in between. I would reduce these figures to about 200 and about 350, but they have the right idea.

Once you are over 3000, try to reach 5000 in one deal. Every deal you play at 120 requirement is a hazard. Keep track of your cash score in melds and canasta bonuses, less estimated cards in hand, and strive to put 5000 in sight before you run for an out.

Another crucial situation in which the score is governing is this: The opponents are close enough to 5000 to win, probably, just by melding; your side needs 50 or 90 for an initial meld. Here you should concentrate to the utmost on going out fast, so as to catch the opponents with a minus score and so give yourselves a breathing spell.

Two-Handed Canasta   This is the prevalent form of Canasta, based on a couple of innovations that I originally introduced: In each turn you draw two cards from the stock and discard only one; and you need two canastas to go out. Otherwise the rules are the same as in four-handed Canasta. The National Canasta Laws Commission adopted these into the official rules for two-hand play.

Most of the time two-handed Canasta is a struggle to get the first big discard pile and control the discard pile thereafter. Once a player loses a sizeable discard pile to his opponent, he must play desperately to go out. Until then, unless he was dealt a freakish hand with a couple of sets of four or five cards, he is almost always better off to play for the pack.

Playing for the pack means safe discarding. Fortunately, drawing two cards in a turn, you get quite a few pairs and an unusually high number of wild cards. The principal value of the wild cards is for safe discards when the going gets tough. As long as you have a chance for the pack, you want to keep as many pairs as possible.

This is one reason why it often pays to break up three- and four-card sets early in the play, discarding one or two cards and saving the pair. If your opponent matches your discards later, thinking they should be safe, you will have a pair and can take the pack. Since your object is to take the pack, holding a set of three keeps a superfluous card in your hand. With that card out of your hand you might have room for an additional pair.

Having no partner to help, you cannot profit from melding except when you think there is danger that your opponent will go out. There is almost no point in making the initial meld from your hand; your opponent will not let the discard pile remain unfrozen for you, but will promptly throw a wild card and freeze it again. If your opponent is an inexperienced player who makes his initial meld early, and if the pack is large enough to be worth taking, you must freeze.

Since you are entitled to draw two cards from the stock, it seldom pays to take the pack unless there are ten or more cards in it. An exception would be found when it has six or seven cards that fit beautifully with your hand and give you one or two early canastas.

Very brief experience will show you how soon in the play you are stuck for safe discards. For this reason you should save your black Threes and other safe discards while the pack is small and not worth taking. Even if your opponent could take your early discard, he will probably disregard it and draw from the stock.

If you were dealt something like three wild cards, a four-card group, and a three-card group, you are usually better off to play for a quick out. The profits will not be nearly so large as when you get a big pack, but there will be a profit, and you will avoid the risk of a big loss.

Any two-handed game has a large factor of psychology in it. You must mix up your play so that your opponent cannot read your early discards. Sometimes throw your unmatched cards first; at other times break up your sets first (if your hand is such that you intend to do so sooner or later). If you acquire fixed habits in discarding, your opponent will soon learn them and frustrate your attempts to trap him.

LAWS OF CANASTA

Players

1. Canasta may be played by two, three, four, five, or six players. It is best for two or four.

2. With two or three players, each plays for himself. With four or more, there are partnerships. With five, two partners are opposed by three, but only two of the three play at a time, rotating so that each of the three in turn sits out. Six-hand may be played in two partnerships of three players each, or three partnerships of two each, or the same as five-hand except that one player on each side sits out each time.

Cards

3. The game is played with two regular decks of fifty-two cards, plus four Jokers, all 108 cards being shuffled together.

4. The Jokers and Twos are wild. A wild card is melded only with natural cards and then becomes of the same rank.

Preliminaries

5. Partnerships may be determined by drawing cards from the deck. The player drawing highest card has choice of seats, plays first in the first deal, and has second highest as partner.

6. In drawing, the cards rank: A (high), K, Q, J, 10, 9,

8, 7, 6, 5, 4, 3, 2. Jokers are void. Suits rank: Spades (high), Hearts, Diamonds, Clubs. Players drawing equal cards must draw again. A player drawing a Joker, or more than one card, or one of the four cards at either end of the deck, must draw again.

7. Partners take places opposite each other.

The Deal

8. The first deal is made by the player who sits at right of the player who drew the highest card. Thereafter the turn to deal rotates clockwise (to the left).

9. Any player who wishes may shuffle the deck. The dealer has the right to shuffle last.

10. After it has been shuffled, the deck must be cut by the player at the dealer's right.

11. The dealer gives eleven cards to each player, one at a time clockwise, beginning with the opponent at his left and ending with himself.

12. The undealt remainder of the deck is placed face down in the center of the table, becoming the stock.

13. The top card of the stock is turned face up beside it, forming the upcard. If the upcard is a Joker, Two, black or red Three, one or more additional cards must be turned upon it until a natural card of ranks Ace to Four appears.

Red Threes

14. A player finding a red Three in his hand must, at his first turn, put it face up on the table and draw a replacement from the stock.

15. A player who draws a red Three from the stock must immediately place it face up on the table and draw a replacement.

16. A player who takes the discard pile and finds a red Three in it must place the Three face up on the table, but does not draw a replacement.

17. Each red Three has a bonus value of 100 points, with an extra bonus of 400 points if all four Threes are obtained

by one side. The value of its red Threes is credited (plus) to a side that has made any meld, or debited (minus) against a side that has made no meld, by the time the play ends.

Order of Play

18. The opponent at left of the dealer plays first. Thereafter the turn to play rotates clockwise (to the left). Each turn comprises: a draw, a meld (optional), and a discard.

19. The player in turn is always entitled to draw the top card of the stock. (In two-hand, the draw from the stock comprises two cards.) He may instead (subject to restrictions in Paragraphs 34–39) take the top card of the discard pile to use it in a meld; having done so, he must take the rest of the discard pile.

20. The discard comprises one card from the hand (never from a meld). All discards are placed in one pile beside the stock (on the upcard if it is still there). The discard pile must be kept squared up, except as examination is allowed under Paragraph 40.

Melds

21. The principal object of play is to form melds, combinations of three or more cards of the same rank, with or without the help of wild cards. (Sequences are not valid melds in Canasta.)

22. A meld is valid if it contains at least two natural cards of the same rank, Ace to Four inclusive, and not more than three wild cards.

23. Jokers and Twos may never be melded apart from natural cards. A set of three or four black Threes (without wild cards) may be melded only in going out.

24. To count plus, a meld must be laid face up on the table, in a proper turn of the owner. All cards left in the hand when play ends, even though they form melds, count minus.

25. A player may meld as many cards as he pleases in his turn, of one rank or different ranks, forming new melds or adding cards to previous melds. (But see restrictions on "Going Out.")

26. All melds of a partnership are placed in front of one member thereof. A partnership may meld a rank already melded by the opponents, but may not make two different melds of the same rank.

27. A player may add additional cards to a meld of his side, provided that the meld remains valid (Paragraph 22). He may not add cards to his opponents' melds.

Canastas

28. A meld comprising seven or more cards is a canasta. Additional to the point values of the cards, a canasta earns a bonus: 500 for a natural, containing no wild card; 300 for a mixed, containing one to three wild cards.

29. A completed canasta is squared up with a red card on top to indicate a natural, a black card on top to indicate a mixed. Additional cards may be added to a canasta to score their point values, but do not affect the bonus except that the addition of a wild card to a natural canasta reduces it to a mixed. (See also Paragraph 22.)

Minimum Count

30. Every card has a fixed point value, as follows:

Each Joker	50
Each Two	20
Each Ace	20
Each King, Queen, Jack, 10, 9, 8	10
Each 7, 6, 5, 4, and black 3	5

31. The first meld made by a side (its initial meld) must meet a minimum count requirement that depends on the accumulated total score of that side at the time, as follows:

ACCUMULATED SCORE	MINIMUM COUNT
Minus	15
0 to 1495	50
1500 to 2995	90
3000 or more	120

32. The count of a meld is the total point value of its component cards. To meet the minimum, a player may meld two or more different ranks. If he takes the discard pile, he may count the top card (but no other) toward the requirement. Bonuses for red Threes and canastas do not count toward the minimum.

33. After a side has made its initial meld, either partner may make any valid melds without reference to any minimum count.

Taking the Discard Pile

34. The discard pile is frozen against a side before that side has made its initial meld. The initial meld unfreezes it for both partners, provided that it is not additionally frozen under Paragraph 35.

35. The discard pile is frozen against both sides when it contains a red Three (turned as upcard) or a wild card. Such a pile is unfrozen only by being taken. (The lowermost freezing card of the pile is turned sidewise to indicate the freeze.)

36. At a time when the discard pile is frozen (against his side or both), a player may take it only to meld its top card with a natural pair of the same rank from his hand. Before touching the discard pile, he should show his pair, together with such additional cards as may be necessary to meet the minimum count for an initial meld.

37. At a time when the discard pile is not frozen against his side, a player may take it: (a) as provided in Paragraph 36; or (b) to meld its top card together with one matching and one wild card from his hand; or (c) to add its top card to a previous meld of his side, including a completed canasta. (But see Paragraph 45.)

38. Having taken and melded the top discard legally, the player takes the rest of the pile into his hand, and may then meld all such additional cards as he pleases.

39. The discard pile may not be taken when its top card is a wild card or black Three.

Information

40. A player may: (a) examine the discard pile before he has made his first discard; (b) call attention to the correct minimum-count requirement if his partner is in the act of making an initial meld; (c) remind his partner to declare red Threes or draw replacements; (d) turn the sixth card of a meld crosswise to indicate that only one more card is needed to complete a canasta.

41. In his own turn to play, a player is entitled to be informed of: (a) the minimum-count requirement or score of either side; (b) the number of cards held by any player; (c) the number of cards remaining in the stock. If his hand is reduced to one card, he may announce the fact.

Going Out

42. A player goes out when he (legally) gets rid of the last card of his hand, by discard or meld. When any player goes out, play ends and the deal is scored.

43. A player may go out only if his side has melded at least one canasta. (In a two-handed game, two canastas.) Failing this requirement, he must keep at least one card in his hand.

44. A player need not make a discard in going out: he may meld all his remaining cards.

45. A player having only one card in hand may not take a discard pile comprising only one card.

46. If able to go out, before or after drawing from the stock, a player may say, "Partner, may I go out?" His partner must answer, "Yes," or "No," and the answer is binding. Before answering, the partner may obtain the information specified in Paragraph 41.

47. A player may not ask, "Partner, may I go out?" after having melded any card or having indicated intention to take the discard pile. But a player may go out without asking permission.

48. A player goes out concealed when he melds his entire

hand in one turn, including at least one canasta, without having made a previous meld and without having added any card to a meld made by his partner. If his partner has not made an initial meld, he must meet the minimum count (without the canasta bonus) if he has taken the discard pile, but not if he has drawn from the stock.

Exhausting the Stock

49. If a player draws the last card of the stock, and it is a red Three, he faces it, may not meld or discard, and play ends.

50. If the last card of the stock is drawn, and is not a red Three, play continues so long as each player in turn takes the discard. In this period, a player must take the discard if it matches a meld made by his side; he need not take it to form a new meld. (For exception see Paragraph 45.) Play ends when the player in turn cannot take or legally refuses the discard.

Scoring a Deal

51. The base score of a side for a deal is determined by totaling all applicable items in the following schedule:

For going out	100
For going out concealed (extra)	100
For each red Three (Paragraph 17)	100
For each natural canasta	500
For each mixed canasta	300

52. The point score of a side is the total point values (Paragraph 30) of all cards melded, less the point values of the cards left in both hands.

53. The score of a side for a deal is the net of its base and point scores. (It may be minus.)

Scoring a Game

54. The score should be recorded on paper, with one column for each side. Each entry should show the scores of the previous deal or deals, together with the accumulated

totals (which determine the initial meld requirements for next hand).

55. The side that first reaches a total of 5000 wins a game. The final deal is played out, even though one or both sides have surely reached 5000. There is no bonus for winning a game. Settlement is made on the difference of the final totals.

IRREGULARITIES

56. *New Deal* There must be a new deal by the same dealer if he departs in any respect from the laws of correct procedure in dealing, or if he exposes a card other than the correct upcard, or if it is discovered during the deal that the cut was omitted. There must be a new deal if it is discovered, before every player has completed his first turn, that any hand was dealt an incorrect number of cards, that a card is faced in the stock, or that the deck contains a foreign card. (If the error is discovered too late for a new deal, a short hand continues short, a faced card is shuffled in the stock, or a foreign card is discarded from the deck and if it was in a hand the player draws a replacement.)

57. *Drawing Too Many* If a player draws too many cards from the stock he must show the excess cards (if they were not placed in his hand) to all players and replace them on the stock. The next player to draw from the stock may, if he wishes, shuffle it before drawing. If excess cards drawn are placed in the hand, the player must forgo drawing in enough successive turns to reduce his hand to the correct number, discarding one card in each turn. Until his hand is correct, he may not meld.

58. *Exposed Card* If a player exposes a card from his hand except as a meld or discard, such card becomes a penalty card and must be left face up on the table. A penalty card counts as part of the hand, and may be duly melded. If not melded, it must be discarded at first opportunity. With two or more penalty cards, the owner may choose which to discard.

59. Insufficient Count If a player puts down an insufficient count for an initial meld, he may correct the error by melding additional cards and may then rearrange the cards melded. If he cannot do this, he must retract all the cards, in which case the minimum-count requirement for his side (for that hand only) is increased by 10 points.

60. Illegal Meld Cards melded illegally, e.g., in an effort to go out when the side has no canasta or when partner has answered, "No," to "Partner, may I go out?" or excess wild cards in a meld, must be retracted. The side is penalized 100 points for the offense. The same penalty applies if a player, having put down an insufficient count for an initial meld, makes it sufficient with additional cards but retracts one or more of those already exposed.

61. Failure to Declare a Red Three If at the end of play a hand is found to contain an undeclared red Three, the side is penalized 500 points. (Does not apply if a player has had no turn, another before him having gone out on first turn, but the red Three counts minus 100.)

62. Condonement If a player makes an illegal meld and the error is not called until the next hand has drawn or indicated intention to take the pack, Paragraphs 59 and 60 do not apply. An initial meld of insufficient count stands as sufficient; an incorrect combination is retracted without penalty.

63. Taking Pack Illegally A player attempting to take the discard pile without having established his right to do so should be stopped at once. There is no penalty if he can then show a valid claim. But if he has taken the pile into his hand before doing so, the opponents may face his whole hand and reconstruct the pile from it. The offender then picks up his cards, draws from the stock, and his side is penalized 100 points.

64. Irregularity in Asking If a player asks, "Partner, may I go out?" after melding any card or indicating intention to take the discard pile, he must if possible go out. If a player asks the question at a proper time, but melds any card before receiving answer, his opponents may decide whether he must go out or not. If a player asks the question, receives the answer, "Yes," and then cannot go out, his side is penalized 100 points.

NOTE: The penalties above for giving information, exposing cards, etc., do not apply to the two-handed game.

SAMBA

TEN THINGS EVERY WINNING SAMBA PLAYER MUST KNOW

1. Avoid discarding Eights, Nines and Tens.

2. Try to make regular canastas in Aces, Kings, Fives and Fours.

3. Always meld a four- or five-card sequence open at both ends; don't meld dead-end sequences (A-K-Q or 6-5-4).

4. Wild cards are expendable—too many may be a handicap.

5. Don't take an unimportant discard pile; the two-card draw is more valuable.

6. Seldom make the initial meld without taking the discard pile, except when you need 150.

7. Pay little heed to safety in discarding unless the discard pile is very large.

8. No discard can be considered safe in Samba except a wild card or black Three.

9. When your partner melds a sequence, you must immediately add any matching card.

10. If your opponents have everything their way, give up sambas, play for regular canastas and out.

SAMBA

I am especially proud of Samba because the game was my own invention and it became the sixth-most-popular game in the country, according to the 1952 survey of the Association of American Playing Card Manufacturers.

Why did I invent Samba? It was to give the public a game that combined a lot of special features they had proved they liked, but that weren't permitted under the official Canasta laws.

They liked to play with three decks, but regular Canasta with three decks wasn't a good game. They liked to meld sequences. They wanted a card that matches a canasta to be a stop card. They wanted to draw two cards at a time. And so on. Samba was the answer, and I was gratified when the National Canasta Laws Commission adopted it and made official laws for it.

Now there is another variation that many Samba players like: You can't go out without at least one samba. This special rule isn't official, but it makes the scoring higher and the game more exciting, so I heartily approve of it for those who try it and like it. However, the discussion that follows is based on the *official rules only*.

Anyone who knows Canasta can learn Samba in five minutes. If you are not already familiar with the game, you can learn how to play it by reading the Canasta rules (Page 186) together with the following explanation of the modifications for Samba. The Canasta rules on irregularities are used in Samba without change.

The points on which Samba differs from Canasta are as follows:

1. The Pack Three regular packs of fifty-two cards each, plus six Jokers, making 162 cards in all.

2. The Deal Each player receives fifteen cards, regardless of the number of players.

3. The Draw In drawing from the stock a player takes two cards. But the discard ending his turn is only one card. (If a player takes the discard pile, he may not also draw from the stock.)

4. Sequences As in Gin and other Rummy games sequences may be melded. A sequence comprises from three to seven cards of the same suit in consecutive rank. A suit ranks from Ace (high) to Four (low). All cards of a sequence must be natural; no wild cards allowed.

5. Sambas A sequence of seven cards is a samba; it is closed, turned face down, and may not be added to, that is, no sequence may ever be extended beyond seven cards. A samba counts as a canasta for the purpose of going out.

6. Wild Cards No more than two wild cards are allowed in a group meld (cards of the same rank). A canasta base is therefore five natural cards. No wild cards may be added to a completed canasta, nor to any sequence whatsoever.

7. Combining Melds A side may make two or more separate melds in the same rank, and either partner may combine them if and when he pleases (but in his turn) if the combined meld would not contain more than two wild cards. Separate sequences may be joined if they make a single valid sequence (not more than seven cards).

8. Taking the Discard Pile The discard pile may never be taken, as in Canasta, with one natural and one wild card from the hand. To form a new group meld, it may be taken only with a natural pair from the hand, whether it is frozen or unfrozen. It may never be taken to initiate a sequence meld with cards from the hand. If not frozen, it may be taken to lay off the top card on an existing minor meld (less than seven cards) whether group or sequence. (The restriction to a minor meld means that the pack may not be taken to lay off the top card on a completed canasta.)

9. Laying Off on Canastas All that may be added to a group canasta are natural cards from the hand, never a wild card. Nothing may be added to a samba.

10. Initial Meld The count required for an initial meld is:

SCORE	REQUIREMENT
Minus	15
0–1495	50
1500–2995	90
3000–6995	120
7000 or more	150

11. Game 10,000 points. As in Canasta, there is no bonus for winning a game.

12. To Go Out A side must have two canastas in order to go out. A samba ranks as a canasta for this purpose.

13. Red Threes A Red Three counts minus against a side that has not completed two canastas when the opponents go out. Each red Three, up to five, counts 100; all six count 1000.

14. Scoring Bonus for a samba, 1500. Bonus for going out, in each deal, 200. No bonus for "concealed hand." All other scores as at Canasta.

Temper of Samba Play The 162-card pack, the fifteen-card hand, and the two-card draw combine to let your hand change character much more quickly at Samba than at Canasta. The effects of this circumstance are:

1. It is much easier to match up all your cards and go out. There are twelve cards of each rank instead of eight, but the size of the canasta is still only seven cards. The number of wild cards is eighteen instead of twelve. This wider scope for canasta building is only partially offset by the increase of the base from four to five cards.

2. You can rarely be caught in a squeeze by opponents who have gained control. In fact, control scarcely exists. The depleted hand is not the horror that it is in Canasta, for in Samba each draw adds a card to it.

3. You can afford, most of the time, to concentrate on building up your hand and melds, without troubling too much about defending the pack. If you decide to try for a quick out as a defensive measure, you have a better prospect of succeeding quickly at Samba than at Canasta. At the same time the play for out does not require such drastic measures, and by getting a pack you may be able to resume the offensive.

Initial Meld Every experienced Canasta player knows that it sometimes pays to make the initial meld from the hand, without taking the pack. This is seldom the case in Samba.

In Samba you can never take the discard pile with only one matching card plus a wild card. To take the discard pile in making a new meld, you always need a natural pair. Hence, putting down an initial meld doesn't make it any easier for you to get the pack later on.

The chief purpose of the quick meld in Canasta is to meet the minimum requirement economically, when your partner might not be able to do so. In Samba don't worry about your partner's ability to meet a minimum count of 50, 90, or 120. Starting with fifteen cards instead of eleven, and drawing two cards at a time instead of one, he will almost always be able to meet the count.

However, the count of 150 is not so easy to amass. If able to meet it with a meld of no more than seven cards, you should usually put the cards down promptly, for here you may relieve your partner of a real strain. Typical ideal melds of 150 are:

Joker Joker A A A   (Ex. 1)
Joker K K   Joker Q Q Q   (Ex. 2)
Joker A A A 2 K K   (Ex. 3)

Except for this situation, wait to make your initial meld until you can take the pack. The disadvantages of melding prematurely are that (a) you inform the enemy what ranks you are saving, and (b) you may use your wild cards unwisely. It is much easier in Samba than in Canasta to collect a natural canasta, for there are twelve cards of each instead of eight. The 500-point bonus is worth striving for and is easily attainable in many instances—so don't meld your wild cards too hastily.

Sambas   The samba bonus—three times that for a natural canasta—is the big prize. On that account some players concentrate on sequences to the exclusion of all else. But a samba is proportionately more difficult to collect than a group canasta. Experience teaches that it is wiser to steer a middle course, trying for a samba only when the effort can be made cheaply, or when the prospects are really good.

There are only five possible sambas in a suit, as follows:

```
4 5 6 7 8 9 10                               (Ex. 4)
  5 6 7 8 9 10 J
    6 7 8 9 10 J Q
      7 8 9 10 J Q K
        8 9 10 J Q K A
```

Observe that for every one of them you have to have an Eight, Nine, and Ten. These, then, are key ranks, to be hoarded on general principle. Just never discard an Eight, Nine, or Ten in the early play. You might later find that you want the card back for a sequence, and in any case you want to keep the card out of adverse hands.

Scarcely less essential are Sevens and Jacks, both necessary for three of the five sequences, and one or the other essential to all. Until the play has developed to the point where you abandon all samba hopes, confine your melding to the end ranks, Four, Five, King, Ace.

Melding Sequences   What kind of sequence offers a good enough prospect of a samba to be worth melding?

Of course, if you are so lucky as to hold a six-card sequence, you put it down at once. Any four- or five-card sequence open at both ends is also good. A four-card sequence open at one end, that is, A-K-Q-J or 7-6-5-4, is usually not worth melding.

The holding of near cards may make a good prospect out of a sequence of only three or four cards. Such melds should be made early, if at all, to forestall the chance that your partner will discard cards that would be useful in the sequence. For example, if you hold:

$$\diamond\ 10\ 9\quad 7\ 6\ 5\quad (Ex.\ 5)$$

meld the $\diamond$ 7-6-5. If your partner can furnish the Eight, you will then be drawing for the Four or Jack. Melding a sequence so close to the end of the suit is so uncommon that your partner will realize you would not do it without some near cards at the other end.

Even without near cards a quick meld of J-10-9, 10-9-8, or 9-8-7 is justifiable. Each such combination, holding at least two of the three vital middle ranks, shows your partner that the hardest hurdle has been vaulted.

When you meld any sequence, you dip into cards that would otherwise help to make group canastas. Sequences thus tend to kill groups. But sequences do not kill one another. Therefore, if you meld a sequence, you will often find it easier to try for one or more additional sambas than to try for groups too. It has been well said that "sambas beget sambas."

Taking the Pack   In Canasta many a pack is worth taking, regardless of the identity of the cards in it, just to get more cards in hand. In Samba there is not the same urgency, for your hand increases anyhow by the draw. The opportunity to see two fresh cards often outweighs the chance to take a moderate pack, getting some useful cards but also some useless ones. Be selective in what packs you take.

Be especially wary of taking a small pack at a time when you are trying to go out. Perhaps you will thereby match up some of the off-cards in your hand, but if you get more than that number of odd cards in the pack, you have simply set yourself back.

In any situation, even when you are trying to go out, a

big pack—say fifteen or more cards—is usually worth taking if only to keep the opponents from getting it. Many of the cards are bound to be useful sooner or later. A big haul may cause you to change your mind about going out, and put you back in the game with a splash.

Defending the Pack　The pack is not of such vital importance in Samba as in Canasta, but it is still important.

Before the first meld of a deal, while the first pack is building up, discard as carefully and on the same principles as at Canasta. After all, a large first pack is a treasure-trove at either game. There is no sense in giving it away freely.

But face the fact that successful defense of the pack is less possible. Don't attempt it at the cost of hurting your own hand. For instance, don't save black Threes in early play, so as to have them as safe discards later on. Better to get the useless black Three out of your hand at once, saving all the cards that may turn into melds.

There is one way, however, in which you ought to defend every growing pack. That is to avoid making it too valuable. Don't give it sequential or near cards of the same suit. You don't want to build up sambas for the opponents.

Another principle of defending—or rather, not defending —is not to begrudge your left opponent a small pack. A player who takes a series of small packs—instead of waiting in the hope of getting the same aggregate of cards in one big pack—pays a price. Each time he takes the pack he misses a chance to get two fresh cards from the stock. This chance is so valuable, potentially, that in fact the experienced player lets many small packs go by him.

Trap Discarding　I have pointed out that in Canasta there are certain limits on trap discarding—discards from matched sets of three or four, made to induce your right opponent to discard a card of that rank and so give you the pack.

In Samba "the lid is off." You can usually afford to make a trap discard without thought of how it depletes your count toward the initial meld. You also need not worry about giving up the beginnings of a canasta base. Hence, the first few rounds of a Samba deal are often a medley of trap and "honest" discards.

Well, go to it. Buffalo your left opponent if you can. But keep this point in mind: You cannot have the same degree of assurance at Samba that your left opponent will have no use for your bait. At Canasta, when you discard from a set of four or five, you figure that your left opponent is unlikely to hold a pair of the rank; there are only eight such cards in the deck. But with twelve cards of each rank at Samba your left opponent often turns up with a pair or more of the same rank.

Melding from the Hand   At Canasta free melding is practically limited to two situations: (a) an effort by one side to go out, as a defensive measure; (b) final cashing of points when the deal will end soon.

At Samba there are additional occasions for free melding.

If you are ever going to meld a sequence, the sooner the better. So, having collected any sequence at all, decide whether it is a good samba prospect, and if it is, put it down promptly. The only occasion to keep a sequence in hand is that it is not yet a good samba prospect, but may become one.

If your side has melded a sequence, you should, of course, add any matching card to it at once.

Exception arises when there is little or no chance of ever building the sequence into a samba. For example, suppose you have previously melded the ♠ K-Q-J-10, and that you have just drawn the ♠ 9. If the opponents have meanwhile melded all three Spade Eights, there is obviously no use in adding the ♠ 9 to the sequence. Even if the opponents have melded only two Spade Eights, your prospect for a samba is so reduced that you should use the ♠ 9 to build toward a canasta of Nines.

Now look at the other side of the picture. Suppose an opponent has melded a sequence, say the ♡ J-10-9-8. You have in hand a set of Sevens including two or three of ♡ 7. You may do well to meld this set, showing your partner that the opponent's samba prospect is slight. This move is especially important if he might otherwise, in fear of the samba, make a misguided effort to go out quickly.

Saving Duplicates In melding groups, particularly at an early stage, give thought to how such melds may dim your own samba outlook. It is amazing and disheartening how many times a card you have melded early turns out to be the very card you need for the completion of a sequence collected later. That is why the tendency in initial melding of groups is to stick to the end ranks.

Another precaution to take as a matter of course is to save duplicates. For example, suppose that you decide to meld a trio of Kings from:

♠K ♠K ♡K ♡K ♣K   (Ex. 6)

Don't just grab the three Kings nearest your thumb. Put down ♠K-♡K-♣K, keeping the two duplicates in hand. While your purpose may be primarily to hold a pair against a freeze, you also serve the purpose of keeping alive your own chance for a Spade or Heart samba.

First Two Canastas It is fairly important to complete two canastas quickly, or at least to get two bases down on the table so that your side knows it can "run for cover" at will. Getting to this position ahead of your opponents often gives you a pronounced advantage. It may induce the opponents to meld sooner than they would have liked, and it always acts as a damper on their samba hopes.

Conversely, if the opponents have this edge on you, don't be too slow about catching up. If your existing melds have turned out to be poor canasta prospects, you had better try out a new rank. Likewise, give consideration to laying off on your existing melds. Suppose you have melded three Kings and kept two in hand (as in Example 6). You may now decide to put the pair on the table, showing your partner the base, and so easing the strain on him.

After Taking the Pack The best time for exploratory melding is when you have taken a large pack.

Melding freely in taking the pack becomes so habitual with

some players that they overlook a situation where you should *not* overmeld. This is in taking the pack for an *initial meld*. You do not yet know what your partner may have in the way of samba prospects. You don't want to kill any possibility. So at this time put down only what you must to make the count, plus any good sequences. Your partner, in his turn, will then plank down all his good sequences, if any, and the way is now cleared for you to meld later if you deem it advisable.

Any time that you take a large pack you give the opponents an incentive to go out fast. Such is Samba play that they may succeed without half trying. Don't hold a huge hand too long.

Signaling for Out   Mark well that in Samba free melding, especially sequences, *does not,* in general, command your partner to try for a quick out. To give such a signal, you have got to do something more drastic than making a simple exploratory meld.

Overmelding in the *initial meld* is sufficiently drastic. As I noted above, the normal procedure is to hoard everything you can, at this time, for the sake of future sambas. Hence the meld of an extra group must be read as an out call.

In any later stage, to call for quick out, you should do any or all of these things: (a) complete canastas with wild cards; (b) meld wild cards prodigally; (c) meld two or more extra sets (not sequences); (d) strip yourself to a few cards.

There is at least one situation in which the urgency of going out as a defense is so obvious that no signal is necessary. This is when the opponents have melded one or two very good samba prospects and you have none. Both you and your partner should meld promptly everything you can spare, complete two canastas, and follow the Canasta principle of discarding for out. Often you will find that your two hands can be fitted together so that one of you can go out, provided that the other expends extra wild cards judiciously to meld odd pairs. The object is, of course, to provide as many different ranks as possible to take care of your partner's odd cards.

Asking Permission As a rule, don't ask your partner, "May I go out?" You can and usually should make the decision yourself. Exception arises only when your partner has a large hand, and (a) he may be able to complete one or more additional canastas, or (b) he may have some good and undisclosed samba prospects to which either you or the pack might contribute.

If you do ask, your partner should say, "Yes," unless one of these situations obtains, and he thinks that there is prospect of gaining on net even though both opponents are given a chance to unload.

Above all, it is nonsensical to deny permission to go out merely to save the deduction for a couple of hundred points left in hand. At Samba such amounts are chicken feed.

SAMBA FOR TWO PLAYERS

Samba for two players is a race to meld out. The player who wins that race usually gets a good score.

Ideally you would make all your melds just before the hand ends, for there is no advantage at all in melding early. This is dangerous, however, because your opponent may meld out while you are still waiting, and then your loss will be very large. Hence your best course is to meld according to a sort of time schedule.

Early Play Meld nothing at all for your first four or five turns. Your opponent will practically never meld out at this stage.

Middle Play Meld natural canastas, if any, during the next four or five turns. Do not put down anything but complete canastas.

Late Play After about ten rounds of play you must expect, or at least fear, the end at each play. Meld all possible canastas—pure or mixed. Put lesser melds down to avoid getting caught with too much. However, never put down a sequence of fewer than seven cards (except when melding out): you mustn't warn your opponent.

At any stage of the play ignore a small discard pile or a middle-sized pile (about ten to fifteen cards) that contains nothing valuable. Take any large pile or any pile at all that gives you an excellent samba prospect or contains several useful cards.

When you have any choice, try to meld in such a way as to save samba possibilities for a later meld. Postpone a meld that definitely breaks up a samba possibility. However, don't wait too long. If the samba doesn't appear by the time you have made about fifteen plays, give it up and settle for ordinary canastas.

PINOCHLE

Three-handed Auction Pinochle

1. Seldom depend on the widow for your melds, but do depend on it for 20 to 30 points in playing strength.

2. Don't risk a sure 300 for a 350, or a sure 350 for 400, unless it's 3 to 1 in your favor.

3. Play a Spade hand if there's an even chance you'll make it, any other hand if it isn't more than 2 to 1 against you.

4. When in doubt whether to play a hand, don't play if the opponents are better than you at the play of the cards.

5. Be bold in pushing an opponent if your weakest suit (or only unstopped suit) is Spades.

6. The Ace of trumps is usually a bad lead unless your next lead will also be a trump.

7. The Queen is a better lead from a flush than the King.

8. The opponents should try to play so as to lead through the Bidder.

9. When the Bidder needs only 50 points or so, the opponents should lead trumps.

10. It is *not* illegal to bury a trump or an Ace, and you don't have to announce it when you do.

PINOCHLE

Pinochle is one of the most popular games in the country, but it is still a troublesome game to write about because it is played in so many different forms. The "money games," however, are three forms of Pinochle: two-handed Pinochle, which has lost a great deal of favor among its former players since Gin Rummy came along; Auction Pinochle, originally a three-handed game that now is most often played by four (with the dealer sitting out), a game that is played mostly in the big cities of the East; and Partnership Pinochle, which is played in all parts of the country.

The two games I will discuss are three-handed Auction Pinochle and Partnership Pinochle. In each case I will take the form of the game that is most played and with which I am most familiar.

Pinochle is a game that can be played very scientifically, and the best Pinochle players are very expert—at least as expert as the best Bridge players are at their game. For this reason the average player is bound to lose unless he knows some of the facts of life about the game. I have used the available space to give the basic principles of each game and to illustrate the situations in which I have most often seen players go wrong.

THREE-HANDED AUCTION PINOCHLE

HAND VALUATION

Pinochle bidding, as I have observed it around the country, is wild and woolly. The average player is inclined to bid, not his cards, but his state of mind, which is usually extreme optimism as to what he will find in the widow.

It is true that this unknown quantity—the cards in the widow—makes bidding less certain in Pinochle than in Bridge. Precisely for that reason, if you want to win, you must steel yourself to play the percentages, not the hunch and the hope.

Curiously enough, the valuation of a hand as it stands (apart from how it may be improved by the widow) is much more precise in Pinochle than in Bridge. Even experienced players are prone to rate a hand in broad terms—a 300 hand, or 350 hand, or 400 hand. Yet it is possible in most cases to rate a hand precisely, as "sure for 300, fair chance for 320, possible for 330." Even close-to-the-vest bidders toss hundreds of points through failure to apply the yardstick.

The estimated value of a hand is the sum of (a) the melds, and (b) the points it will win in play.

Playing Strength   Most hands strong enough to bid are most easily valued by counting the points that the opponents can take on the tricks they will win.

Let us consider first the count in nontrump suits. If your holding in a plain suit is entirely losing cards, count by the table on Page 212.*

* There are three ways of counting the points in Pinochle. In the original and traditional way, still insisted upon by all players of serious three-handed Auction Pinochle (the game under discussion here), the value count is: Ace 11, Ten 10, King 4, Queen 3, Jack 2. A simplified count, used by some players of three-handed Auction Pinochle and by nearly all players of Partnership Pinochle, is: Ace 10, Ten 10, King 5, Queen 5. Finally there is the still more simplified method of counting 10 points each for the Ace, King, and Ten. Any card that has a point value is called a counter; other cards count nothing. In this discussion of three-handed Auction Pinochle we will assume that the original, 11-10-4-3-2, count is used, but for purposes of simplicity, we will estimate scores in even fives and tens. The table we give for counting losers would not vary much regardless of the method it is based on. Only if the bidder must estimate his losses within a point or two is it important to him whether one loser will cost him 20, 21, or 22 points. Whichever method is used, all the counters together total 240 and the last trick counts 10, making a total of 250 to be won in cards.

1 loser	20
2 losers	40
3 losers	50
4 or more losers	60

The basis of this table is the average loss. Obviously the opponents may pile Ace-Ace on the first loser, Ten-Ten on the second, and so on. Actually their cards may not be so divided as to permit them to get the maximum count, or they may make slips in the defense losing their maximum.

The foregoing is a basic count; it may need correction in any or all of three ways, as follows:

1. Add to the loss any counters that you must contribute to the adverse tricks. Thus a singleton Nine counts as 20 lost, but singleton King is 25 lost and singleton Ten is 30.

2. Subtract from the loss (in a long suit) an Ace or other sure trick, together with anything it will collect by force. For example, a holding of K-Q-J-9 counts as 60 points lost, but A-Q-Q-J-9 is only 50, since you can cash the Ace.

3. Subtract from the loss (in a long suit) the counters you bury or that you can save as long cards to be cashed after trumps are out. If you hold the ◇ 10-10-K-Q-J and bury the Tens (Spades being trumps), your maximum loss is clearly 40, not 50. To illustrate the point about long cards, look at this hand.

♠ A 10 K Q J 9   Bid: 320
♡ A K Q   Meld: 200
◇ —   Need: 120
♣ A 10 K Q 9 9   Buried: ◇10 ◇9 ♡J   (Ex. 1)

The plan of play is to lead the ♣A and then the ♣9. With normal breaks you will force out trumps by leads of three or four losing Clubs, plus a lead of the ♠A at the strategic moment. You will survive the Diamond forces, and so will eventually be able to cash your ♣10, giving the opponents only 40 in the suit.

Trump Loss   What points to reckon as lost in trumps depends on the plan of play. In the majority of cases the proper plan is to force out the adverse trumps by plain-suit leads (as in Example 1). You must therefore count that the opponents will save all their trump counters. Thus in Example 1 you count that 30 must be lost in trumps.

In the exceptional hand, where the proper plan is to lead trumps, count the exact stoppers the opponents may have, together with the counters that may or must fall on these tricks.

♠ A 10 10 K Q J J   Bid: 350
♡ K Q   Meld: 170
◇ A   Need: 180
♣ A A 10 10 Q   (Ex. 2)

Losing 50 in Hearts, you cannot afford to lose more than 20 in the black suits. The only chance is to lead the ♠ K (after cashing the ◇ A), giving up a 20-point trick at once. Then your trumps should be solid. Pull the adverse trumps and lead the Clubs from the top down, hoping for a 4-3 split. If by any chance the opponents have cashed their Hearts before forcing you back with a Diamond, and have failed to take more than 55 in Spades and Hearts together, you can indulge in a lead of the ♣ Q first. By giving up 15 points you protect against an otherwise fatal split in Clubs of 5-2 or 6-1.

Suit Splits The direct count of winners in a suit you seek to establish depends not only on the high cards at large but also on the splits.

All that you need to know about abstract probabilities is this:

If the number of cards outstanding in a suit is odd, the chance of the most even possible split is well over 50%. Assume this split in valuing a hand, though of course in the play you should take out insurance against a bad split when you can do so.

If the number of cards outstanding in a suit is even (and more than two), an even split is only the second most probable; the first most probable is the split where one opponent holds two cards more than the other. But the relative frequencies are fairly even. Therefore you have to reckon with both in the bidding as well as in the play.

The exact figures, if you want them (I don't!), are as follows:

CARDS OUT	SPLIT	PROBABILITY (%)
2	1–1	52
	2–0	48
3	2–1	78
	3–0	22
4	3–1	50
	2–2	40
	4–0	10
5	3–2	67
	4–1	29
	5–0	4
6	4–2	48
	3–3	34
	5–1	15
	6–0	3
7	4–3	61
	5–2	31
	6–1	7
	7–0	1

Expectation of the Widow Now we come to the crux of the matter: What should you expect to find in the widow?

If you want a simple rule that will save you thousands of points, here it is: DON'T EXPECT TO FIND A NEW MELD; DO EXPECT TO FIND AN INCREASE OF 20 TO 30 POINTS IN PLAYING STRENGTH.

Large sums are paid out annually by Pinochle players who hoped to find the ◊ J or the fourth King or the trump Ten in the widow. The only cure for this virulent malady is daily exercise in facing the inexorable facts. Here they are:

A card missing from your hand which, if supplied by the widow, would give you a new meld, is a "place open." The odds on buying at least one such card are as follows:

PLACES OPEN	ODDS
1	5 to 1 against
2	2 to 1 against
3	even
4	3 to 2 for
5	2 to 1 for

Look at what this means in terms of an actual hand. Suppose you pick up:

♠ K Q J 9
◇ A K J
♡ A K 9
♣ A K Q J 9   (Ex. 3)

The hand melds 190 at Clubs. The average player will bid 300 without a second look. He sees that if he buys the ♣10 or ♠A he can claim 300 without play, and could actually make 350 or more. He notes that if he buys a ♡J or a red Queen he melds 230 or 210, leaving "only" 70 or 90 to be won in play. Add 20 to 30 points for the increase of playing strength by the widow, and there you are!

This is all a hallucination! Forget the ♡J and the red Queen. Any of these would score a new meld, but would impair the playing strength. You would have to buy also another trump to get any appreciable gain. And even the tyro knows that bidding to buy two right cards is sheer madness.

No, the hand boils down to a straight two-place hope for the ♣10 or ♠A. If you are going in for that hope you may as well bid 350 as 300. But the odds are 2 to 1 against you. You can't make money bidding against the odds.

Even a three-place buy, at even chances, is not worth bidding on in itself. It is sometimes worth a risk in order to boost an opposing bidder, and it sometimes figures as added insurance when you need a full 30 points help in playing strength from the widow.

You seldom get a hand that offers four or more places open. True, you can concoct such hands as Example 3, where you might buy the filler to any of five or more melds. But plain marriages, pinochle, and 40 Jacks don't help a hand much: the cards you have to hold to score them are mostly losers. The increments that count for bidding purposes are flush, 100 Aces, 80 Kings, possibly 60 Queens. The conclusion is that you don't bid to buy a new meld.

Playing-Strength Increase It is a different story as to buying additional playing strength from the widow. Rare is the hand that will not be improved by the chance to bury some cards —losers or unguarded Tens. For example:

♠ 10 9
♡ 10 9
♢ A 10 K Q Q J 9
♣ A 10 K K Q Q   (Ex. 4)

At Diamonds this hand counts to lose 45 in Spades, 45 in Hearts, 25 in Diamonds, and 30 in Clubs, a total of 145. It melds 200, and therefore is a bare bid of 300—without the widow. But the worst it can buy is something like ♠J, ♡J, ♡J. By burying both Tens and ♡J you pare down the Spade-Heart loss from 90 to 70.

Furthermore an additional card in trumps or your long side suit almost always saves 10 or 20 points. With Example 4, if you buy any Diamond or Club with two worthless Hearts or Spades, you save another 20 points through the ability to void yourself of one of these weak suits.

Here are some figures that show the range of the chances:

CHANCE OF BUYING AT LEAST ONE CARD OF A GIVEN SUIT

When you have 5 cards	19 to 13 in favor
" " " 6 "	6 to 5 in favor
" " " 7 "	3 to 2 against

CHANCE OF BUYING A CARD IN EITHER OF TWO SUITS

When you have 9 cards (in the two suits together)

	7 to 1 in favor
10	6 to 1 in favor
11	5 to 1 in favor
12	4 to 1 in favor

This last table is the important one. Most biddable hands

have length in two suits, and the odds are overwhelming that the widow will lengthen at least one of them.

The Safe Bid Suppose the player at your right deals and you pick up this hand:

♠ A 10 K Q J
♡ A Q 9
◊ 10 Q J
♣ A Q 9 9   (Ex. 5)

At Spades you can meld 250. If played as it stands, its counted loss is 30 in Spades, 45 in Hearts, 60 in Diamonds, and 50 in Clubs, a total of 195. That leaves 55 points for you (assuming you get last). Actually you see that you can bury the ◊ 10, and if you make nothing more than 30 in trumps plus the side Aces you will take 60 points. That gives you 310 points. Add 20 or 30 for expected improvement by the widow, plus the counters your trumps are bound to pick up from the adverse hands—isn't it a good bid of 350?

Such is the argument of the average Pinochle player, and it pays the rent for his expert opponents.

You might well go to 350, if pushed, on this hand, but you should start at 300, or 310 or 320 if 300 is bid ahead of you. If there is any one rule of winning at Pinochle, it is: Make the safe bid; don't stretch the hand to reach the higher bracket.

While it is true that you should take account of the expected improvement from the widow in valuing a hand, you should regard that primarily as a safety factor. In voluntary bidding just bid what the hand is worth as it stands, leaving the 20 or 30 points from the widow as a margin of safety against bad breaks.

Furthermore, if you start with the highest bid you have any prospect of making, you can't stand a boost, or you take a boost and go bête most of the time. In either case you are duck soup for alert opponents.

The best way to deal with an inveterate booster is to let

yourself get boosted, on occasion, into the higher bracket—
and make your bid. And you can do that only if you have
started with the rock-bottom safe bid.

Here is a type of hand on which overbidding is a common
and costly practice:

♠ A Q Q
♡ K K Q J
◇ Q 9
♣ A 10 K Q J 9   (Ex. 6)

This is a sound bid of 300. Suppose you make the usual
bid of 350, ten times running. Two or three times someone
will boost with 360 when he would have let you play 330.
You sell, and while you will usually collect from the booster,
even then you'd have been better off to collect 300 from all
players than 360 from one. Once or twice you'll buy a worthless widow and have to concede. Perhaps five or six times
you'll make your 350. Now add it all up and you'll find that
you would have done better to collect ten times on a 300 bid.

♠ A 10 J 9
♡ A Q 9
◇ A 9 9
♣ A 10 K Q J 9   (Ex. 7)

This is a dream hand—flush and Aces—on which the average player bids 400 automatically. Let's say that the odds are
3 to 1 you will make 400. But figure it out—if you lose the
hand at 400 once in four times, you are a little worse off
than if you had collected four times at the safe 350.

Competitive Bidding   You lose by willful overbidding, but
you also lose by letting the other fellow play cheaply. You
are bound to compete in the bidding beyond your own safe
bid, both to force an opponent beyond his margin of safety,
and so collect some bêtes, and also to buy the bids that are
yours by right.

Of course you will give to the limit of your own margin of
safety, if necessary, in competitive bidding. You must at times

go 10 or 20 points more to boost an opponent into the next
bracket. For example:

♠ A 10 Q 9 9
♡ 10 9
♢ A 10 K Q J 9
♣ 10 9   (Ex. 8)

The safe bid on this hand is 300, and 330 can very probably be made. If pushed you should go to 340, possibly 350.
This is still in the region where you need to buy only playing strength, not a meld.

A great danger of this sort of stretching is that once you
get going you find yourself unable to stop. Take the precaution of making up your mind in advance just how far you
will go, and when you come to that point, stop.

Bidding on the Widow   I have laid it down as a rule, cal-
culated to save you thousands of points, not to bid in hope
of picking up a new meld from the widow. This rule applies
to all the ordinary hands where you have no more than two
places open for a meld big enough to count for anything.
But don't overlook that there are occasional hands with three
or four places open. On such a hand, having an even chance
or better to fill, plunge, if you must, to boost an opponent or
to overcall a booster. For example:

♠ A Q
♡ A 10 Q J
♢ A K Q J 9
♣ 10 K Q 9   (Ex. 9)

This hand melds 170 at Diamonds, yet would have to
struggle to make a minimum bid of 250 (if that is your minimum). However, it has three places open (the ♡K, ♢10,
♣A) to increase the meld to at least 270. If the bidding is
competitive, you may as well bid this hand to 350—you
need a new meld in any event.

Psychological Factors   It cannot be too much emphasized
that the most important rule of competitive bidding is: Know
your opponents! Only when you have some knowledge of

their bidding habits can you figure any percentages in boosting or standing a boost.

The dangerous man to try to boost is the perennial optimist. This may sound like a paradox, but the explanation is simple. The optimist tends to go the limit of his hand on his first bid. He is the fellow that always bids 350 with Example 6 and 400 with Example 7. If you overcall him he is apt to sober up, look at his hand a second time, and realize that he has got to sell out.

The easiest fellow to push up is the one that follows "the book"—including this one!—slavishly. He always leaves himself a wide margin of safety, and your job is simply to make him use it up. He will always go 20 points higher, usually 30, and often 40.

To avoid being typed yourself, vary your style. Bid "the works" occasionally, stretching a safe 300 to 350 or a safe 350 to 400. Then, when a booster overcalls, pass. Start with an underbid occasionally, letting yourself be "forced" into the higher bracket. The bids you make this way, and the bêtes suffered by would-be boosters at other times, will save you competition at many times when you cannot stand it.

MELDING AND BURYING

Melding   Usually you meld everything you can, leaving as little as possible to win in play. But the cards that make up the cheaper melds—plain marriages and 40 Jacks—are mostly losers, and you will sometimes gain in playing strength more than what you lose by discarding them. For example:

♠ A 10 K Q 9 9
♡ A K Q
◇ A K J 9   Bid: 350
♣ A J   Widow: ◇ K ◇ 9 ♣ 9   (Ex. 10)

The melds (with Spades as trumps) total 220. If you bury the ♣J, ♣9, ◇9, your losers count: Spades 30, Hearts 45, Diamonds 50, a total of 125. This is too much. Now count it with a discard of the ♡K, ♡Q, ♣J. The loss in Hearts drops to zero, in Diamonds to 45, a gain of 55. This more than offsets the loss of 20 points in meld and 20 points by

keeping ♣9. The expected winning is 355 instead of 345.
And the hand is actually much more playable because of
the extra Diamond you can keep.

The Discard You meld what you can (or must); keep all
trumps and Aces, and all of a long plain suit (five or more)
if you can. That usually leaves you few choices of discard.
Here are some tips on what to do when choice offers.

The foremost advantage of the discard is that it allows you
to save a Ten that otherwise would go to the opponents. For
example, having a doubleton ♣A-10 (Spades are trumps),
you lay away the ♣10 automatically.

The second advantage is that you can get rid of some losers
in short suits. Having, say, the ♣J-9 (Spades are trumps),
you must count a 40-point loss with these cards in hand. By
burying them you reduce the loss to zero.

Nine times out of ten the right cards to bury all come
from a short holding. The distributionally strong Pinochle
hand is the two-suiter—at least five cards each in trumps and
a plain suit. From such a hand as the following the discard
is obvious: the ♠10, ♠J, ♡9.

> ♠ A 10 J 9
> ♡ A 9
> ◇ A Q J J 9 9
> ♣ A A 10 K Q 9   (Ex. 11)

Saving Guards to Aces The normal policy of short-suiting
yourself often calls for blanking an Ace. Then you have to
cash the Ace, to save it, before starting your long suit. You
thereby leave yourself open to immediate forces—and also
tell the opponents what is the forcing suit. This policy is correct when your trumps are long enough to stand the forces.
With a mere five-card trump suit, you are sometimes better
off to save a low guard to an Ace, so that you can retain
it as a stopper. For example:

> ♠ A 9   Bid: 400
> ♡ A 10 K Q J   Meld: 250
> ◇ A A 10 10 K J 9 9 Need: 150
> ♣ A 10 9   (Ex. 12)

If you woodenly bury the ♣10, ♣9, ♠9, you have to cash both black Aces before starting on the Diamonds. Then, unless the Diamond and trump splits are exactly right for you, the opponents may overtake you in the pumps (forcing you to trump) and your trumps may last long enough to gather only about 100 points.

The right discard is ♣10, ◇A, ◇10. You can then start the Diamonds at once, and the opponents will have to knock out one of your black Aces before they can start forcing. Even against poor splits in your suits you have good chances to bring in the long Diamonds and make the bid.

If forced to keep a guard to an Ace, you will find that it often pays to keep a Ten with it, as a potential second stopper. For example:

♠ A 10 K Q 9	Bid: 320
♡ A 10 9	Meld: 190
◇ A Q J 9 9	Need: 130
♣ A 10 10 K J	(Ex. 13)

Though you must name Spades, this hand is really what in Bridge is called a No-Trumper. To blank the ♡A is unthinkable. That being so, you may as well keep the entire Heart holding, as a possible double stopper. Bury the ◇Q-9-9. Since you have melded the ◇J for pinochle, besides the 100 Aces, the opponents may tackle Hearts instead of Diamonds in feeling for your short suit. The other Ace may come out on the first lead, leaving you in complete command.

To Play or Drop   If you play a hand and fail to make your bid, you lose double bête. If you concede without play, you lose single bête. The question whether to play or drop depends on the chance of making, together with the particular scale of scoring values.

To illustrate the method of calculating chances of making, let us take a very simple case:

♠ K Q	Bid: 360	
♡ K	Meld: 180	
◇ A A 10 10 K J	Need: 180	
♣ A A 10 10 K Q	Buried: ♠9 ♡J ♡9	(Ex. 14)

What are the chances of making 180 in play? The plan is, of course, to yank out trumps, cash the solid Diamonds, and concede merely the three tricks in the off-suits. At most these tricks will cost 50 in Spades, 25 in Hearts. This is 5 points too much. You can afford to lose only 70.

Other than a defensive mistake (which you cannot expect when your meld and the early play will mark every card in your hand), the only chance is to pare down the Spade loss to 45. This will occur if one hand has three of the four top Spades, so that his partner can contribute only a 5-point card on the second round.

By reference to the table, Page 214, you will see that the chance for a 3-1 split of four outstanding cards is just 50%. So you have an even chance of losing only 45 in Spades.

But you must reckon one other factor. To win the last trick, you must have two long trumps. When you finally lead Spades, after taking out trumps, you will have to take one force before you can get rid of your remaining off-card. Any 5-1 or 6-0 split in trumps will beat you. While the chance of a trump split no worse than 4-2 is very good—72%— this is not 100%. The compound chance of the needed good breaks in trumps and Spades is 72% times 50%, or 36%. This means that you have about a one-third chance of making, or the odds are 2 to 1 against you.

Should you drop? To answer this question, we must go into the scoring.

Suppose that the value of a bid in the 350-390 bracket is five chips, and that bids of 350 and above settle also with the kitty. Suppose that three times you have this sort of hand, with the odds 2 to 1 against making. If you play all three, and lose twice, you pay out sixty chips in the double bêtes. Once you make, and collect fifteen, a net loss of forty-five. If instead you drop all three times, you pay out forty-five in single bêtes. Thus you have gained nothing by dropping. It is better, then, to play, for lucky breaks may reduce the expected loss.

When Spades pay double, the same method of figuring shows that you should play a Spade hand if the chances of making are even or better, but should toss it in if the odds are against you.

The foregoing assumes that the kitty is paid and pays just like a player. But the practice varies in different circles. If you pay the kitty for bêtes, but do not collect when you make, you should play a non-Spade hand with a 3-to-2 chance or better in your favor, and a Spade hand only with a 6-to-5 chance.

BIDDER'S PLAY

Forcing Since the normal type of hand after the discard is a two-suiter, correct play is usually to open your long side suit, and continue at every opportunity. For example:

♠ A 10 Q J 9 9	Bid: 300
♡ Q	Meld: 160
◇ A A K Q J 9 9	Need: 140
♣ Q	Buried: ♡9 ♡9 ♣9 (Ex. 15)

Counting 50 lost in Hearts and Clubs, you must hold the loss in your long suits to 60. Lead the ♠A and continue with the ♠9. If the Spades split 3-3, you can then take out trumps to cash the ♠10-Q. If the split is 4-2, you will force one opponent to trump twice, and that will very probably leave your trumps solid. In either case you lose no more than 35 in Spades and 20 in trumps.

Avoiding Smears The count of losers is in one way a maximum count. For example, you count two losers in a suit as costing 40 points, on the assumption that the opponents can and will pile A-A-10-10 on the tricks. Yet 50% of the time they will be unable to do so, because their tops are split 3-1 instead of 2-2.

But in another way this count is optimistic. It assumes that you will win every counter remaining in a suit as soon as you are void of it. This is true only so long as your trumps last. However, you take that into account by bidding only with a trump suit long or strong enough to outlast the opponents. The constant danger, which a valuation system cannot take into account directly, lies in *smears*. An opponent who is able to smear an Ace or Ten to his partner thereby deducts 10 points from your counted winnings.

On all close hands, therefore, the play revolves around the bidder's effort to avoid giving opportunity for smears, and the opponents' efforts to get such chances.

To illustrate, let's replay Example 15 badly. Suppose that, with the idea of holding down the trump loss to 10 points, you start by leading both Diamond Aces, probably taking out all trumps but one ◇ 10. Your opponent leads ◇ 10, and his partner tosses him ♣ 10 or ♡ 10. There go 20 points. When you continue Spades, you find a 4-2 split (more probable than 3-3). On two Spade tricks won by one opponent the other gets two more smears. There go another 20 points. With the 30 they take in Spades, the opponents bête you.

The point of leading your long plain suit before taking out trumps is to bump the stoppers in this suit and in trumps together. This process concedes the opposition no more than your counted loss in the two suits (with normal splits), and often pares down the trump loss by putting you in position to yank out the rest after one or two forces.

Even if you are able to extract trumps without loss of a trick, it may be fatal to do so. For example:

♠ A A 10 10 K Q J 9	Bid: 400
♡ K Q J 9 9	Meld: 260
◇ K	Need: 140
♣ K	Buried: ♣ J 9 9 (Ex. 16)

With 50 to lose in Diamonds and Clubs, you must hold the loss in the long suits to 60. All you can hope to salvage out of the Hearts is 5 points, for a long card. But you can give away 55 in Hearts, and 5 in trumps. Therefore lead the Hearts straight out. With a 4-3 split no metal can touch you, for at worst a ♠ K goes on the fourth round. If you were to take out trumps, a 10-point smear on the fourth round would bête you. (Of course, the defense is to lead trumps on such hands.)

Leading Trumps The typical hand in which you should

take out trumps before leading your long side suit is one in
which the danger of smears is less than the danger of giving
away too many points in your long suits. For example:

♠ A K	Bid: 400
♡ A 10 10 K K Q	Meld: 240
◇ A 10 10 K Q	Need: 160
♣ A K	Buried: ♠9 ♣J ♣9 (Ex. 17)

Having 50 to lose in the black suits, you must give away
no more than 40 in the red. Obviously you cannot afford to
pump the opponents with Diamonds, giving them 30 or 40
points in the suit. The right plan is to try to clear each suit
with the loss of only one 20-point trick. Start with the ♡Q
to force the Ace out at once. When you get back with a
black Ace, lead two top trumps, then the ◇K.

Another type of hand where the opening trump lead is
correct is one without a long side suit but with general
strength. For example:

♠ 10 K Q Q 9	Bid: 320
♡ K Q	Meld: 250
◇ A K Q 9	Need: 70
♣ A A K Q	Buried: ♡10 ♡10 ♡9 (Ex. 18)

Needing to catch only 20 points besides making your Aces,
lead a ♠Q and wait. Lead trumps again when you are in
next. Let them lead to you.

OPPONENTS' PLAY

Reading Bidder's Hand As an opponent, you know much
more about the Bidder's hand than he knows about yours.
You have seen the widow and the melds. You know some or
many of the cards the Bidder has kept, and often can infer
what else he has—cards he will keep if he has them and
cards he must have to elect to play. Also, you know some of
the cards he hasn't got from what he doesn't meld.

Knowing most of the Bidder's hand, you also know most
of your partner's hand. Finally, any residual uncertainty
about the holdings is often cleared up by the first trick or
two.

For example, the bid is 310 and the widow is the ♡A, ♡J, ◊Q. The Bidder melds the ♠A-10-K-Q-J and ♡K-Q for 170. He leads the ♡A, then ♡Q. Your partner follows with the ♡Q and ♡10. Your Heart holding is the ♡A-10-K-9; your Spades are the ♠A-10-J. You proceed to figure:

Hearts are obviously the Bidder's long side suit. My partner had just two Hearts and I four; the Bidder has six. He cannot have more than six trumps, or he would have another meld. Therefore, he has three or four cards in Diamonds and Clubs. Such information is valuable in the later play.

Pumping Bidder Against what I have called the normal hand, the two-suiter, where the Bidder tackles first the plain suit, the routine defense is to pump the Bidder with the suit in which he is weak or void. Especially when the Bidder has to make a lot in play, try to run him out of trumps as quickly as possible.

The Bidder sometimes has to confess his weak suit by cashing a blank Ace first. At other times his weakness is perfectly obvious by his melds and lead. But there are instances where you have to guess between the off-suits, and here you and your partner should co-operate to pick the right one.

Try to win the lead if you are in position to spot the Bidder's weakness and your partner is not. Let him win the trick if you don't know—especially if he sits under the Bidder. Let us return to the 310 bid shown earlier in this section. Your complete hand is:

> ♠ A 10 J
> ♡ A 10 K 9
> ◊ K K J J
> ♣ A 10 K Q

You sit at the Bidder's right. With the play as described, to the first two leads, you can see that your partner will be uncertain whether to lead Diamonds or Clubs, unless he happens to hold double Ace in Diamonds. You yourself don't know which is the Bidder's void, but you do know that a Diamond lead through him cannot hurt your cause. So over-

take your partner's ♡ 10 with the Ace and lead ◊ K. Then
if the Bidder has the ◊ A-10-9 you will pick up his Ten,
whereas if your partner led Diamonds he would give the
Bidder his Ten.

If you are stuck in the lead, at the left of the Bidder, and
have to make a sheer guess, pick the off-suit in which you
hold double Ace or none, rather than the one where you hold
single Ace. With double Ace you are safe because the Bidder
would not have kept a Ten in hand anyhow. With no Ace
you probably can never catch his Ten if he has it.

Leading Trumps If the Bidder's long side suit is badly split
against him, with several stoppers outstanding, the defense
should give thought to the advisability of leading trumps
rather than punching the Bidder.

The usual object of leading trumps is to clean them out of
one hand so as to allow smears by that hand on tricks in the
Bidder's suit won by the other opponent.

I cannot give you any general rule about leading trumps,
simply because you are bound to have particular information
about the actual situation that is a better guide than any rule.
Here is an example:

$$
\begin{array}{l}
\spadesuit\ K\ J \\
\heartsuit\ 10\ Q\ 9\ 9 \\
\diamondsuit\ A\ A\ 10\ 10\ K \\
\clubsuit\ K\ Q\ Q\ 9 \qquad \text{(Ex. 19)}
\end{array}
$$

You sit at the left of the Bidder. He melds the ♠ A-10-K-
Q-J-9, the ◊ K-Q-J, for 220 on a bid of 370. The widow
was the ◊ Q, ◊ 9, ♡ A. The Bidder leads ◊ J, which you
take with the ◊ A, and your partner drops the ◊ 9. He would
give you the ◊ Q if he had it; therefore the Bidder has all
the missing Diamonds and you are going to win five straight
tricks in the suit.

Crediting the Bidder with six Diamonds besides six trumps
and two Hearts (the ♡ A he picked up in the widow, plus a
guard, for he did not cash the ♡ A) leaves only one card in
doubt. This is probably the other ♠ A.

On this reading you can let your partner get rid of his

trumps in time to smear high Clubs on your Diamond tricks. Lead the ♠J, letting him play the ♠Q (the reading gives him the ♠10-Q-9, and you don't want to force the Ten by lead of the King). Then he can ruff the second Diamond round with the ♠10 and lead his ♠9, later getting three smears.

The one time when trump leads are virtually obligatory is when the Bidder is playing for a small number of points, having melded many losing cards. One by one he must lead these cards and relinquish the lead. If you then lead another of the nontrump suits, you will help him to do the one thing that may be necessary to the making of his bid: to save his trump length and get the last trick. If you lead trumps, all his trumps may be gone before he has been able to lead his last losing melded cards, and he cannot get the last trick. Your trump leads may also prevent him from trumping your counters.

Suppose the bid is 450 (these situations arise most frequently on high bids) and the meld is as follows:

	♠ A 10 K Q J
(South)	♡ K Q
	◇ K Q J
	♣ K Q

Melding 390, he needs only 60 to make his bid. He decides to play and starts with the Queen of Hearts. This is your hand:

	♠ 10 K Q 9
	♡ A 10 K
	◇ A 10 Q J
	♣ A K J 9

You win—whether with the King or Ten makes no difference, since the Bidder cannot be supposed to hold the Ace. The Ten is slightly preferable just on the off-chance that he might. Your lead now must be a trump. The King is best, because your partner must have the Ace. He cannot have a Ten, and you want your highest-scoring available card to go on your partner's Ace. Having won this, your partner must lead a Spade back. If you are permitted to win this, you lead still another Spade; if not, you duck the next lead to your partner so he can lead a trump again. South has six more tricks to lose, and you will be able to make him trump with his last trump long before he has lost the last of his losers. This will assure you of the last trick, and with 35 points at most in the trump suit South cannot expect to make his contract without the last trick, something he cannot win, as all his trumps are gone.

Getting Maximum   Reading the pattern of the Bidder's hand is important not only to find the suit in which you can punch him, but also to take the maximum possible in his short suits.

As the Bidder, you count some such holding as the ♠ J-9 for a loss of 40 points. As the opponent, don't forget that to collect the full 40 you have got to pile A-A-10-10 on these two tricks—if you can.

A well-established convention of defense is "Ace calls for Ace." If your partner (at the left of the Bidder) leads the Ace of an unopened plain suit, and you have the other one, put it on. By the same token, don't lead an Ace in this position unless you are willing to have your partner toss in the second Ace. Having to make a blind lead in feeling for the Bidder's weak suit, prefer to lead a topless suit rather than one headed by a single Ace without a Ten.

Keep Bidder in the Middle   The defense is easiest when you can "keep the Bidder in the middle"—lead from his right rather than from his left. The urgency of going through him is likely to be greatest on the first defensive lead, especially when there is doubt about his weak suit or when a trump lead is indicated. If you are at his left, therefore, try to keep out of the way and let your partner in the lead unless your hand is such that you can afford to take command and dictate the defense.

LAWS OF AUCTION PINOCHLE

1. Number of Players   The game of Auction Pinochle is played by three, four, or five players, of whom only three are active players at any one time.

2. The Pack   Forty-eight cards, two each of A, K, Q, J, 10, and 9 in each of four suits, Spades, Hearts, Diamonds and Clubs.

3. Rank of Cards   A (high), 10, K, Q, J, 9.

4. The Draw   Each player lifts a portion of the pack, taking no more than half the cards remaining. The last player to cut must leave the bottom card on the table. When all have cut, each shows the bottom card to the portion he cut. The lowest card determines the first dealer, the next lowest sits at the dealer's left, and so on. If two players draw cards of equal rank, they cut again.

5. The Shuffle   The dealer shuffles the pack and places it on the table, face down, at his right.

6. The Cut   The player at the dealer's right lifts no fewer than five nor more than forty-three cards from the top of the pack. The dealer picks up the remainder of the pack. The player who cuts then places his portion face down on the table and the dealer places his portion on top of it, completing the cut.

7. Order of the Game   Each player's turn in dealing, bidding, and playing come to him in rotation, which is to the left. There are three active players, who receive cards in the deal. When there are four players, the dealer receives no cards; when there are five players, the dealer and the player second from his left receive no cards. These players are inactive and may give neither advice nor information to the active players.

8. The Deal   The dealer deals three cards to each player in turn, beginning with the player at his left, then deals three cards to the center of the table, then deals the remaining cards three at a time to each active player in turn until each has fifteen cards. All cards are dealt face down. The three cards dealt to the center are termed the widow.

9. Bidding   Each active player in turn, beginning with the player at the dealer's left, must make a bid or must pass. A bid is expressed in points only, in multiples of 10 points. The player at the dealer's left must bid 300 or more.* Each successive bid must be higher than the last preceding bid. Having passed, a player may not thereafter bid. When two players have passed the auction is closed. The highest bid becomes the contract. The player who made the highest bid becomes the Bidder. The two other players jointly are the Bidder's opponents.

10. Looking at the Widow

a. If the contract is 300, the Bidder may decline to expose the widow, and must pay the basic value of that bid (Section 21b) as a forfeit to the kitty, after which the deal passes to the next player in turn.

b. In any other case the Bidder then turns the three cards of the widow so that all players may see them, after which he takes them into his hand.

11. Melding

Only the Bidder may meld. Melding consists in announcing or showing certain combinations of cards which have value in points. At the request of any player, the Bidder must show his melds. The following combinations have values as melds:

SEQUENCES

A K Q J 10 of trumps (flush)	150
K Q of trumps (royal marriage)	40
K Q of any other suit (marriage)	20

GROUPS

♠A ♡A ◇A ♣A (100 Aces)	100
♠K ♡K ◇K ♣K (80 Kings)	80
♠Q ♡Q ◇Q ♣Q (60 Queens)	60
♠J ♡J ◇J ♣J (40 Jacks)	40

SPECIAL

♠Q ◇J (pinochle)	40
9 of trumps (dix, pronounced deece)	10

* There are many variations of this. In many games the minimum bid is 250; in a few games it is as low as 200. Still others play that the first man may play at 250 or 200 if he does not look at the widow, though it still counts among his tricks.

A card which is part of a meld under one heading may be counted as part of a meld under another heading, but may not be counted as part of another meld under the same heading.

12. Burying After melding, and preferably before picking up any cards he shows upon the table, the Bidder must bury, or lay away, face down, any three cards which he has not melded, to reduce the number of the cards in his hand to fifteen. The cards laid away will count to the credit of the Bidder after the cards are played.

13. Concession

a. The Bidder may concede defeat (single bête) after looking at the widow but before leading a card. A concession offered by the Bidder may not be withdrawn if either opponent has thereafter exposed any card or if both opponents have discarded their hands.

b. Either opponent may propose that the Bidder's contract be conceded to him, and if the other opponent agrees that the contract is made; but the other opponent may decline to concede.

14. First Lead The Bidder always leads to the first trick. He may lead any card.

15. Announcement of Trump Before leading to the first trick the Bidder must name the suit which will be trump. The Bidder may change his meld, the cards he buries, and the trump suit as often as he wishes before he leads to the first trick, but not thereafter. If the Bidder names the trump and both opponents concede, he may not then change the trump.

16. Objects of Play The objects of play are to win tricks containing cards which have scoring values and to win the last trick. The scoring values of cards taken in tricks won, and of the last trick, are:

Each Ace	11
Each Ten	10
Each King	4
Each Queen	3
Each Jack	2
Last Trick	10

The Nines have no scoring value when taken in tricks.

17. The Play The card led to a trick and the two cards played in turn by the other two players constitute a trick. Any trick containing a trump is won by the highest trump. Any trick not containing a trump is won by the highest card of the suit led. Of two cards of identical suit and rank played to the same trick the one played first is the higher. The winner of each trick leads to the next, and may lead any card.

Each player must follow suit to the card led if able. If void of the suit led, he must play a trump if able. If able neither to follow suit nor to trump, he may play any card.

If the card led is a trump, each player must, if able, play a higher trump than any previously played to the trick. This is called playing over. (He need not overtrump in playing to a plain-suit lead that the player before him has trumped.)

18. Result of Play The Bidder gathers all tricks he wins into a pile, face down, at the bottom of which are the cards he buried. Either opponent similarly gathers in all tricks won by his side. When the last trick has been completed the two sides ascertain and agree on the number of points they have respectively taken in.

19. Means of Settlement Settlement may be made with chips at the end of the play of each deal, or a score may be kept of the respective points won and lost by the players in the game.

20. The Kitty A separate score, or a separate pile of chips, is maintained for an imaginary extra player called the kitty, who solely receives payment when a bid of 300 is conceded without exposure of the widow, who receives payment the same as an opponent when the contract is bête, and who pays the same as an opponent when the contract is 350 or more. The kitty is the joint property of all players in the game. If the kitty has a deficit, they must supply it equally. When the game ends, or when a player leaves the game, each player takes his proportionate share of the kitty.

21. Settlement
  a. In settlement the Bidder pays to or collects from every

other player, active or inactive and including the kitty as provided in Section 20.

b. If the point value of the Bidder's melds plus the points he wins in play equal or exceed the amount of his bid, or if the opponents concede, the Bidder's contract is made and he collects from each other player.

UNITS (R CHIPS)

Bid	Basic Value	Value if Spades are Trump
300–340	3	6
350–390	5	10
400–440	10	20
450–490	15	30
500–540	20	40
550–590	25	50
600–640	30	60
650 or more	35	70

c. If the Bidder conceded after looking at the widow but before leading to the first trick, he pays to each other player the basic unit value of his bid, regardless of what suit he named as trump.

d. If the Bidder led to the first trick, and the sum of the point values of his melds plus his tricks do not at least equal the amount of his bid, the Bidder is double bête and pays to each other player: twice the basic unit value if Spades were not trump; four times the basic unit value if Spades were trump.

22. Scoring

a. When chips are used, each player pays or collects the value of his contract at its determination.

b. When a score is kept, each player has added to his score any units he has won in each deal, and has subtracted from his score any units he has lost in each deal. One player is designated as scorekeeper, but every player is equally responsible for the correctness of the score. The totals of those players who are plus must equal the totals of those players who are minus at the end of every deal.

IRREGULARITIES

23. Misdeal   There must be a new deal by the same dealer:

a. If the pack was not properly shuffled or was not cut, and if a player calls attention to the fact before the widow has been dealt;

b. If, in dealing, the dealer exposes more than one card of any player's hand;

c. If any card of the widow is exposed in dealing;

d. If at any time before the cards are shuffled for the next deal the pack is found to be incorrect (that is, not precisely as defined in Section 2). Scores made with the same pack in previous deals are not affected.

24. Exposure of the Widow

a. If a player sees a card in the widow before the auction closes, he may not make another bid.

b. If at any time before the auction closes a player handles the widow and in so doing exposes a card, there must be a new deal by the next dealer in turn, and (penalty) the offender must pay to each other player, including the kitty and every inactive player, the unit value of the highest bid last made prior to his offense.

25. Incorrect Hand   If any player has too few cards and another player, or the widow, has too many:

a. If it is discovered before the widow has been properly exposed by the Bidder, the hand with too few cards draws the excess, face down, from the player or widow having too many;

b. If it is discovered at any time after the widow has been properly exposed by the Bidder, and if the Bidder's hand contains the correct number of cards, the Bidder's contract is made; if the Bidder's hand contains an incorrect number of cards, he is single or double bête, depending on whether or not he has led to the first trick;

c. If the widow has too few cards, there must be another deal by the same dealer.

26. Illegal Card Exposure   If a player drops, or names, or

otherwise exposes any card in his hand, except in leading or
playing it:

a. If the player is or becomes the Bidder, there is no
penalty.

b. If that player is or becomes an opponent, the penalty
is that on the first lead or play at which he could legally play
that card the Bidder may either require or forbid him to
play it.

27. *Exposure of More Than One Card*   If either or both of
the opponents of the Bidder exposes more than one card after
the first lead has been made, the Bidder's contract is made.

28. *Bid Out of Turn*   A bid out of turn is void without
penalty, but the other two players (or either of them, if the
other has passed) may treat it as a correct bid by bidding or
passing over it.

29. *Insufficient Bid*   If a bid out of turn is not high enough
to overcall the last preceding bid:

a. If the offender has previously passed, the bid is void
without penalty.

b. If the offender has not previously passed, he is deemed
to have passed; but the other two players (or either of them,
if the other has passed) may treat it as a correct bid by
bidding or passing over it.

30. *Impossible Bid*   If a player bids less than 300, more
than 650, or any figure not expressed in multiples of 10
points, his bid is void.

31. *Played Card*   A card is played when its holder places
it upon the table with apparent intent to play, or when he
names it as the one he intends to play. A card once played
may not be withdrawn, except to correct an irregularity when
permitted by these laws.

32. *Improper Burying*   If, after the Bidder leads, it is ascertained that he buried a card he melded, or buried too many
or too few cards, and as a result has an incorrect number of
cards in his hand, he is double bête.

33. *Information as to the Auction and Meld*

a. Until an opponent has played to the first trick, the opponents may ask or state the number and nature of the cards melded by the Bidder, the point value of the meld, the amount of the bid, and the number of points the Bidder needs to win in cards.

b. After either opponent has played to the first trick, any player may ask what the trump suit is; but if any opponent names the trump suit except in response to such a question, or if an opponent asks or gives any information as to the amount of the bid, the nature or value of the meld, or the number of points either side has taken or needs, play ceases and the Bidder's contract is made.

c. A player has no redress if he acts on incorrect information given in response to a question, or if he does not know what suit is trump.

34. Looking at Turned Card

a. The Bidder may turn and look at the card he buries, at any time before he leads or plays to the second trick. If he does so thereafter, he is double bête.

b. Any player may turn and look at a trick until his side has played to the next trick. If the Bidder turns and looks at a trick thereafter, he is double bête; if an opponent does so, the contract is made.

35. Trick Appropriated in Error   A trick taken in by the side not winning it may be claimed and must be restored at any time before it is covered by cards taken in on a subsequent trick; unless so claimed and restored it remains the property of the side that took it in.

36. Revoke   A player revokes if, when able to play as required by law, he:

a. fails to follow suit;

b. fails to play over on the lead of a trump;

c. fails to play a trump when he has no card of the suit led;

d. fails to play an exposed card when directed by the Bidder to play it.

The Bidder may correct a revoke at any time before he has led or played to the next trick; there is no penalty. An opponent may correct a revoke at any time before he or his partner has led or played to the next trick; play continues and if the Bidder does not make his contract the deal is void and he neither pays nor collects. A player may withdraw a card played after an opponent's revoke and before it was corrected.

Unless a revoke is corrected in time, play ceases, and if the offender is the Bidder, he is double bête; if he is an opponent, the contract is made.

If both sides revoke, the penalty applies to the offense to which attention is first called; if attention to both revokes is drawn simultaneously, the penalty applies to the offense which was committed first.

37. Lead Out of Turn

a. If the Bidder leads when it was an opponent's turn to lead, there is no penalty; the opponent whose lead it was may choose to treat the lead as a correct one, or may require that the card be withdrawn unless either opponent has played to it.

b. If an opponent leads when it is not his turn to lead, the offense is treated as a revoke under Section 36.

38. Claim or Concession   If at any time after the first lead is made:

a. The Bidder concedes that he is bête, or an opponent exposes or throws in his cards or expressly concedes that the contract is made, play ceases and the concession is binding.

b. An opponent suggests concession, as by saying to his partner, "Shall we give it to him?" the concession is not valid and play must continue unless said partner agrees.

c. The Bidder claims that the contract is made, or an opponent claims that the Bidder is bête, play ceases and all unplayed cards are taken by the side which did not make the claim.

39. Error in Count of Meld

a. If, after the Bidder leads to the first trick, he is found to lack a card essential to a meld he announced but did not show, he is double bête.

b. If an incorrect point value was agreed upon for the Bidder's meld, correction may be made at any time before settlement is completed.

40. If an inactive player is first to call attention to an irregularity by the Bidder, no penalty may be exacted for such irregularity.

41. Error in Settlement

a. Chips paid and corrected as a result of an erroneous agreement on the result of a bid, or on its unit value, are not returned.

b. A score entered by a scorekeeper based on an erroneous agreement by all active players as to the result of a bid, or its unit value, may not be corrected after the cards have been mixed for the next shuffle.

c. A score incorrectly entered by the scorekeeper—that is, not entered in accordance with the agreed suit or value of the bid—may be corrected whenever it is discovered.

PARTNERSHIP PINOCHLE

TEN THINGS EVERY WINNING PINOCHLE PLAYER MUST KNOW

(*Partnership Pinochle*)

1. Don't depend on your partner for a meld of more than 20 unless he's bid.

2. The average total of melds around the table is only 130 to 140.

3. When you've won the bid, name your own suit—don't try to guess your partner's.

4. The better your own hand in high cards, the less should be expected from your partner's.

5. Make the conservative bid and you'll score more in the long run.

6. Cash your Aces fast—especially when you have four or more cards in the suit.

7. A 100 Aces are worth at least 200 points all by themselves.

8. The Bidder's first lead should usually be a trump.

9. Bid conservatively when you meld, and tricks will count almost as much at somebody else's bid as at your own.

10. Never forget the score—and remember that the Bidder's score is counted first.

PARTNERSHIP PINOCHLE

There are so many different forms of Partnership Pinochle that you might almost say the game is not played exactly the same in any two cities. However, in every form there are four players, each holding twelve cards, and playing in two partnerships. Therefore, many of the problems of play are common to all the games.

In the oldest form of Partnership Pinochle there was no bidding. The dealer's last card was turned as the trump card, establishing the trump suit for that deal.

All the modern forms, however, are bidding games. Usually the player at the dealer's left is the first bidder, and each player has exactly one bid. The highest bidder names the trump.

In my native Philadelphia, and in many other cities, this is called Firehouse Pinochle because it is the game firemen used to play while sitting around their station houses waiting for an alarm. There are some special rules and conventions played in Philadelphia that I will tell you about later. At the start I will discuss the game most widely played.

In this game eldest hand must bid at least 100. (This is equivalent to a pass; he or someone else almost always bids more.) However, the next-higher bid is 200, and after that the bids go up in units of 10 points. Each player has exactly one bid. No matter which side gets the bid, *eldest hand always leads first*.

Basic Problems of Bidding There is usually a considerable difference between bidding as first or second hand, and bidding as third or fourth hand.

Generally, however, each bid must be a compromise. The player wants to get the bid, because he wants his best suit to be trump; therefore, he wants to make a high bid. But he doesn't want to risk a bête, so he doesn't want to overbid unnecessarily.

As between these two extremes, it is better to be conservative in most cases. The penalty for an overbid is great, and a few bêtes will be much more costly than the loss from the few times that the opponents will overcall your bid and make their contract.

With a hand like this:

♠ A J
♡ A K K
♢ A 10 K Q J
♣ A 9   (Ex. 1)

with 250 to meld, the hand is virtually a laydown for 350. Should this conservative bid be made, risking the danger that an opponent will overcall, or should a higher bid (up to 400) be made in order to shut the opponents out?

The decision should always be in favor of a 350 bid. With only four Aces among the other three hands, there is little danger that any single player will have a powerful hand. If your partner has no meld and is weak in Diamonds, the combined hands may not take more than 100 or 110 points.

On this hand you can meld 120 even if an opponent takes the bid away from you, and win four or five tricks—perhaps more. If you overbid, you risk a large loss only for the benefit of making Diamonds trumps and scoring 130 extra for the Diamond flush. It is not worth risking 200 to 250 sure points (plus the additional danger of going down) for an extra 150 or thereabouts.

The circumstances are different with a hand like the following:

♠ A A Q
♡ A A 10 K K Q 9
♢ J
♣ K   (Ex. 2)

This hand melds only 90, but must almost surely take 180 in cards if Hearts are trumps, and probably will take 190 or more (because the opponents will hardly have the cards and distribution of cards required to load the maximum number of points on the three losing tricks). If an opponent takes the bid away on this hand, the loss to the holder will be 30 points in melds and probably 150 in play. For this reason it is worth while to take a chance in order to make Hearts the trump suit. The hand justifies a bid of 300 (unless this would violate a bidding convention being used in the game), an overbid that requires a meld or perhaps an Ace and a Ten from your partner. This is not too much to expect.

The first and second bidders have this advantage: Their partners will still have a chance to bid. If you underbid and are overcalled at your left, your partner can bid again, based on the strength shown by your bid. But this is dangerous. He will not know what trump you intended to name, and may make a very costly guess.

Because of this fact a series of conventional first- and second-hand bids have grown up in most circles that play Partnership Pinochle. The exact meaning of bids varies in different places (later on I will give one such schedule), but so long as the partners understand them they probably come to about the same thing.

Another thing that affects your bidding is the distribution of your hand. If you have a balanced hand, for example, 4-3-3-2, you may bid quite conservatively in first and second positions; whatever trump suit your partner may name, you will have some support for it. If you have a freak, like Example 2 above, you must bid the maximum—or, if your schedule of conventional bids contains one, you should make some bid that warns your partner that you have a one-suit hand.

Third hand has nothing to fear except from the dealer. He will judge on the basis of his hand as to how likely the dealer is to overcall a conservative bid. If he does not expect the dealer to be very strong (for example, if he has stoppers in two or three suits, so that dealer is unlikely to have anything but melding values), then he should make the most conservative bid possible. Why take any chance on a bête if it is unnecessary?

The condition of the score often controls the choice between a conservative bid and a high bid.

If the opponents are far ahead, bid aggressively. You cannot risk letting them get the contract cheaply. If you are far ahead, you can afford to be very conservative—the points you score even when they are the bidders will usually get you to 1000 ahead of them. When the score is very close, you should usually be conservative unless both sides are so close to game (being around 800 each) that the Bidder is almost sure to win; in such cases you should be ultrabold.

Bidding Valuation While in various games of three-hand Auction Pinochle players cling to the 11-10-4-3-2 scoring schedule, in Partnership Pinochle it has become almost the universal custom, even among the strongest players, to use the simplified schedule whereby each Ace or Ten counts 10 points and each King or Queen counts 5.

The simplest method of hand valuation is to count your winning tricks, multiply the number by 20 points, and add that total to your meld. That is the playing value of your own hand. You must add what you may expect your partner to contribute; but as you will see later, such expectancy is extremely slight.

As tricks in your own hand count 1 for each Ace, 1 for each trump over three (in addition to any Aces and other sure winners you may hold in the trump suit), and 1 for a four-card side suit if you have five trumps. Don't count more than one trick in any suit of four or more cards unless it is the trump suit, or unless a long solid suit of your own is going to be trumps. (With six high trumps a five-card side suit is worth an extra two tricks.)

Now you count what you may expect in your partner's hand. As mentioned above, in melding this may not be much. The total meld of all four players averages only about 130, and 20 of these are always the two dixes. A marriage is about the most you can expect from your partner, and you should not risk much of an overbid even in expectation of that.

What you can expect your partner to win in the play depends partly on the strength of your own hand. In Examples 1 and 2 above, in each of which you hold four Aces, you can hardly depend on your partner to win more than one trick. If your hand were weaker, with more outstanding strength to be divided among the other three hands, you could depend on your partner for more.

The following rule of thumb is sound mathematically as well as practically: Take the number of tricks you do not expect to win in your own hand, divide by three, and that is your partner's share. At 20 points per trick you may usually add this share to your bidding values.

> ♠ A Q
> ♡ Q J 9 9
> ♢ A K Q J
> ♣ A K   (Ex. 3)

Count three tricks for the three Aces, and one for the fourth trump, a total of four tricks, which we estimate as 80 points. That leaves eight tricks to be won by the other three players. Your partner's share is two or three of those tricks, 40 to 60 points. Your total of 160 plus his low expectancy of 40 gives you a sound 200 bid, and an overcall strength of 210 or 220 if the player before you has bid. As first or second hand, you have the added advantage of being able to support whatever suit your partner may name both with melds and with trumps.

A few combinations like 10-10-K can be counted as a trick in your hand (but not 10-10-K-J-9, which is too long for a nontrump suit unless you have another long suit in your hand that will be trumps). It is a dangerous gamble to assign any value to the Ten in a holding such as A-10-9. Though the Ten may work out to win a trick almost half the time, the economics of Pinochle is such that you cannot afford to overbid on a 50% chance. You lose too much when you lose.

Competitive Bidding While conservatism is the rule in making the first bid, you must be aggressive when an opponent has made a bid ahead of you. This principle should not be misunderstood. You still do not bid more than the value of your hand, but you do bid the maximum of your hand. You must be optimistic, and not pessimistic, as to what you will find in your partner's hand and what the suit breaks will be.

However, your aggressiveness depends on what you have by way of defense and what you can score even if the opponents play the hand.

Take Example 3, the last one shown. We have shown that the optimistic valuation of this hand is 220 points. If an opponent has bid 210, you may overcall with 220. It would be stupid, however, to try to push as high as 250, especially since you have a meld of 60 and your trick-taking strength will be about the same if the opponents get the bid. In a case like this:

♠ A A K Q 9
♡ K Q Q
♢ A J J
♣ A   (Ex. 4)

you count six tricks for 120, plus your meld of 110, giving you a total of 230. If your partner had his share of the six tricks that must be won by the other players, he would have two tricks and you could add 40 to your estimate. But when an opponent has bid 250 ahead of you, the strength he shows plus the four Aces in your hand should make you doubt if your partner can win those two tricks, or indeed if he can win any tricks at all. On that basis your limit is your basic 230 and you are not strong enough to overcall the bid of 250.

Necessarily in the bidding you are often in competition with your partner. You cannot tell, even when he has bid, whether it is better for him to play the hand or for you to play it.

Sometimes, of course, the situation is clear-cut. In Example 2 you had a hand that practically demanded to play at its own suit:

HOW TO BE A CONSISTENT WINNER

♠ A A Q
♡ A A 10 K K Q 9
◊ J
♣ K   (Ex. 2)

Whether the previous bid was your partner's or an opponent's, on this hand you overcall it to the limit of your ability so that you can name Hearts. If the bid was your partner's, it is possible that he had an equally good suit, but it is so unlikely that you should not risk it.

To overcall your partner's bid just to shut out the dealer is very dangerous. Unless you have a high-grade trump suit of your own, by taking the bid away from your partner you will confront yourself with the problem of guessing what trump suit to name.

Usually there is nothing more dangerous than trying to guess your partner's suit. The fact that you have a weak suit is no proof that that was his suit. There are occasional exceptions like this:

♠ K Q J J
♡ 10 10 Q
◊ Q J
♣ K Q Q   (Ex. 5)

If your partner has made a high bid like 320, showing a probable flush, and it has been overcalled by the next player, you with your 140-point meld can afford to bid over any conceivable intervening bid, knowing that your partner has a Diamond flush. You have all of the other three suits stopped. But you should shiver as you do it. After all, your right-hand opponent had to have something, or he could not have bid over 320. If it turned out that he, and not your partner, had the Diamond flush, while your partner had a freak like this:

♠ A 9
♡ A A K Q J 9
◊ A
♣ A 10 J   (Ex. 6)

you would take quite a beating.

It is problems like this that have led to the establishment of so many conventional bids, which we will discuss next.

Partnership Conventions The following are conventional in most Partnership Pinochle games:*

200—an average hand with a meld of about 100 points and reasonable playing strength; no particular information about the suit. This is usually a balanced hand, and if your partner gets the bid, he simply names his best suit and will usually find reasonable support for it.

210 or 310—a one-suit which should be undisturbed unless your partner has a self-sustaining suit of his own.

250—a flush. This is justified by the fact that the flush melds 150, and even a reasonably weak playing hand, combined with your partner's average expectance, and with the trump length and strength that a flush contains, will win 100 points in the play.

260—Aces. The 100-point meld, plus the playing strength of the four Aces (which, even as four tricks, we value at 80 points, and which are actually worth somewhat more because of the control they exert), will usually be accompanied by another meld, a fair trump suit, or additional playing strength. Players have a tendency to undervalue 100 Aces. The information given by this bid is tremendous, because the Aces are tremendous support for any strength your partner may have, both in their melding value and in their playing strength.

In many games, especially where bonuses are paid for bids of 300 or more, 290 is used as a conventional bid to show Aces with a marriage or two, or perhaps a pinochle, outside. Your partner must bid at least 300 and name his suit.

Except in games with continuous bidding, conventions are employed only by first and second hands. With continuous bidding there may be additional conventions used in responses to your partner's bid.

* Conventional bids are different in Firehouse Pinochle; see Page 254.

THE PLAY

The play is about the same in any form of Partnership Pinochle where there is any bidding at all. (In the old-fashioned game, when the trump card was turned instead of being named by the Bidder, the primary object of the play was to find out who had the trumps; but in the bidding games, it is safe to assume that the Bidder has at least four or five trumps, even if he had no meld in his trump suit. He may have more, depending on the amount of his bid.)

Information from the Melds   The first information comes from the cards melded; and very often from melds that were not made.

While every Pinochle player watches and remembers the melds, and bases his play on his positive knowledge that certain cards are in certain hands, far too few players bother to figure out the placing of cards from what was not melded. This is something that usually requires conscious thought at the time, but it is worth while.

For example, your right-hand opponent melds 80 Kings. Your left-hand opponent melds 40 Jacks. If you have a Queen of Spades, you know your partner has the other; if you have no Queen of Spades, you know your partner has both of them. Your right-hand opponent could not have had one, or he would have had a marriage in Spades; your left-hand opponent could not have had one or he would have had a pinochle. That is a simple and obvious example, and some of them require more thought and a bit of guesswork, but the point I am trying to stress is that so many players fail even to notice such things.

As the play progresses, and more cards show up, it is worth stopping occasionally to check up on the melds that were not made. The opportunity arises every time a King or Queen is played by a player who did not meld a marriage. His play of the Queen, for instance, definitely marks any missing King of the suit as being in one of the other hands. For an intelligent player it is often enough simply to notice that fact, and the location of the missing King will become clear. Every additional bit of information about the location of an outstanding card will help you in the play.

Leading In Partnership Pinochle eldest hand always leads first, no matter who is the Bidder. In Firehouse Pinochle the Bidder leads first, an influence taken from three-handed Auction Pinochle; this custom is spreading somewhat in Partnership Pinochle games. However, we will assume that eldest hand leads first, that still being the custom in the majority of games.

In Partnership Pinochle there is almost an even chance that someone will have a singleton in a suit. Therefore, a player must usually begin by cashing his Aces (except trump Aces, and except that when you have both Aces of a suit there is generally no hurry about taking them). If your Ace is blank, then, as in any Pinochle game, you must cash it before you relinquish the lead. If your Ace is in a suit of four or more cards, you must lead it yourself; otherwise an opponent may get in and take the other Ace of the suit, leaving yours to be trumped on the second round.

When you have only two cards of a suit, you need not cash your Ace—the danger that your Ace will be trumped is slight. (However, you usually cash it anyway if you are the Bidder's partner.) When you have three cards of a suit there is somewhat more danger, but if you want to retain control of the suit you may occasionally take a chance on waiting.

The same principle controls your play in a suit someone else leads. With four cards or more headed by an Ace, you put up the Ace at once; you usually do with three; and you must with two, or your Ace might be trapped next time by the lead of the other Ace.

From a suit headed by 10-10, one of the Tens is the best lead even if it goes against the grain. You cannot save them both, and leading one of the Tens is the best way to save one of them. This is an undesirable lead, of course, if there is anything better.

A suit headed neither by Ace nor by double Ten should

usually be opened by leading a King or Queen rather than a lower card.

When the Bidder leads he should usually lead trumps. The exception is when his trump suit is weak and he has a long side suit. In such cases he wants the opponents to waste their trumps on his side suit, leaving him with his trump length for control and for getting last.

♠ A K Q Q 9
♡ A 9
◊ A K K J J
♣ —————   (Ex. 7)

This hand, played in Spades, will usually produce the most points if the Ace of Diamonds is opened and Diamonds continued, forcing all three of the other players eventually to trump. Even if they find the Club suit on their first lead, your Spades will probably outlast theirs and get the last trick for you. If they lead Hearts, you will have time for another round of Diamonds without having your trump length shortened.

Of course, if your side suit is solid, you can start trumps from even a weak suit.

♠ A K Q Q 9
♡ A 9
◊ A A 10 10 J
♣ —————   (Ex. 8)

With Spades trumps you are better off to lead trumps and risk a bad break rather than have your high Diamonds trumped, which will be costly in terms of points. There is a fair chance that the opposing Spades will break 3-2-2, and that you will have complete control of the hand (with only one trump outstanding) after you have led two rounds. (You start with the Nine or Queen.) Even if your partner has only one Spade, and your opponents have three each, you are in no danger. And if you find, after leading two rounds of Spades, that there is danger that an opponent still holds two trumps, you can then shift to Diamonds and retain your trump superiority.

Signals Partnership play requires some signals. In Partnership Pinochle these are not the same as those used by Auction Pinochle players, previously described. For example, the two partners in Auction Pinochle play that "an Ace calls for an Ace"—that is, if one leads an Ace, the other should throw an Ace on it. In Partnership Pinochle you don't throw your Ace on your partner's unless you are a defender and think that is the only trick you are going to get in the suit.

The play of a Nine (or of the player's lowest card) on your partner's lead of an Ace shows the other Ace (unless, of course, it is a singleton or 9-9). When the Bidder's partner makes this play, he shows control of the suit and suggests a shift to trump. Very often an opponent of the Bidder cannot give this signal because he must not lose the chance to play a counter. For example, with A-10-K-9, the Bidder's partner would play the Nine, but an opponent would usually have to play his Ten for fear of losing it.

As an opponent holding A-10-10-9 you should play the Ace on your partner's lead of the Ace. But the Bidder's partner plays the Nine so as to retain full control of the suit. The only exception is when the Bidder's partner cannot stand a shift to trumps; in that case he "lies" by playing a Ten.

The Bidder's first lead from A-A-10 of trumps is the Ten; then he shifts to his side Aces to see if his partner can signal a suit that can be run after trumps are pulled. His partner may be unable to give such a signal, but by playing high-low on the first two rounds of trumps he shows that his hand nevertheless contains a solid suit.

In discarding, strength is shown by an unnecessarily low discard of the suit on a trick won by the partner. A negative signal is given by a high discard in a suit.

It is common in all forms of Pinochle to play cards you have melded instead of cards you have not melded. This withholds information from the opponents. When a player in Partnership Pinochle plays an unmelded card ahead of a melded one, he often does so to signal in the suit to his partner. Having melded a pinochle, and so being placed with the Queen of Spades, he would show control of the suit by playing the Jack.

FIREHOUSE PINOCHLE

This is the game popular in Philadelphia, played with slight variation in many other big cities, that I have referred to in the preceding pages.

It is a four-handed Partnership Pinochle game with twelve cards dealt to each player as in regular Partnership Pinochle. In the scoring we count 10 points each for Aces, Tens and Kings and nothing for Queens, Jacks and Nines.

Eldest hand has the first bid, but any one of the first three players may bid or pass. If all three pass, the dealer must bid at least 200 (we call it 20, since we drop the superfluous zero off of each score), and of course he may bid more if he wishes. Game is 1000, and the score of the bidding side is always counted first.

Bonuses are paid for bidding and making contracts of 300 or more. Bidding and making exactly 300 is 1 extra point, 310 is 2 extra points, and so on, so that 400 is worth 11 extra points. If the bidding side holds 100 Aces, and makes its bid, it gets a bonus point; if it is bête, the bonus point goes to the opponents. If a side takes all the tricks, it gets 2 bonus points, and in addition the opponents lose their meld. Winning the game counts 5 bonus points, with an extra point if the opponents have not reached 500, and still another point if they end with a minus score.

Because the dealer will make his compulsory bid only about two thirds of the time, while his opponents get whatever they make regardless of which side is the Bidder, there is little bid against the dealer's side except in two cases: when his opponents can bid 300 or more and earn a bonus; and when the score makes it proper, as when there is a Bidder-out condition (with both sides approximately 800 or more toward the game, so that whichever side gets the bid will probably win the game).

The dealer's partner usually bids 200 (regardless of meld)

if he has a five-card suit or better, since, if he passes, his partner will almost always have to bid and may pick an inferior suit.

There are many bidding conventions to get a partnership to its highest safe score and earn the biggest possible bonus. These bidding conventions, used only by first and second bidders, are as follows:

210—A very strong trump suit (such as A-A-10-K-Q-9)

220—About 100 to meld, plus two Aces

230—Same as 220, plus a five-card suit

240—About 160 to meld, plus two Aces

250—100 Aces

260—100 Aces with an extra 20 meld (or, as some play, a five-card suit)

270—100 Aces with at least 40 more to meld

280—100 Aces with at least 60 more to meld

290—A roundhouse or the equivalent

300 and up—A flush and a hand of strength appropriate to the bid

340—A roundhouse and a pinochle, or the equivalent, such as 100 Aces, 80 Kings and a couple of marriages, or a pinochle.

LAWS OF PARTNERSHIP PINOCHLE

1. Number of Players The game of Partnership Pinochle is played by four players, in two partnerships.

2. The Pack Forty-eight cards, two each of A, K, Q, J, 10, and 9 in each of four suits, Spades, Hearts, Diamonds, and Clubs.

3. Rank of Cards A (high), 10, K, Q, J, 9.

4. The Draw The pack is spread face down on the table and each player draws a card, but not one of the four cards at either end of the pack. The players drawing the two highest cards play as partners against the other two. If two players draw equal cards, both must draw again to determine which is higher.

The highest card determines the first dealer. Partners sit

opposite each other, each having an opponent at his left and right.

5. The Shuffle The dealer shuffles the pack and places it on the table, face down, at his right.

6. The Cut The player at the dealer's right lifts no fewer than five nor more than forty-three cards from the top of the pack. The dealer picks up the remainder of the pack. The player who cut then places his portion face down on the table and the dealer places his portion on top of it, completing the cut.

7. Order of the Game Each player's turn in dealing, melding, and playing comes to him in rotation, which is to the left (clockwise).

8. The Deal The dealer deals three cards at a time to each player in turn, beginning with the player at his left, each player thus receiving twelve cards. (In many games the cards are dealt one at a time.)

9. The Bidding Eldest hand bids first; he must bid 100 unless he chooses to bid 200 or more. Each player in turn thereafter must make a bid or pass. All bids must be multiples of 10, and the lowest bid allowed is 200. There is only one round of bidding. The highest bidder (the Bidder) names the trump suit.

10. Melding After the bidding is ended, each player places face up on the table any melds he may hold, as follows:

SEQUENCES

A-K-Q-J-10 of trumps (flush)	150
Double flush	1500
K-Q of trumps (royal marriage)	40
K-Q of any other suit (marriage)	20

GROUPS

♠ A- ♡ A- ◇ A- ♣ A (100 Aces)	100
All eight Aces	1000
♠ K- ♡ K- ◇ K- ♣ K (80 Kings)	80
All eight Kings	800
♠ Q- ♡ Q- ◇ Q- ♣ Q (60 Queens)	60

All eight Queens	600
♠J-♡J-◇J-♣J (40 Jacks)	40
All eight Jacks	400

SPECIAL

♠Q-◇J (pinochle)	40
Double pinochle	300
9 of trumps (dix, pronounced deece)	10

A card that is part of a meld under one heading may be counted as part of a meld under another heading, but may not be counted as part of another meld under the same heading.

A memorandum is made of the total points melded by each side, but its total is not credited to a side unless and until it wins a trick.

11. First Lead After the melds are shown and totaled, each player replaces his melded cards in his hand and the play begins. Eldest hand makes the first lead.

12. Objects of the Play The objects of the play are to win tricks containing cards of scoring value, and to win the last trick. The scoring values of cards taken in tricks won, and of the last trick, are:

Each Ace	10
Each Ten	10
Each King	5
Each Queen	5
Last Trick	10

Jacks and Nines have no scoring value when taken in tricks. The total of points to be divided in play is 250.

13. The Play The card led to a trick and the three cards played in turn by the other players constitute a trick. All the tricks won by a side are gathered by one partner. A trick containing a trump is won by the highest trump. A trick not containing a trump is won by the highest card played of the suit led. Of two cards of identical suit and rank played to the same trick the one played first is the higher. The winner of each trick leads to the next, and may lead any card.

Each player must follow suit to the card led if able. If void of the suit led, he must play a trump if able. If void of both the suit led and of trumps, he may play any card.

If the card led is a trump, each player must, if able, play a higher trump than any previously played to the trick. This is called playing over.

14. Scoring One score is kept for each side. If the Bidder's side wins in melds and tricks at least the amount of the bid, it scores all it makes; if not, it is set back by the amount of the bid. The opposing side scores whatever it makes in melds and tricks.

15. Game The first side to reach a score of 1000 wins the game. The score of the Bidder's side is counted first.

IRREGULARITIES

16. Misdeal There must be a new deal by the same dealer:

a. If the pack was not properly shuffled or was not cut, and if a player calls attention to the fact before looking at his hand and before the last card is dealt.

b. If more than one card is exposed in dealing.

17. Wrong Number of Cards If one player has too many cards and another too few, and if:

a. The error is discovered before either of these two players has looked at his hand, the player with too few cards draws the extra cards from the hand with too many.

b. The error is discovered after one of the players has looked at his hand, all players meld, and then the player with too few cards draws the extra cards from the unmelded cards of the player with too many; the card drawn may then be used by the former in melding, and he may change his meld.

c. The error is discovered after the first lead, play continues; the last trick or tricks comprise only three cards each after the short hand is exhausted, and excess cards remaining in the long hand after the twelfth trick are dead; a side that held an incorrect hand may not score for points won in tricks or for the last trick, but may score its melds if it won a trick.

18. Incorrect Pack If at any time the pack is found to be incorrect (not in accordance with Section 2), play ceases and no points for cards or melds score in that deal, but the results of previous deals are not affected.

19. Exposed Card A card dropped face up on the table, named by a player as being in his hand, or otherwise exposed except in melding and correct leading and playing, is an exposed card. An exposed card must be left face up on the table and must be played at the first legal opportunity. If the card is still unplayed at the first turn thereafter of the partner of the owner to lead, either opponent may name the suit which he must lead.

20. Lead or Play Out of Turn If a player leads or plays out of turn, the card so played becomes an exposed card and is dealt with under Section 19.

21. Revoke As required by the laws, a player revokes if he fails when able to follow suit to a lead; to trump; or to play over on a trump lead. A side that revokes may score nothing for points taken in tricks or the last trick in that deal, but does not necessarily lose its melds.

(The revoke penalty is by agreement sometimes applied to the exposure of a card and to leads and plays out of turn.)

22. Played Card A card is played when its holder places it upon the table with apparent intent to play, or when he names it as the one he intends to play. A card once played may not be withdrawn, except in correct of a lead or play out of turn.

23. Information As to Cards Played

a. Until his side has played to the next trick a player may require all four cards of a trick to be turned face up and the holder of each to be indicated.

b. Except as provided in Section 23a above, no player may ask or give information about any cards previously played. If a player gives information to his partner in violation of this law, his side incurs the penalty for revoke, Section 21.

24. Trick Appropriated in Error A trick taken in by the side not winning it may be claimed and must be restored at any time before it is covered by cards taken in a subsequent trick; unless so claimed and restored, it remains the property of the side that took it in.

25. *Error in Count* A player is entitled to the full value of any melds he shows on the table, even if he announces their value incorrectly. A side is entitled to all the points actually in its tricks, even though less is claimed by reason of miscounting. Erroneous announcements as to the value of melds and trick points must be corrected on demand of any player if made before the score of the deal has been agreed upon by both sides and entered on the score sheet (or settled in chips).

26. *Error in Entering Score* A score incorrectly entered by the scorekeeper—that is, not entered in accordance with the agreed result or value, or an arithmetical error in adding scores—must be corrected on the demand of any player if made before the winner of a game is agreed upon.

BLACKJACK

TEN THINGS EVERY WINNING BLACKJACK PLAYER MUST KNOW

Gambling House Game

1. Take another card if you have 16 or less and dealer's showing card is 7, 8, 9, 10, or Ace.

2. Stand with as little as 13 if dealer's showing card is 2, 3, 4, 5, or 6.

3. Stand even on 12 if dealer shows a 4, 5, or 6.

4. Never split a pair of Fours, Fives, Tens, or picture cards.

5. Always split a pair of Eights or Aces.

6. Always take "one down for double" to 11 unless dealer shows an Ace.

Home Game

7. The dealership is worth conservatively about three times the amount of the maximum bet.

8. Make the maximum bet with any Ace, Ten, or face card.

9. Bet the minimum on any card from the Four to the Eight.

10. The best seat is at the dealer's right.

SUMMARY OF BLACKJACK STRATEGY
(CASINO GAME)

Depending on Card Shown by Dealer

DRAWING (HARD COMBINATIONS)

12	Hit vs. 2, 3, 7, 8, 9, 10, A
	Stand vs. 4, 5, 6
13 to 16	Hit vs. 7, 8, 9, 10, A
	Stand vs. 2, 3, 4, 5, 6
17 to 21	Always stand

SPLITTING PAIRS

YOU HOLD	ACTION
A–A	Always split
2–2	Split vs. 2, 3, 4, 5, 6, 7
	Otherwise hit
3–3	Split vs. 2, 3, 4, 5, 6, 7
	Otherwise hit
4–4	Hit (never split, never double down)
5–5	Never split
	Double down unless dealer has 10 or A
6–6	Split vs. 2, 3, 4, 5, 6, 7
	Otherwise hit or stand (see above)
7–7	Split vs. 2, 3, 4, 5, 6, 7
	Otherwise hit or stand (see above)
8–8	Always split
9–9	Split vs. 2, 3, 4, 5, 6, 8, 9
	Stand vs. 7, 10, A
10–10	Never split, always stand

DOUBLING DOWN (HARD COMBINATIONS)

11	Double down except vs. A
10	Double down except vs. 10 or A
9	Double down vs. 2, 3, 4, 5, 6, not vs. 7, 8, 9, 10, A

DRAWING AND DOUBLING DOWN (SOFT COMBINATIONS)

A–2	Double down vs. 5, 6
	Otherwise draw
A–3	Double down vs. 5, 6
	Otherwise draw
A–4	Double down vs. 5, 6
	Otherwise draw
A–5	Double down vs. 5, 6
	Otherwise draw
A–6	Double down vs. 3, 4, 5, 6
	Otherwise draw
A–7	Double down vs. 4, 5, 6
	Hit vs. 9, 10, A
	Stand vs. 2, 3, 7, 8
A–8 or A–9	Always stand

BLACKJACK OR TWENTY-ONE

This is a doubly popular game. It is the only card game that is played in virtually all American gambling houses.* It is equally popular as an informal home game. But there are many differences between the casino game and the home game.

In either game, the dealer has an advantage. A casino game always has a house dealer, against whom everyone must bet, and to make the game more attractive to its patrons the casino places severe restrictions on the dealer. In the home game, any player may be dealer; usually the right to deal passes any time a player gets a blackjack (also called a natural), which is a count of 21 in the first two cards—Ace and face card or Ten. In the casino game the betting limit may range from one dollar—or even less—to $500; the home game is usually played for pennies or quarters, or at most for dollars.

I will discuss the two games separately, beginning with the casino game.

THE CASINO GAME

Let us understand one thing clearly: When you play Blackjack (or Twenty-One, as it is often called) in a gam-

* An American casino derives its profit primarily from dice games, where the big-money bettors play. Slot machines and roulette, though profitable, are designed to keep the ladies amused while their menfolk are doing the big betting elsewhere. Blackjack used to be in this category but in the last few years it has become a major gambling game and quite a source of income to the casinos.

bling house, you figure to lose. This is true of any game played in a gambling house. If the odds were not against you, the house would not bank the game.

Yet a situation has developed in Blackjack—and it may not last very long—when for the first time in history gambling houses are banking a game in which the odds may be very close to even rather than for them. If this is so, the gambling houses will soon change the rules; because without a mathematical advantage they cannot pay the rent and salaries and other overhead expenses. It is right that gambling houses should have the edge, because they furnish recreation to their patrons. The smart gambler does not begrudge this advantage to the "house" but he tries to keep the percentage against him to a minimum. Then, with a little luck, he can win.

Mathematical Calculations   Before we had electronic calculating machines, Blackjack was such a complicated game to figure out with pencil and paper that no one knew the exact odds. All calculations were based on experience and observation, and all published advice—including my own!—was wrong.

Then came the UNIVAC and other giant calculating devices. A group of young Air Force men, whose names I have credited in the Foreword to this book, took the time and trouble to develop a method of play for Blackjack, based on the best mathematical figuring. Some others, especially my friend Dr. Allan Wilson, a computer scientist, carried the process even farther; as I write this, Dr. Wilson is preparing his own exhaustive book on Blackjack play.

Casinos used to say that their edge over good players was about 2½% and over poor players it could be almost anything. The new knowledge of Blackjack that has been given to us by the electronic calculators reduces the house advantage to little more than one-half of one per cent (about 0.6%) and a player who watches and remembers the cards can bring it down to practically an even game. At craps, which previously had been the most favorable game for the player, the house advantage is 1.4%.

How the Casino Game Is Played With only minor differences, the following customs prevail in all professional games.

A regular 52-card pack is used. Before dealing, the dealer shows and burns one card (or in some places he places a blank card on the bottom of the deck).

Each player against the house must place his bet before the dealing begins. A single player may elect to play two or more hands. If he wishes to play at least four hands, the house will usually "close the table" (not permit anyone else to play at it)—especially if the player is a good customer who makes a sizable bet on every hand.

A player may split any pair, such as two Fours or two Jacks, playing them as two separate hands. He places on the split card as much as he bet originally on the first card, in effect doubling his bet. If he splits a pair of Aces he may draw only one card to each Ace and is not paid extra if he gets a blackjack; if he splits any other pair he may draw as often as he wishes to each hand. Most houses permit any two 10-point cards, such as a Queen and Jack, to be split; but this is a sucker trap, because pairs of 10-point cards should not be split anyway.

If a card dealt to a split pair results in a new pair—for example, if you split Eights and draw another Eight to one of them—you may split again.

You may also "double down," also called "taking one down for double." This means that you turn up your two original cards, regardless of what they total, and the dealer gives you one more card—only one card, no more, no less—and you must stand on the total you get in the three cards. To do this, you must double your original bet.

Some houses, but not many, permit you to take one down for double after your first *three* cards. Some permit you to double down after splitting a pair: For example, you split Eights and draw a Three to one of the Eights; you may double your bet on that combination and take one card down.

If you get a blackjack against the dealer, he pays you 1½ times the amount of your bet and you win immediately. If the dealer gets a blackjack he wins immediately but he collects only the single amount of your bet. Two blackjacks are a stand-off.

You may hit or stand on any total up to 21, but the dealer may not. The dealer must hit 16 and must stand on 17. Even if the dealer has a "soft" 17 (Ace plus Six-spot), he must stand. Some casinos give the dealer an option on a soft 17, but it is always unpopular with the customers to give the dealer any option. Some casinos, but not many, require the dealer to hit a soft 17, which is an advantage to the house.

The dealer gives two cards face down to each of his opponents but deals himself one card down and one card face up.

If the dealer's up-card is an Ace or face card or Ten, he looks at his face down card to see if he has a blackjack. If his up-card is anything else, he may not look at his face down card until he has finished dealing to all his opponents.

These are the basic conditions of the casino game—with one exception, "insurance," which I will discuss later—and all calculations are based on them.

The Dealer's Advantages and Disadvantages   The biggest advantage of the dealer is that if one of his opponents "busts" —goes over 21—the dealer wins the bet, even if later the dealer too goes over 21. By the system of play that once was almost universally followed, about one opponent in four busted before the dealer's turn came, giving the dealer a decisive 25% advantage at the start.

With this advantage the dealer would be a sure winner except that casinos balance by imposing three disadvantages on the dealer. First, the dealer pays 1½ to 1 for his opponents' blackjacks and collects only singly himself. Second, the dealer cannot use his own judgment in standing or drawing, based on what his opponents show; he must hit 16 and stand on 17. When he hits 16 it is about 8 to 5 that he will go over and lose to all hands that have not previously gone over themselves. Sometimes he must stand on 17 when he knows it is probably a losing number. If given the full option as to when to stand and when to draw, the dealer would be a sure winner.

Third, and most important among the dealer's disadvantages, one of his cards is dealt face up so his opponents can see it. Nearly every decision a player has to make is based on his knowledge of the dealer's up-card. Nearly always the up-card controls a player's decision on doubling down and on splitting pairs—extra advantages to the player that once were thought to be unimportant but now are known to have a great effect on his winnings or losses. Often the up-card decides the question of when to stand and when to draw, which is the subject I will discuss next.

When to Stand, When to Draw This is the most frequent problem in Blackjack. The proper plays are worth committing to memory so that you can make them automatically. Much depends on the dealer's up-card and on whether you have a "hard" combination (not including an Ace) or a "soft" combination (one that includes an Ace).

With a hard combination, you stand on anything from 17 (such as a Nine-Eight) up to 21, regardless of what dealer's up-card is.

You hit a hard 13, 14, 15, or even 16, when dealer's up-card is a 7, 8, 9, 10 (face card), or Ace. But you stand on any of these counts when dealer's up-card is 2, 3, 4, 5, or 6.

With 12 you should stand when dealer shows 4, 5, or 6, but you should hit against any other card that dealer might show.

With 11 or less you always draw, unless it is proper to double down or split, according to the advice I will give later.

It is quite a new idea in Blackjack ever to stand on as low a count as 12, but there are even more startling departures from the old strategy in the play of soft combinations (those including an Ace).

The easiest way to remember the strategy of the soft combinations is this:

On combinations that total *more than 18*—that is, on A-8 (=19) and A-9 (=20)—you always stand.

On combinations that total *less than 18*—that is, on A-2 (=3 or 13) through A-6 (=7 or 17)—you always hit, unless it is better to double down, as I will explain later.

Only on the soft A-7 combination, totaling 8 or 18, do you have a wide choice of plays. With A-7 you should double down if the dealer's showing card is 4, 5, or 6; you should stand if the dealer's card is 2, 3, 7, or 8. But—an action unheard of until recently—if the dealer's card is 9, 10, or Ace, you should draw to A-7 even though you would have a count of 18 if you stood. Whatever you do against dealer's 9, 10, or Ace, you figure to lose in the long run; but you will lose less if you draw than if you stand.

A prominent casino player told me not long ago that he would be willing to give a player a count of 18 every time and undertake to beat him. (Of course, in this case the dealer can draw to 17.)

Splitting Pairs Once it was thought that no pair could profitably be split except Aces and Eights—and casinos did not permit a player to split Aces. Now it is known that the decision to split pairs depends largely on what up-card the dealer shows, and that pairs should be split more often than not.

Aces should always be split, even though the house rules forbid drawing more than one card to each Ace and they do not pay the blackjack bonus, but only even money, if you draw a 10-point card.

Eights should always be split, even though dealer shows an Ace—advice that will surprise many experienced players.

Tens, Fives, and Fours should never be split.

Nines, Sevens, Sixes, Threes, and Twos should be split, or not split, depending on what the dealer's up-card is. The summary is:

Nines: Split if dealer shows 2, 3, 4, 5, 6, 8, or 9. Do not split against 7, a 10-point card, or an Ace.

Sevens, Sixes, Threes, and Twos: Split if dealer shows 2, 3, 4, 5, 6, or 7. Do not split if dealer shows any other card.

If a card drawn to one of a split pair produces another pair, split the new pair.

If a card or cards drawn to one of a split pair produces a combination that it pays to "double down" (which I will explain in the next section), you should double down if the house rules permit.

As for the decision to hit or stand, follow the principles I previously stated, applying them to each hand separately.

Taking One Down for Double This is called "doubling down" in some circles. When you double down, you turn up both of your first two cards, the dealer gives you one card face down, and you must stand on these three cards.

In doubling down, much depends on whether your original count, in your first two cards, is "hard" (not including an Ace) or "soft" (including an Ace).

It has always been agreed that you should not double down to a hard count of 12 or more, because drawing a Ten or face card would bust the hand. Similarly, everyone has always agreed that you should nearly always double down when your count is exactly 11. There have been differences of opinion on two-card combinations counting 10 or 9, and few players ever doubled down to any count lower than 9.

The new advice is:

HARD COMBINATIONS

12 to 20: Never double down.

11: Double down unless dealer shows an Ace.

10: Double down unless dealer shows an Ace, Ten, or face card.

9: Double down only if dealer shows 2, 3, 4, 5, or 6.

8 or lower: Never double down.

SOFT COMBINATIONS

A-9 or A-8: Never double down.

A-7: Double down only if dealer shows 4, 5, or 6.

A-6: Double down only if dealer shows 3, 4, 5, or 6.

A-5, A-4, A-3, or A-2: Double down only if dealer shows 5 or 6.

A-A: Don't double down; split.

Watching the Cards   Anyone who, in addition to playing as I have suggested, can remember every card that has been played, will have an excellent chance of being a winner. However, few players are capable of doing this and even fewer are willing to go to the trouble, so I will confine this section to hints on how to make counting easier.

Assuming an average of four players against the dealer, an average of fourteen cards will be dealt for each hand. This includes the hands of the four players plus the dealer's hand. After three hands have been dealt, forty-two cards will have been used and there will be ten cards left to start the last deal.

In each of the first three deals, there should be four or five 10-point cards (Tens and face cards) and one or two Aces dealt.

It is not difficult for a keen player to notice the total number of cards used for each hand, the number of Aces that have shown, and the number of 10-point cards that have shown.

When the undealt portion of the pack contains an unusually high number of 10-point cards and Aces, the pack is said to be "rich." With a rich pack, the player should make a relatively high bet, because the dealer's advantage is considerably reduced.

When the undealt cards contain relatively few 10-point cards, the pack is said to be "lean." The advantage is with the dealer, because he is less likely to bust or to deal a blackjack, and the player should bet the minimum.

The pack is not rich, even when it contains many 10-point cards, if it does not contain at least two Aces, because the chance of blackjacks is slight. One advantage of a player playing several hands against the dealer, when the pack is rich, is that if blackjacks occur it is 4 to 1 that one of the opposing hands, rather than the dealer, will get a blackjack.

Even when the pack is lean and the player does not bet high, he profits from knowing that the pack is lean. He can increase his chances in the play by hitting hands on which he would customarily stand.

For example, the player's count is 13 or even 14 and dealer shows a Six. Ordinarily the player would stand. But if the player has watched the cards and knows that in ten remaining cards there are only two 10-point cards, the player should draw. The odds heavily favor his improving rather than going over.

In this same situation a player should not double down nearly so quickly, since his drawing a 10-point card to perfect his hand is unlikely.

When the pack is rich, it affects a player's strategy of play in this way: If he has 16 or even 15 and dealer shows a high card (Seven to Ten)—normally a draw situation—he stands instead of drawing. The high percentage of 10-point cards still to be dealt might too easily bust him, and there is an excellent chance that the dealer, if he must draw, will bust.

Insurance   The "insurance" bet offered by gambling houses is often more of a delusion than a bargain.

Whenever the dealer's up-card is an Ace, you are permitted to take insurance. This means that the house will bet you 2 to 1 that the dealer does *not* have a blackjack. You can take this bet up to half the amount of your original bet, and if the dealer's hole card is a 10-point card, giving him a blackjack, the house will pay you.

As an example: You have bet $50 on your regular hand. Dealer shows an Ace. You can take an insurance bet of $25. If dealer's hole card is a ten or face card, the house pays you $50. If it is not, you lose your $25 insurance bet.

As with every other bet you place against a gambling house, there is a percentage against you on an insurance bet. There are sixteen 10-point cards in the pack—four Kings, four Queens, four Jacks, four Tens. There are thirty-six cards that are not 10-point cards. Even though you have seen one of the other thirty-six—the dealer's Ace—and perhaps your own two cards, neither of which is a 10-point card, there are still thirty-three cards that will beat you and only sixteen cards that will win for you. The odds against you are 33 to 16 and the house offers you 32 to 16 (2 to 1).

Out of every $49 that you bet, you figure to get back only $48, leaving the house with a $1 profit. Therefore the house edge is slightly more than 2%, compared to its 1.4% advantage on a line bet in craps.

There is one deceptive situation where insurance gives you a sure profit. Suppose your bet was $50 and you have a blackjack in your first two cards. Dealer shows an Ace. If dealer does not have a 10-point hole card, you will be paid $75. If you make a $25 insurance bet you will surely win $50. If dealer has a blackjack, you win $50 on your insurance bet while your main bet becomes a stand-off. If dealer doesn't have a blackjack, you win $75 on your main bet but lose back $25 on your insurance bet.

The insurance bet may be a way to escape possible disappointment, but in the long run you would make slightly more by not taking the insurance; the insurance bet will average to cost you 2% of $25, or 50 cents every time you make it.

Nevertheless, the insurance bet in Blackjack is the only case I have ever seen where a player may have an advantageous bet against the house.

If you watch the cards closely, as I have suggested, you may occasionally know that there is an exceptionally high number of 10-point cards still to be dealt. Perhaps in the last fifteen cards there are six 10-point cards. In that case the odds are only 9 to 6, which is 3 to 2, that the dealer's hole card is a 10-point card. When you take a bet at 2 to 1, you have the better of it. I have seen some freak cases where a player could take an insurance bet with the odds as high as 2 to 1 in his favor.

General Rules for Good Play   This section on Blackjack has given all the fine points of expert play that have been discovered by computing machines and by the finest computer scientists in the country. By careful study and by memorizing every fine point you will be able to play Blackjack in casinos and have very close to an even chance.

However, I know that most players don't have the patience,

time or memory to make the perfect mathematical play every time. So here are six basic rules to follow; they should not be too much trouble to remember and they will improve your game tremendously.

1. Draw to 16 or less if dealer shows 7 or higher.
2. Stand with 12 or more if dealer shows less than 7.
3. Stand with "soft" 18 or more.
4. Double down with 11 always—with 10 if dealer shows less than 10.
5. Split Aces and Eights.
6. Don't take out insurance.

These rules may not make you a consistent winner, but they will help make you less of a consistent loser.

THE HOME GAME

I said that mathematical calculations are complicated in the gambling-house form of Blackjack; if so, they are virtually impossible in the home game. The gambling-house dealer is rigidly limited in his play; playing against him, you can base your decision on the knowledge that he will have to hit 16 and stand on 17. In the home game the dealer is not so restricted. Since you cannot be sure what he is going to do, you cannot prove the correctness of any decision except by its results.

For this reason advice on family Blackjack has to be a matter of opinion. The advice I am going to give you here is based on long experience in hundreds of games.

General Rules of Play While there are even more different ways of playing the home type of Blackjack than the casino type, the following customs prevail in many home games:

Only one pack of cards is used. The dealer gives each player, including himself, one card face down. Then each player makes a bet after looking at his card; this bet may range from a minimum of perhaps one chip to a maximum of perhaps four or five chips. The dealer may then double all bets if he wishes, and if he does double, any player may redouble. One more card is then dealt to each player, including the dealer, face up. After that, the dealing proceeds to each player in turn in accordance with the rules. However, when the dealer's turn comes, he may stand or draw as he pleases, the same as a player. In settlement, ties pay the dealer.

Blackjack pays 2 to 1, whether a player has it or the dealer has it. The first player against the dealer to get a blackjack becomes the next dealer after the completion of the current hand.

No other bonuses are paid to the dealer. In fact, I am against paying the dealer the blackjack bonus, though it is quite customary.

Pairs may be split, and when Aces are split the player may draw as many cards as he wishes. It is customary to pay him double on blackjacks dealt to one or both of his split Aces.

Doubling down is permitted on any two or three cards totaling exactly 11.

Betting and Doubling A player should always bet the maximum on an Ace, near maximum on a 10-point card, minimum on all cards from the Four to the Eight, and a middle-sized bet on a Two, Three, or Nine. Optimists bet maximum on 10-point cards and near maximum on Two, Three, Eight, or Nine. The reason for betting above the minimum on a Two or Three is because of the special bonus, which I will cover later.

The dealer should double invariably when he has an Ace. It usually pays the dealer to double when he has a 10-point card, unless there are one or two known conservatives against him who have made the maximum bet; since such players may be known to bet the maximum only when they have Aces, the dealer would put himself at a disadvantage by doubling and would also risk a redouble.

In deciding to double the dealer should be guided by the number and size of the bets against him. If all the players have made low or minimum bets, the dealer should invariably double on a Ten and some will double on a Nine. The dealer has an advantage to start with and should double whenever he thinks that his first card is at least as good as the average of the cards against him. But if in a six-handed game two careful players have bid the maximum, and the other four the minimum, the dealer may have more to lose than to gain if he doubles even on a Ten.

When the dealer does double, a player should redouble only if he has an Ace.

Value of the Bank The dealer's advantage in home Blackjack may run more than 25%. His great advantage stems from four things: The players must draw first; he is paid the blackjack bonus; he may double the bets; and—most important—he wins all ties.

Because of this, many players will pay well for the privilege of becoming the next dealer; and since the rules permit a player to sell his right to deal, there is often spirited bidding for it.

However, players generally pay too much to become the dealer. Despite the great advantage, the price may be exorbitant, because on the very first hand a blackjack may be dealt and the dearly bought dealership will be lost. However, a blackjack is dealt about once in twenty hands. In a fair-sized game, that is, one in which there are four or more players besides the dealer, I would estimate the dealership to be worth buying at about three times the amount of the maximum bet. That is, if the maximum bet is $1.00 and the minimum bet 25 cents, you can afford to pay $3.00 to become the next dealer.

Drawing Cards The advice given for the casino game applies generally to the home game as well as to the casino game, but it must be modified by certain information and certain factors that do not exist in the casino game.

For judging when to draw and when to stand, the following things must be taken into consideration:

1. The dealer's up-card.
2. Did he double?
3. What does your own up-card give away?
4. What are the bets at the table?

If the dealer doubled and now draws an Eight, you know that his score is almost surely 18 and may very well be 19. In such cases you would hit even 18 because you cannot win by standing on it.

If a conservative dealer doubled, you would even hit 18 because you are "dead" if you don't. Conversely, you would stand on 17 or 18 if you were doubled by the wild-betting type of dealer.

Another guide would be if dealer doubled in spite of some large bets. Then you would have to draw to 17 or 18. But if he doubled when everyone was betting small, you would stand on 17 or 18 and hope for the best.

Another tip: "Know thy dealer." His temperament, conservative or wild, may be a most helpful clue in close situations.

The dealer's failure to double is significant, especially when his upcard is a 10-point card. In such a case you would surely stand on 16 and have a slightly better chance than if you drew.

The same considerations are effective when the dealer doubles and gets a 4, 5, or 6. You can figure his having most likely 14, 15, or 16 respectively. If, for example, he has a Four showing, you can profit from standing on 15 because the odds are against your improving if you draw, and the odds favor his going over 21 when he draws.

Another factor that influences your draw is this: If your 15 was composed of a Ten or Nine up and a Five or Six in the hole, you would stand. The dealer may draw when actually he can beat you. If you had your Five or Six up and your Nine or Ten in the hole, you would draw. If possible avoid giving a sure thing to the dealer, except in this situation:

If two or three players made big bets and have stood on hands that appear likely to be 18- to 20-point scores, the dealer is virtually forced to try for a high score against them. An important part of the winnings of a good Blackjack player comes from the free rides he gets in such cases, by simply standing on a 14 or 15 total and collecting when the dealer goes over 21.

There are many more bonuses in the ordinary home game than in the casino game. If you get a total of five or more cards without going over 21, you collect extra—double your bet for five cards, four times if you get a sixth card, eight times if you get a seventh card, and so on, doubling each time. Of course, this is such a rare occurrence that it seldom pays to play for it; but if in your first four cards you have a 17 that does not figure to win, it is certainly better to draw than to stand, since you may lose anyway if you stand, and you will be paid double if you get a low card and win.

However, you seldom play unnaturally in order to try for a bonus. You don't make a big bet on a Two or Three, or split a pair of Twos or Threes, to give yourself a start toward this bonus for five cards and under.

Seldom risk one bonus to earn a larger one. If you already have five cards and under, don't draw to anything higher than 12, even though six cards and under pays four to one. An exception is when you have seen an unusually large number of 10-point cards; then you might draw to 13.

My advice on splitting pairs is to split Aces, Nines, Eights, and Sevens, if the dealer shows no better than an Eight; and if the dealer has doubled, I would not split my Eights or Sevens but would draw a card instead. If the dealer shows a Nine, Ten, or Ace, whether or not he has doubled, I would split only Aces.

Players should not double down on 11 quite so quickly in the home game. However, I would double down if dealer's up-card is a Seven or less. If dealer has doubled, I would double down only if his card is Six or less.

Dealer's Play The dealer has an advantage not only in the rules, but also in the play. Having complete freedom of action, he can almost always judge his proper play by what has happened before.

As I mentioned above in passing, the dealer should consider not only the probable scores against which he must compete, but also the amounts of the bets on them. He may have to sacrifice two, or even three minimum bets to improve his chances of winning a couple of larger ones. At other times he may take a small loss rather than risk losing all bets, because, though he may be sure of losing to a player who bet the maximum, he will get back part of it by collecting from smaller bettors whose hands are probably worse than his.

Just as the players against him can judge the dealer's hand by his doubling or failing to, he should be able to estimate the probable holdings of the various players by the amount of their bets.

LAWS OF BLACKJACK (TWENTY-ONE)

The Casino Game

1. Number of Players   As many as can sit at the table; but usually seats are provided for no more than six players besides the dealer.

2. The Pack   The regular 52-card pack. In addition the dealer in some places uses a joker or blank card which is never dealt, but is faced up at the bottom of the pack to mark the location of the last of the shuffled cards.

3. The Shuffle and Cut   The dealer shuffles. Any player may cut the pack. The dealer then burns a card (shows it, then places it face up on the bottom of the pack), or uses the extra card for this purpose if that is the custom.

4. Betting   Before the deal begins each player places a bet, in chips, in front of him on the table; usually minimum and maximum limits are placed upon betting, so that, for example, no player may bet less than one chip or more than ten.

5. The Deal   When all players have placed their bets, the dealer gives one card face down to each player in rotation, including himself; then another card face down to each other player, and a card face up to himself. Thus each player except the dealer receives two cards face down, and the dealer receives one card face up and one card face down.

6. Object of the Game   Counting any Ace as 1 or 11, as he wishes, any face card as 10, and any other card at its pip value, each player attempts to get a count of 21, or as near to 21 as possible, without going over 21.

7. *Naturals* If a player's first two cards are an Ace and a face card or Ten, giving him a count of 21 in two cards, he has a natural or blackjack. If any player has a natural and the dealer does not have a natural, the dealer immediately pays that player one and one-half times the amount of the player's bet. If the dealer has a natural, he immediately collects the bets of all players who do not have naturals, but no player need pay any more than he bet originally. If the dealer and any other player both have naturals, the bet of that player is a stand-off (he takes back his chips, and neither pays nor collects).

If the dealer's face-up card is a Ten, face card or Ace, he may look at his face-down card to see if he has a natural; if his face-up card is anything else, he may not look at his face-down card until his turn comes to draw.

8. *Drawing* If the dealer did not have a natural, when he has settled all bets involving naturals he turns to the player nearest his left. That player may stand on the two cards originally dealt him, or may require the dealer to give him additional cards, one at a time, until after receiving any such card he stands on the total already dealt to him if it is 21 or under; or the player busts (goes over 21), in which case he immediately pays the amount of his bet to the dealer. The dealer then turns to the next player in turn to his left and serves him in the same manner.

When the dealer has thus served every player, he turns up his own face-down card. If his total is 17 or more, he must stand. If his total is 16 or under, he must take a card and must continue to take cards until his total is 17 or more, at which point he must stand. If the dealer has an Ace, and counting it as 11 would bring his total to 17 or more (but not over 21), he must count the Ace as 11 and stand. (There are some exceptions: A few casinos require the dealer to draw to a soft 17; a few give the dealer the option of standing or drawing.)

9. Settlement   A bet once paid and collected is never returned. If the dealer goes over 21, he pays to each player
who has stood the amount of that player's bet. If the dealer
stands at 21 or less, he pays the bet of any player having a
higher total; collects the bet of any player having a lower
total, and is at a stand-off with any player having the same
total.

10. Reshuffling   As each player's bet is settled, the dealer
gathers in that player's cards and places them face up on
the bottom of the pack. The dealer continues to use the
originally shuffled pack until he comes to the face-up card,
which signifies the end of the shuffled cards. At this point he
interrupts the deal, shuffles all cards not in play, has them
cut by any player or players, again burns a card or places the
blank card face up on the bottom, and continues the deal.
Before any deal, if the dealer does not think there are enough
cards to go around in the next deal, he may gather up all
cards for a new shuffle and cut.

11. Splitting Pairs   If a player's two first cards are of the same
denomination—as two Jacks, or two Sixes—he may choose
to treat them as two separate hands. The amount of his
original bet then goes on one of the cards, and he must place
an equal amount as a bet on the other card. When this player's
turn to draw comes, the dealer first gives him one card face
down to each hand. If one of these cards is paired again, he
may split again. The player may then require the dealer to
give additional cards, face up, to either hand, in whatever
order he wishes, until he has gone over or stood on both
hands. The hands are treated separately, the dealer settling
with each on its own merits. When a player splits Aces, he
may draw only one card to each and is paid only singly if
he is dealt a natural. (Some casinos permit a player to split
any two 10-point cards as though they were a pair.)

A player may double his bet and receive one card face
down (called "one down for double" or "doubling down").
He may not then draw another card. (In some casinos, a
player may double down after he has been dealt three cards.

In a few casinos, a player may double down on a hand when he splits a pair.)

There is no penalty for any irregularity, but an irregularity must be corrected if discovered before the bet has been settled; after the bet has been settled, there can be no correction. If the dealer has a natural, but fails to announce it before dealing an additional card to any player, his hand constitutes a count of 21 but can be tied by the hand of any other player whose total is 21 in three or more cards.

The Home Game

1. *Number of Players* Two to fourteen.

2. *The Pack* Fifty-two cards.

3. *Values of Cards* Ace, 1 or 11 (at holder's option); any face card, 10; any other card, its pip value.

4. *Determining the First Banker* Any player picks up the pack and deals the cards in rotation, face up, until a blackjack (Spades or Clubs) falls to any player. That player is the first dealer.

5. *The Shuffle and Cut* The dealer shuffles the pack and any other player may cut. The dealer then turns up the top card of the pack, shows it to all players, and places it, face up, at the bottom of the pack; this is called "burning" a card, and when that card is reached in the deal there must be a new shuffle and cut before dealing continues. If an Ace is turned, the pack must be shuffled and cut again.

6. *First Round of Dealing* Dealer gives one card face down to each player in rotation, including himself.

7. *Betting* After looking at his card each player places a bet which may not be less than the minimum or more than the limit established for the game. After all players other than the dealer have bet, the dealer may require that all bets be doubled. Any player may then redouble his bet.

8. Completion of the Deal   The dealer then gives one card face up to each player in rotation, including himself.

9. Blackjacks   If the dealer has a blackjack (Ace, and face card or Ten) every player pays him double the amount of his bet, except that another player having a blackjack pays nothing. If any other player has a blackjack and the dealer has not, the dealer pays that player double the amount of the player's bet. (In many games, a "virgin" blackjack— both cards in the same suit—pays triple.)

10. Drawing Cards   If the dealer does not have a blackjack, he starts with the player nearest his left and gives each player in turn as many cards as that player requests, one at a time, until that player goes over 21 and pays, or stands.

When all players have gone over or have stood, the dealer turns up his face-down card and may draw cards until he wishes to stand. The dealer is not bound by rules to stand on or draw to any total. If the dealer goes over 21, he pays all players who have stood; if the dealer stands on a total of 21 or less, he pays all players who stood with a higher total, and collects from all players who stood with the same or a lower total—"ties pay the dealer."

A player against dealer may split a pair or take "one down for double" to 11, in each case doubling his bet.

11. Bonus Payments   Any player who forms one of the following combinations collects immediately from the dealer, and cannot later lose his bet even if the dealer has a higher total:

a. If a player has five cards and his total is 21 or under, he collects double his bet; with six cards totaling 21 or under, four (in some games, three) times his bet; and so on, doubling for each additional card.

b. A player who makes 21 with three Sevens receives triple the amount of his bet (some pay 10 or 20 to 1).

c. A player who makes 21 with Eight, Seven and Six of the same suit receives ten times the amount of his bet.

d. The dealer does not collect any bonuses except for a blackjack. He does not necessarily win if he has five or more

cards with a total under 21, but pays any player who has a
higher count.

12. Changing the Bank   The dealer continues as dealer until
another player is dealt a blackjack and the dealer has no
blackjack; in this case, after all bets in the current deal
have been settled, the player who had the natural becomes
the next dealer. If two or more players have naturals and the
dealer has none, the one nearest the dealer's left becomes
the next dealer. A player entitled to deal may, if he wishes,
sell the privilege to another player.

IRREGULARITIES

13. If the dealer fails to burn a card, he must, on demand,
shuffle the remainder of the pack and burn a card before
continuing the deal.

14. If the dealer fails to give any player a card on the first
round of dealing, he must on demand supply that player
from the top of the pack unless attention is called to the
error after the dealer begins the second round of dealing,
in which case the player lacking a card stays out for that
deal.

15. If the dealer gives any player his first card face up, that
player must still make his bet, but the dealer must give him
his next card face down. If the dealer fails to give him his
next card face down, the player may withdraw his bet and
drop out for that deal.

16. Any player who stands must expose his face-down card
as soon as the dealer has stood or gone over. If that player
has in fact a total of more than 21, he must pay the dealer
even if the dealer has gone over. (Some play that he must pay
the dealer double.)

17. If the dealer gives a player two cards on the first round
of dealing, that player may choose which card to keep and
which to discard; or may keep both cards, play two hands,
and place a bet on each. He may not, however, play both
cards as belonging to the same hand.

18. If the dealer gives a player two cards on the second round of dealing, the player may choose which to keep.

19. If a card is found faced in the pack, it is dead and is placed face up on the bottom of the pack.

20. If the dealer gives a card to a player who did not ask for it, that player may keep the card if he chooses, or may refuse it, in which case it is a discard and is placed face up at the bottom of the pack. The next player in turn may not claim it.

HEARTS

1. Never pass a Spade lower than the Queen.

2. Pass the Spade Ace, King, or Queen if you have three Spades or less; hold them if you have four or more.

3. The Queen of Spades is safer in your hand than out.

4. Aces and Kings may work for you; Eights and Nines may ruin you.

5. Pass to protect your hand, not to hurt your neighbor.

6. Don't be afraid to take a few Hearts if you're playing to get out of the lead.

7. Most slams are made by cunning, not by having the necessary cards.

8. Don't play for slams if you can help it.

9. Count the cards—you can win in most Hearts games just by knowing how to count 13.

10. Don't try to beat every opponent; play the other fellow's game if it helps you too.

HEARTS

Hearts is not played as a money game nearly as often as other games in this book, but when it is, the game is tough and the competition is likely to be very strong. For that reason the player who is interested in Hearts needs the advice given in the following pages.

The real game of Hearts is a cutthroat game. When the game is played as a partnership game, it is just a reverse sort of Whist. This is contrary to the spirit of Hearts, and I have disregarded it. I treat Hearts as a four-handed game, with everyone playing for himself, and with the features that have been almost universally adopted into the game—the Queen of Spades as a penalty card that must be played at the first legal opportunity; and the passing of three cards to an opponent so as to improve your own hand. Played this way, Hearts is a game that is almost unsurpassed for the application of skill in reading the meanings of plays and planning your own play so as to make the most of what you know about the other players' hands.

THE PASS

Pass Your Troubles   The first question you have to meet is: What shall I pass?

We shall assume throughout that you pass three cards to

your *left*. Many experts consider it a fairer game if you pass to your right, but the pass to the left is much more generally played.

The right to pass any three cards to your neighbor is, above all, an opportunity to get rid of your worst troubles. Suppose you pick up:

♠ Q 3   ♡ A K   ◊ Q 10 6 4   ♣ A J 9 4 2   (Ex. 1)

No problem here! You thankfully hand your left neighbor the ♠Q, ♡A-K. Of course, you may receive from your right neighbor something like this: the ♠A-K, ♡Q. If so, say kismet! You did what you could to get out from under.

Few hands are so simple as this. Much of the time you would have to pass more than three cards to feel really safe. Sometimes you have only one or two troublesome cards, giving you a real choice—and an opportunity to go wrong, in addition. And once in a while you have the ideal hand, which you would like to hold pat. Here your sole thought is to prepare against the worst of troubles that the man on your right may hand you.

Black Maria   If dealt Black Maria—the Queen of Spades— your instinct should be to keep her if you possibly can. She is safer in your hand than out—you cannot discard her on your own trick. But she is better passed if you do not have enough additional Spades to stand repeated Spade leads. You need at least three other Spades, whether high ones or low ones. Likewise, the Spade Ace and King are dangerous if insufficiently guarded.

Spade Safety   What is a safe Spade suit? In a four-hand game take it as a rule that any five-card Spade length, whatever you have at the top, is safe, and that any three-card length with one or more tops is unsafe. Thus, with the ♠A-K-Q-J-10, don't pass any Spades. The odds are overwhelming that you cannot be forced to take your ♠Q on a Spade lead. But with the ♠A-x-x, ♠K-x-x, ♠Q-x-x, or the like, pick out the top Spades or Spade to pass as a matter of routine. (Exception noted later.)

The four-card length is the borderline holding. As an abstract proposition, where the x's are all very low cards, such holdings as A-x-x-x, K-x-x-x, Q-x-x-x are dangerous. You should usually pass the top Spade unless you have more acute troubles elsewhere. But with intermediate cards—♠J, 10, 9—below the top Spades, the four-card length is less dangerous because you have a prospect of winning an early Spade lead and switching suit. Thus A-10-8-4, K-J-8-7, Q-J-9-5 are all less dangerous than the foregoing examples. By the same token, if you have the ♠Q, one of the higher tops is a powerful guard. With the A-Q-x-x, usually keep the holding intact. Should you pass the ♠A-Q, then receive the ♠K, you would have bitter regrets.

An important point with these borderline holdings is the position of the opening lead. If this comes from your immediate left, you may well keep intact such holdings as the A-x-x-x, K-x-x-x, even A-x-x and K-x-x. The idea here is that an opening lead of a Spade would clear up your trouble at once. Contrariwise, if the opening lead is to come from your right neighbor, don't be dogmatic about holding such combinations as the Q-J-9-5, A-Q-x-x, etc. One lead through you may clear up everybody else's "Spade trouble." Then, if the Spades do not split 4-3-3-3, repeated Spade leads will eventually force you to take your Queen.

Another form of Spade trouble is to receive just one or two small Spades in the deal. Receipt of top Spades from your right-hand opponent will be unpleasant. The natural reaction is to shorten the hand in some other suit, hoping for the opportunity to discard such Spade tops. For example:

♠ 85   ♡ A K 7 4   ◇ Q 7 4 2   ♣ J 8 6   (Ex. 2)

Pass the ♣J-8-6 automatically.

When you pass the ♠Q, without the Ace or King, and have no other danger spots to serve, you should pass two additional cards of different suits, not two of the same suit. Then you are prepared in at least two side suits to put up a high card on the first trick, with assurance that you cannot gather the ♠Q.

Heart Trouble Second to "Spade trouble" is "Heart trouble" —the possession of unguarded top Hearts. Here the question of what constitutes a minimum guard cannot be answered in general terms. It is a statistical fact that Hearts are led less frequently, on average, than any other suit. In some deals they are never led; in others, they are led five or six times. So far as one can generalize, two low Hearts are adequate protection for one or two high Hearts. From such holdings as the ♡A-x-x, ♡J-10-x-x, don't pass high Hearts except as a luxury when you have no trouble elsewhere.

You naturally like to get rid of the tops from such holdings as the ♡A-x, ♡K-J-x, ♡10-9. But even here there may be reason in the rest of the hand for keeping them. We will return to this matter later.

Neutral Suits In the neutral suits, Diamonds and Clubs, the top cards are not dangerous, but lack of low cards may be fatal. Rejoice on seeing such an array as the ◇A-J-7-4-2, but quail before the ♣K-10-9-7.

The matter of exit is peculiarly governing in the neutral suits for the reason that you must look to these suits, as a rule, to get you and keep you out of the lead toward the end of a hand.

Further, a Diamond or Club holding with which you cannot duck a trick when you want to is a prime target for the man who holds the ♠Q and wants to discard it.

Suppose you hold:

    ♠ A 10 8 4   ♡ K 7 3   ◇ 5 2   ♣ K 10 9 7   (Ex. 3)

The Spade and Heart holdings are only "borderline dangerous," while the Club holding is wholly in the danger zone. You should pass ♣K-10-9, or ♣K-10 and ♡K (dependent on the playing habits of your opponents).

Short holdings—one, two, or possibly three cards—are not dangerous as they stand, no matter how high, but may be promoted to killers by what you receive. Thus with:

    ♠ Q 10 7 3 2   ♡ J 5   ◇ Q 10   ♣ K 7 5 4   (Ex. 4)

pass the ◇ Q-10 because you can afford this luxury. Keeping them will spell trouble if you receive two or three more high

Diamonds. (Of course the third card you pass is the ♡J.)

Passing for a Slam   A slam—the taking of all thirteen Hearts and the ♠Q by one player—is usually the result of two circumstances, a number of top cards dealt to this player plus the receipt of some helpful cards. In a good share of instances the player had no intention of trying for slam when he passed, or even after he received, but fell into it as a defensive operation.*

When you pick up more troubles than you can resolve by passing three cards, you naturally speculate on a slam. For example:

♠ K 7 6   ♡ A Q 9 7   ◇ A 9 8 6   ♣ K 10 9   (Ex. 5)

The receipt of high cards in any suit but Diamonds would fix you, should you pass, say ♠K and ♡A-Q, or ♠K and ♣K-10. You may well pass something like ◇9-8 and ♣10, trying for a slam.

Now let's change just one card, giving you:

♠ K 7 6   ♡ K Q 9 7   ◇ A 9 8 6   ♣ K 10 9   (Ex. 6)

It is a virtual certainty that you cannot make a slam unless you receive the ♡A. This is too forlorn a hope. If the lead is at your left, pass the ♡K-Q-9 or ♡K-Q and ♣10. With the lead elsewhere try the ♠K and ♡K-Q. It is important to give both top Hearts. The point is to encourage a possible slam by your left neighbor. Despite your remaining tops, he could have slam prospects with the ♡A, together with the high Hearts and Spades.

The ideal hand, of course, is one with which you have a two-way play. If things go your way in the beginning, you can play for a slam; if not, you can get away clear.

This is often a hand with which you can control the Heart suit—top and bottom—and it is just a question of whether you get Black Maria early.

* Under the laws a slam gives no score for anybody for that deal. It thus may be sought by a player who has been "painted," to wipe out his debit. In some circles a slam is rewarded by a credit score, and therefore is often planned at the outset.

Examples of Passing Here are some deals illustrating various points in the question of what to pass. (South is always the dealer, West the opening leader.)

Example 9

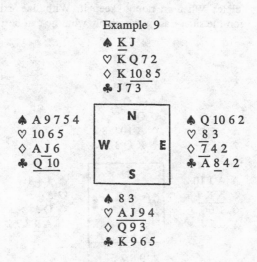

♠ K J
♡ K Q 7 2
◇ K 10 8 5
♣ J 7 3

♠ A 9 7 5 4
♡ 10 6 5
◇ A J 6
♣ Q 10

♠ Q 10 6 2
♡ 8 3
◇ 7 4 2
♣ A 8 4 2

♠ 8 3
♡ A J 9 4
◇ Q 9 3
♣ K 9 6 5

South: ♡ A-J-9. This is an arbitrary choice among alternatives, others being the ◇ Q-9, ♣ 9 and ◇ Q, ♣ K-9. The hand shows no acute danger spots, but might be hurt by your right opponent's pass.

West: ◇ J, ♣ Q-10. Routine. The Clubs go, to mitigate the danger that you might receive three high Clubs from your right opponent. The ◇ J is passed, rather than the ◇ A, because a sure entry often proves valuable. This point is illustrated many times in these example deals.

North: ♠ K, ◇ 10-8. An alternative is to give the ♡ K-Q instead of the Diamonds. With acute Spade trouble, North naturally wants to try to short-suit himself. But to give the ♣ J-7, leaving a singleton instead of a doubleton, leaves the hand perilously short of exit cards.

East: ♡8, ◇7, ♣8. The Spade holding is just on that
borderline that gives legitimate choice whether to
keep or to pass the Queen. We incline to the principle: When in doubt, keep it. With fine exit suits
on the side, East picks simply what he can best spare.

Example 10

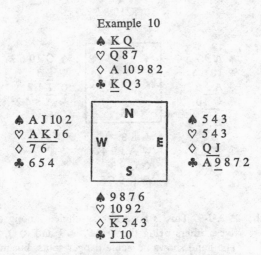

```
                    ♠ K Q
                    ♡ Q 8 7
                    ◇ A 10 9 8 2
                    ♣ K Q 3
        ♠ A J 10 2          N          ♠ 5 4 3
        ♡ A K J 6                      ♡ 5 4 3
        ◇ 7 6           W       E      ◇ Q J
        ♣ 6 5 4                        ♣ A 9 8 7 2
                            S
                    ♠ 9 8 7 6
                    ♡ 10 9 2
                    ◇ K 5 4 3
                    ♣ J 10
```

South: ♡10, ♣J-10. Routine.
West: ♡A-K-J. Routine.
North: ♠K-Q, ♣K. In a sense the ♣K is the optimistic
choice; the pessimistic would be the ♡Q. If he
passes the ♣K, he hopes to have Club exit and to
avoid winning Heart leads. If he passes the ♡Q, he
prepares to get rid of the ♡8-7 by simply leading
them.
East: ◇Q-J, ♣9. Routine. Note the point of saving the
♣A on general principle.

Example 11

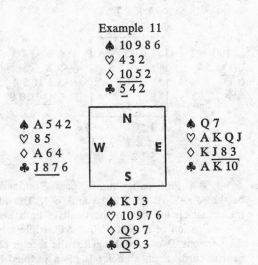

```
                    ♠ 10 9 8 6
                    ♡ 4 3 2
                    ◇ 10 5 2
                    ♣ 5 4 2

 ♠ A 5 4 2         N          ♠ Q 7
 ♡ 8 5                        ♡ A K Q J
 ◇ A 6 4      W        E      ◇ K J 8 3
 ♣ J 8 7 6                    ♣ A K 10
                    S

                    ♠ K J 3
                    ♡ 10 9 7 6
                    ◇ Q 9 7
                    ♣ Q 9 3
```

South: ♠K, ◇Q, ♣Q. The alternative is to pass two Diamonds or two Clubs with the ♠K.

West: ♣J-8-7. More or less a guess as to what your right opponent will give.

North: ◇10-5, ♣5. An ideal nullo hand, which can but be impaired by any pass. Of course North picks what he can best spare.

East: ◇J-8-3. Believe it or not, this hand was dealt and played! Obviously the only hope to escape a huge debit is to make a slam. Happily the prospect of success is very great.

Example 12

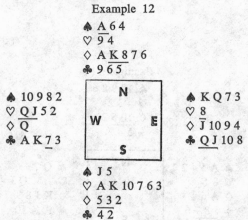

♠ A 6 4
♥ 9 4
♦ A K 8 7 6
♣ 9 6 5

♠ 10 9 8 2
♥ Q J 5 2
♦ Q
♣ A K 7 3

♠ K Q 7 3
♥ 8
♦ J 10 9 4
♣ Q J 10 8

♠ J 5
♥ A K 10 7 6 3
♦ 5 3 2
♣ 4 2

South: ♦ 5-3, ♣ 4. Perhaps a "hunch" pass! Routine would be the ♥ A-K-10 or ♥ K-10 and ♣ 4. The idea of the actual choice was to short-suit in both neutrals, in anticipation of receipt of the ♠ Q, while retaining the precious Two in each against the receipt of high neutral cards. Such a choice is often justified by the known passing habits of your right opponent.

West: ♥ Q-J, ♣ 7. An odd-looking choice. Routine would be something like the ♦ Q and ♣ K-7. Yet this choice is based on an astute idea. If West does not receive the ♠ Q, he wants to open Spades and continue the suit at every opportunity. He therefore saves his neutral entries. If he receives the ♠ Q, he wants all the top command he has in the neutral suits to manipulate a "grand exit."

North: ♠ A, ♦ K-8. North decides to mitigate the somewhat dangerous Diamond suit rather than concentrate on the Spade danger by giving the ♣ 9-6 or ♥ 9-4.

East: ♥ 8, ♣ Q-J. A dangerous hand all around for lack of enough low cards. The Heart void is established as a matter of course, in the hope of getting rid of the ♠ Q on a Heart lead. The ♣ Q-J are picked to shorten the holding worst equipped as to exit cards.

Example 13

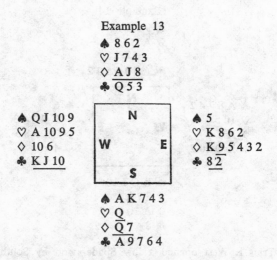

♠ 8 6 2
♡ J 7 4 3
◇ A J 8
♣ Q 5 3

♠ Q J 10 9   N   ♠ 5
♡ A 10 9 5   ♡ K 8 6 2
◇ 10 6   W   E   ◇ K 9 5 4 3 2
♣ K J 10   ♣ 8 2

         S

♠ A K 7 4 3
♡ Q
◇ Q 7
♣ A 9 7 6 4

Routine short-suiting by all hands. South: ♡Q, ◇Q-7. West: ♣K-J-10. North: ◇A-J-8. East: ◇9, ♣8-2.

THE PLAY

Normal Spade Opening It is to the interest of each player not holding the ♠Q to force that card out by Spade leads, lest he himself catch it as a discard. The normal opening lead is therefore a Spade, unless the leader has "Spade trouble" or can afford to pursue some special plan. The play of Example 14 typifies the normal course. After the pass the hands are:

Example 14

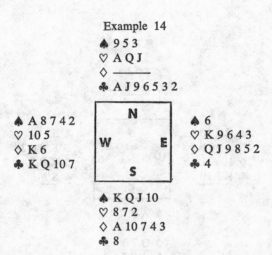

Trick 1. West opened a low Spade, won by South with the King.

Trick 2. South led the ♣8. He naturally wished to establish a Club void to get rid of his ♠Q by discard. West won the trick with the ♣Q.

Trick 3. West led another Spade, won by the Jack.

Trick 4. South led the ♡7. North won with the ♡A.

Trick 5. North led his last Spade, won by the ♠A.

Trick 6. West led the fourth Spade, knowing that at last South would be forced to play the ♠Q.

Leading from Spade Trouble The "normal" reason for failing to open Spades is possession of a top with less than four guards. Take Example 15. After the pass:

Example 15

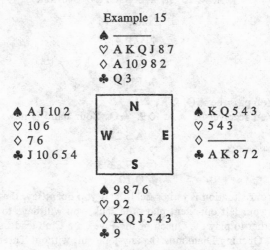

```
              ♠ ————
              ♡ A K Q J 8 7
              ◇ A 10 9 8 2
              ♣ Q 3

♠ A J 10 2           N           ♠ K Q 5 4 3
♡ 10 6                           ♡ 5 4 3
◇ 7 6           W       E        ◇ ————
♣ J 10 6 5 4                     ♣ A K 8 7 2
                      S

              ♠ 9 8 7 6
              ♡ 9 2
              ◇ K Q J 5 4 3
              ♣ 9
```

West does not want to risk a Spade opening. The choice of lead is governed by two considerations: First, it is safer to open blind a short suit than a long. Second, if you want to place the lead at your left, lead a neutral suit rather than Hearts. Second hand may jump in with a high Club or Diamond, but not with a high Heart unless he has acute "Heart trouble."

West therefore led the ◇ 7. North played the Ace, and East shed the ♠ Q. But North was then able to cash all the Hearts and make a slam.

The point of trying to put your left opponent in the lead when you have Spade trouble—the ♠ A or ♠ K, but not the ♠ Q—is, of course, that he may lead Spades and resolve your trouble. But if you have passed him the ♠ Q and received a top, without sufficient guards, you know that he probably will never lead Spades. Yet, so long as he leads, you will never gather the ♠ Q. Even one lead from his hand may disclose enough about his hand to show you a method of salvation. Therefore, try to put him in at once. For example:

You are dealt:

Example 16

♠ Q 6 2
♡ K 9 4
◊ A 8 6 3
♣ J 10 5

You pass the ♠Q, ♡K, ♣J.
You receive the ♠A, ◊9, ♣Q. Your hand is now:

♠ A 6 2
♡ 9 4
◊ A 9 8 6 3
♣ Q 10 5

Your situation is rather ticklish. If you open, say, the ♣10, and your left opponent plays the Jack, you will have to guess whether to play the Queen or the Five on a Club lead through you. Opening Diamonds (as any long suit without Three-Two or Four-Two at bottom) is a wild gamble. Your best course is to open with the ♡9. You may take four Hearts, but then you will surely get out with the ♡4. So long as your left opponent holds up the ♡K, you know Heart leads are safe for you. Just possibly you may force him in on the first or second Heart round. Finally, by resolving some other player's Heart trouble you may win the co-operation of a third Heart lead, giving you a chuck of the ♠A.

Position of the Lead The player of any experience at all knows that it is advisable to save exit cards—Twos, Threes, Fours—for later rounds of a suit, playing the high cards, if need be, on the first and second rounds, when all other players are likely to follow suit.

With some such holding as the ◊A-K-Q-J-2 the only question is whether to save the Two for the second, third, fourth, or fifth round. This is, of course, a matter of inferring the Diamond split, reading the location of the ♠Q, and so on. Before we go into this complex business, let's take note of another principle of equal importance in the early play.

Before the opening lead all that you know about the three opposing hands is three cards of your left opponent's hand, plus whatever you can infer of your right opponent's hand by what he chose to pass you. The play begins as a fumble in the dark. Everybody tries to avoid giving up his exit cards prematurely. But this idea must not be pressed to the point of failing to take advantage of fortunate placements of the lead.

At any early stage you are happiest when your left opponent has the lead. If you have any trouble suit at all, you are unhappiest when your right opponent has the lead. Sometimes you would rather have to lead yourself than let your right opponent or even the opposite player come through your trouble suit.

Take, for example, the play of the deal from which Example 16 (West's hand in the following example) was quoted. After the pass the hands were:

Example 17

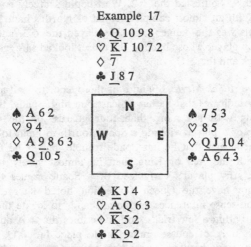

```
                 ♠ Q 10 9 8
                 ♡ K J 10 7 2
                 ◇ 7
                 ♣ J 8 7

   ♠ A 6 2            N            ♠ 7 5 3
   ♡ 9 4                           ♡ 8 5
   ◇ A 9 8 6 3    W       E        ◇ Q J 10 4
   ♣ Q 10 5                        ♣ A 6 4 3
                     S

                 ♠ K J 4
                 ♡ A Q 6 3
                 ◇ K 5 2
                 ♣ K 9 2
```

Trick 1. West led the ♡9 and won the trick.

Trick 2. West led the ♡4, and North won with the ♡10. North, of course, saved his ♡2 for eventual exit.

Trick 3. North led the ◇7, bringing out the Ten, King, Ace. Both South and West played high, since neither wanted to leave the lead with his right opponent, who might embarrass him with a Spade lead.

Trick 4. West led the ♣10. He knew that this lead was safe, since he had passed North the ♣J and ♠Q. North played the ♣J, and East won with the Ace.

Trick 5. East led a Spade, and North won with the ♠8.

Trick 6. North led the ♣8, West winning with the Queen. West was unhappy at having to get in again, but considered it more dangerous to let South's ♣9 hold.

Trick 7. West risked a lead of the third Club, and was delighted to find North stuck in with the ♣7.

Trick 8. North led the ♡J. With only the Ace and Queen still in play he knew this was a forced exit. South put up the ♡A, knowing that West could not have the ♡K. But if West produced the ♡2, South could then force North back in by leading the ♡Q to his blank King. But West shed the ♠A.

Trick 9. South led the ◇2. West could scarcely go wrong now! With an almost complete count of North's hand he saw that this was the danger trick. He played the ◇3, and East, the only player whose hand at the outset looked safe, gathered the trick and the ♠Q.

Locating Black Maria   Failure of the opener to lead a Spade usually indicates that he has at least one high Spade, the Ace or King with not more than four guards, or the Queen. Failure of a player winning a Spade fourth in hand to return the suit argues that he has Spade trouble, and if he did not win with the Ace or King then he almost surely has the Queen. Any player's early lead of a Spade argues that he does not have the Queen (exception noted later). These common-sense inferences enable all hands to locate the ♠Q, usually within a few tricks, and sometimes the ♠A and ♠K as well. It is, of course, important to place the ♠Q, for its location may show you how best to protect yourself from taking it.

As a simple example, suppose that after the pass your Spade holding is the ♠A-K-5. You were not dealt the ♠Q. You sit South, and West opens a Spade, letting you get rid of one honor. You exit with a Club and North wins. North leads a Spade and East plays low. Clearly you can put up the other Spade honor with great assurance; the ♠Q is marked in East's hand.

When the hand holding the ♠Q gets in, his choice of lead is likely to be very revealing. Since he must usually expect to get rid of the ♠Q by discard, he will usually break his shortest side suit. Or, if he breaks a suit in which he subsequently reveals himself long, he is preparing for the "grand exit." Once in a while, however, he must try to get his left opponent in for continued Spade leads—his left opponent having once led Spades without bringing out the ♠A or ♠K. This procedure is usually a resort of desperation by a hand holding the ♠Q without sufficient guards.

Hearts Is Collusion It has been well said that "Hearts is perforce a game of tacit collusion." The interest of two or three players may coincide at a certain juncture—e.g., in desiring Spade leads—whereupon they would more or less consciously strive in partnership toward this end. At the outset there is usually an opposition between two sides, neither of which has yet identified its own members, between the players with "Spade trouble" and those without. But the play of a single trick may, and often does, so change the situation that interests shift, and new temporary partnerships are formed.

For you as an individual this means that you must be alert to detect who, if any one, will give you help at the moment.

Suppose that after the pass you hold:

Example 18

♠ K 7 3   ♡ Q 8 4 3   ◇ J 10   ♣ A J 8 3 2

You passed the ♠A and ◇ 8-6, receiving the cards under-lined. You sit South. West opens the ♣K, on which the others play the Queen and Ten. You let him hold the trick. He continues with the ♣7, and again both other players follow. You take your ♣A.

You know that West has Spade trouble. He apparently is voiding himself in Clubs to get discards. Help him along! If his trouble is the ♠A only, then he will lead Spades after getting rid of it (if he ever gets in the lead), and that will resolve your own Spade trouble. If West has the ♠Q as well as the ♠A, then the ♠Q may go on the third Club, and you are saved. So you naturally return the ♣2 instead of embarking on some such procedure as getting rid of your Diamonds.

The Grand Exit I have spoken several times of the "grand exit" and it is high time to explain this term.

The grand exit is a whole campaign executed by a player so unfortunate as to hold the ♠Q together with a hand so poor in low cards that it is in danger of being stuck in the lead at the end and forced to cash the ♠Q. The campaign consists in protecting the exit cards at all costs (taking Hearts freely), getting rid of all forced-entry cards before executing the final "grand exit" that gets the hand out of the lead forever. Here is an example:

Example 19

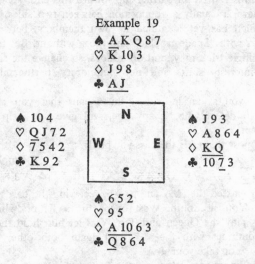

Trick 1. West led the ♠10, East winning with the ♠J.
Trick 2. East returned the ♠9, North winning with the Ace.

Trick 3. North led the ♠8. An unhappy outlook for him! His only sure exit card was the ♡3. To avoid being stuck in at the end with "stiff" cards, he had to plan to get rid of all his entry cards before finally exiting with the ♡3. The first move was to bail out the remaining Spades.

Trick 4. North led the ◇9, won by the Ace. The order of breaking suits was dictated by North's high cards. The constant danger in a grand exit is that the opponents may hammer at the suit of your exit card and force it out prematurely. The general policy is therefore to start the suit in which your tops are weakest, saving your tops to hold command.

Trick 5. South led the ♡5. North won with the ♡10, of course saving his King for command.

Trick 6. North led another Diamond and East was in with the ◇Q.

Trick 7. East led a low Heart, forcing North's King. North weathered this attack on the Hearts by virtue of his top command of the neutral suits.

Trick 8. North cashed the ◇J, which was high.

Trick 9. North cashed the ♣A.

Trick 10. North led the ♣J, which held.

Trick 11. North exited with the ♡3, West winning with the ♡J.

Trick 12. West led the ♣2, won by South with the ♣4 and gathering the ♠Q.

Score: West, 3; North, 10; East, 0; South, 13. The grand exit saved North probably 10 to 12 points.

The Slam There is seldom much play for slams unless the maker gets a plus score; but since this is a widely played variation, this section will assume that the maker of a slam scores +26.

At times a slam is made by connivance of all four players. One player who would otherwise be stuck with many Hearts and possibly the ♠Q as well seeks salvation in a slam. Each of the others decides he cannot interfere without risk of catching the ♠Q.

Example 20

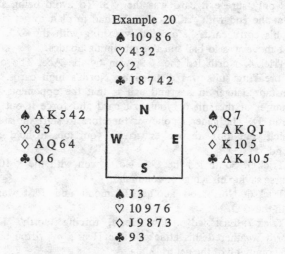

```
                    ♠ 10 9 8 6
                    ♡ 4 3 2
                    ◇ 2
                    ♣ J 8 7 4 2

  ♠ A K 5 4 2          N           ♠ Q 7
  ♡ 8 5                            ♡ A K Q J
  ◇ A Q 6 4     W           E      ◇ K 10 5
  ♣ Q 6                            ♣ A K 10 5
                        S

                    ♠ J 3
                    ♡ 10 9 7 6
                    ◇ J 9 8 7 3
                    ♣ 9 3
```

Trick 1. West led the ♣Q, East winning with the Ace.

Trick 2. East led the ◇10, won by West's ◇Q.

Trick 3. West led the ♣6 and East won with the ♣10.

East was now in a precarious spot. He had passed for a possible slam, which at this juncture looked dubious. He had losing cards in both neutral suits. He decided to go for the slam by bailing out the Hearts, so that none could be discarded on his Diamond and Club losers.

Four leads took out all the Hearts. West could see that if he tried to block the slam he would probably get the ♠Q himself on a Spade or Diamond lead. So he co-operated by ditching his ♠A-K on the Hearts. East then cashed the ♠Q to complete the slam.

If opportunity arises to kill an incipient slam at no cost, you should of course do so, to debit the opponents at your expense. The play of Example 12 illustrates how attention to detail may pay off. The cards after the pass:

Example 21

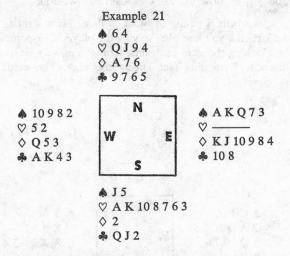

    ♠ 6 4
    ♡ Q J 9 4
    ◇ A 7 6
    ♣ 9 7 6 5

♠ 10 9 8 2   ♠ A K Q 7 3
♡ 5 2   ♡ ———
◇ Q 5 3   ◇ K J 10 9 8 4
♣ A K 4 3   ♣ 10 8

    ♠ J 5
    ♡ A K 10 8 7 6 3
    ◇ 2
    ♣ Q J 2

Trick 1. West led the ♠10 and South won with the ♠J.

Trick 2. South returned the Spade and East was in with the Ace.

Trick 3. East led the ◇8. Seeing that he might have to try for a slam for lack of exit cards, East decided to find out if the ◇A would come out promptly and leave him a solid suit. But West held the trick with the ◇Q, North holding up in order to let West continue Spades.

Trick 4. West led a Spade, won by the King. North discarded the ◇A. This discard of course gladdened East, who now set about getting rid of his Clubs.

Trick 5. East led the ♣8, won by West with the Ace.

West knew at this juncture that East was probably trying for a slam, since if he were merely trying to exit he would have bailed out the Spades first. To lead the fourth Spade now might let East back in a handful of solid Spades and Diamonds. West decided to try to spoil the slam.

Trick 6. West led the ♡2, won by North with the ♡4 and taking the ♠Q.

The reward of West's foresight was a zero score, North and East splitting the points 16 and 10.

It is worth 6 points to block a slam. (If a slam is made against you, you lose 6½, leaving the player a ½-point gainer by blocking the slam as against letting it make.) Example 13 illustrates how this fact affects the play. The cards after the pass:

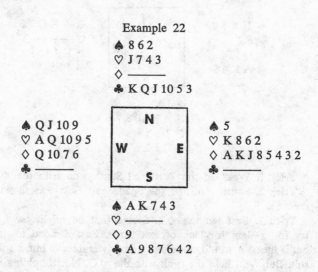

Example 22

♠ 8 6 2
♡ J 7 4 3
◇ ——
♣ K Q J 10 5 3

♠ Q J 10 9   ♠ 5
♡ A Q 10 9 5   ♡ K 8 6 2
◇ Q 10 7 6   ◇ A K J 8 5 4 3 2
♣ ——   ♣ ——

♠ A K 7 4 3
♡ ——
◇ 9
♣ A 9 8 7 6 4 2

Trick 1. West led the ◇ 10, which held, North shedding the ♣ 10.

Trick 2. West led the ◇ 7, which held, North letting go the ♣ J and South the ♠ K.

Trick 3. West led the ♡ Q, again winning. North got rid of the ♣ K and South shed the ♠ A.

Trick 4. West led the ♡ A. North played the ♡ J. East, fortified by the ♡ 2, held up the King. It would have been craven to help West to the slam.

West continued with the slam try as his only hope, leading his ◇ 6, ♠ 9-10-J, hoping that the ♡ K would be discarded. But East sat tight, won the tenth trick with the ♡ K, and threw West back in with the ♡ 2. East took three Hearts, painting West with the other 23 points.

Card Reading It goes without saying that to win money at Hearts you must keep track of every card played, who played what, and the order in which the cards fall. This is a much tougher proposition than in Bridge, where you see at least one other hand and can frequently draw inference about the unseen hands from the bidding. If you cannot keep track of all the cards, train yourself thus: First try counting the number of cards played in each suit. This is fairly easy, as chiefly you have to note discards on tricks not all of one suit. Next practice watching the spots so as to know the exact rank of the unplayed cards. Finally, practice remembering the exact order of the play, and draw all possible inferences therefrom.

Here is a typical example of what may happen if you do not pay sufficient attention to detail. You are dealt:

> Example 23
> ♠ J 9 6 3
> ♡ A K 5 3
> ◇ K 5 2
> ♣ Q 6

You elect to pass the ♡K, ◇K, ♣Q. After receipt your hand is:

> ♠ J 9 6 3
> ♡ A Q J 9 5 3
> ◇ 5 2
> ♣ 6

So with your "impregnable" hand you take 14 points! Why? Because you held onto the Spades, discarding Hearts. Was the outcome foreseeable? Yes!

You sit East. The play goes as follows:

Trick 1. West opens the ♠10. All hands follow, South winning with the Ace.

Trick 2. South cashes the ◇K, all following suit.

Trick 3. South cashes the ◇9, all following suit.

Trick 4. South cashes ◇Q, West shedding the ♡8 while you let go the ♣6. North follows suit.

Trick 5. South cashes the ◇7. You and West discard Hearts.

Trick 6. South cashes the ♣Q. You discard another top Heart. The others follow suit.

Trick 7. South leads the ♣5, won by North with the ♣K, and you let go another top Heart.

Trick 8. North leads the ♡6, on which you play the ♡9, South the ♡K, and West the ♣8.

Trick 9. South leads the ♡4 and wins when North produces the ♡2 and you the ♡3, West letting go the ♣A.

Trick 10. South leads the ♠8 and wins, North discarding the ♡10.

Trick 11. South cashes the ♠K.

Trick 12. South leads the ♠2, and you are forced in with the ♠3.

Trick 13. Your ♡5 is the only Heart left, and it gathers South's ♠Q.

Your instinct is to save low Spades above all else because they provide you leads on which you cannot gather the ♠Q. But when an opponent is bent on a grand exit, you don't want to get stuck in with nothing but high or long cards. To provide against that outcome, you get rid of your entry cards if possible. Just realize that Spades can be the sticking suit as well as any others.

You can see by the play from Trick 4 on that South is trying for a grand exit. You happily know that you have nothing to fear from the first round of Hearts, as you passed the ♡K to South. Hearts might be his exit suit, e.g., if he has the ♡K-2, with or without more Hearts; when the time comes his King may take out all the Hearts left in West and North and the ♡2 sticks you in. If this is the situation, you probably can do nothing about it because you cannot hope to get rid of five Hearts by discard. The stick-in would not hurt you, but since your only other suit is Spades you would have to count on the ♠3 to stand as an exit on the fourth Spade round.

You have a tip that the Spades are massed, by the breaks in the other suits. If Spades are the suit South counts on for exit, you can protect yourself surely by discarding one or two Spades on the neutral suits.

LAWS OF HEARTS

1. Number of Players Three to seven; best for four. Each plays for himself.

2. The Pack Fifty-two cards.

3. Rank of Cards A (high), K, Q, J, 10, 9, 8, 7, 6, 5, 4, 3, 2.

4. The Draw Draw or cut; low deals first, and thereafter the deal passes to the left.

5. The Shuffle and Cut Any player may shuffle, the dealer last. The player at the dealer's right cuts.

6. The Deal The cards are dealt one at a time as far as they will go equally; any remaining cards are placed on the table, face down, and are taken in by the player who wins the first trick; no one may look at them during the play.

7. The Pass After looking at his hand each player selects any three cards and passes them face down to his left-hand neighbor. The player must pass the three cards before looking at the three cards he receives from his right. (Some pass to the right; some to the player sitting across the table.) In six- and seven-hand play, only two cards are passed.

8. The Play Eldest hand makes the opening lead. Each hand must follow suit to a lead if able; if unable, a hand may discard any card. But the player dealt the ♠Q must discard it at his first opportunity. A trick is won by the highest card of the suit led.

The rule that the ♠Q must be discarded at the first opportunity is often set aside in social play.

9. Object of Play To avoid winning in tricks any Heart or the ♠Q (called Black Lady or Black Maria).

10. Scoring A separate count is kept for each player. At the end of each hand the points taken in tricks by each player are totaled and entered in his column. The counting cards are:

Each Heart counts . . .   1

The ♠Q counts   13

In many localities if a player wins all thirteen Hearts and

the ♠Q there is no score for that deal; in other localities the player is credited with 26 points.

When a table breaks up all columns are totaled, and each player settles with every other on the differences of their totals. One way to determine the payments is to determine the average of all scores and the difference by which each player exceeds or falls below the average. For example:

Player	Final Total	Difference from Average
W	42	+3
X	71	+32
Y	19	−20
Z	24	−15
	4) 156	(39 average)

Since the object of play is to take the least points, Y and Z collect 20 and 15 points respectively, W paying 3 and X 32.

If desired, the individual scores may be kept as running totals, so that a player may see at a glance how he stands relative to the others. The aggregate of all scores at any time must be a multiple of 26.

11. Scoring Variants

a. Variant No. 1. Each player pays one chip for each Heart, thirteen chips for the ♠Q, and lowest score for the deal takes all. Players that tie split the pool, leaving any odd chips in the pool for the next deal.

b. Variant No. 2 (Sweepstakes). Each player pays one chip for each Heart, thirteen chips for the ♠Q. If one player alone scored zero, he takes the pool; if two or more players made zero, they split the pool. If every hand was painted (took one point or more), the pool remains as a Jack for the next deal, or until it is eventually won.

IRREGULARITIES

12. *Misdeal* If the dealer exposes a card in dealing, or gives one player too many cards, another player too few, the next player in turn deals.

13. Play Out of Turn   A lead or play out of turn must be retracted if demand is made before all have played to the trick; after all have played, a play out of turn stands as regular without penalty.

14. Quitted Tricks   Each trick gathered must be placed face down in front of the winner and tricks must be kept separate. If a player so mixes his cards that a claim of revoke cannot be proved, he is charged with all 26 points for the deal, regardless of whether the alleged revoke was made by him or another player.

15. Revoke   Failure to follow suit when able, or to discard the ♠Q at the first opportunity (where this rule is in force), constitutes a revoke. A revoke may be corrected before the trick is turned and quitted; if not discovered until later, the revoke is established, play is immediately abandoned, and the revoking hand is charged with all 26 points for the deal. If revoke is established against more than one player, each is charged 26 points. But the revoke penalty may not be enforced after the next cut after the deal in which the revoke occurred.

16. Incorrect Hand   A player discovered to have too few cards must take the last trick (if more than one card short, he must take in every trick to which he cannot play).

CRIBBAGE

TEN THINGS EVERY WINNING CRIBBAGE PLAYER MUST KNOW

1. The best thing to save in your hand is a run.

2. Never give a Five to the opponent's crib.

3. Subtract the count you give away from the count you save, and keep the cards that net you the most.

4. With a bad hand save low cards to score by a go.

5. Don't give near cards to the opponent's crib.

6. A Five, if you can spare it, is the best card you can put in your own crib.

7. Don't be afraid to lead a "tenth card"—it's often good.

8. Don't play "on" with no chance for a run.

9. The safest lead is a Four.

10. Always watch the score—it affects nearly every play.

CRIBBAGE

Cribbage is unique. There is no bidding or declaring, and the method and purpose of play are unlike that of any other game. It all seems like simple arithmetic, and in fact Cribbage is one of the favorite games for children. But don't imagine that it is child's play! It is one of the few games both popular and skillful enough to call into being its own clubs and leagues. I do not know how far the cult of this English game has spread to the Western U.S., but I do know that New England is honeycombed with Cribbage clubs, and that they are in the process of establishing a national organization to supervise sectional and national tournaments.

The basic game is two-handed, but it is often played by three or four.

DISCARDING TO THE CRIB

A large proportion of the hands you hold offer no problem as to what to discard to the crib. You keep all the cards that can make a count, and ditch the extra. Or, if you have to break up something, you keep as much as you can, help your own crib or balk your opponent's, save the best prospects for improvement—and so on, under clear-cut principles that are fairly easy to apply. Let's go into these principles.

Keep Full Count The following hand contains 5 points, and still has them if you discard the K-3. So that is your discard, regardless of who has the crib.

K J 10 9 6 3   (Ex. 1)

Keep a Low Card   In some cases your entire count is contained in two or three cards. You have a choice among loose cards. A point to keep in mind is that a low card is apt to be of more value in the play than a high. Thus, with:

K 10 7 7 6 3   (Ex. 2)

you want to keep 7-7-6. Save the Three also, for a possible go.

Tenth cards (cards counting ten—Kings, Queens, Jacks, and Tens) are on the whole the safest you can give your opponent's crib. The least likely card a player will give his own crib is a Five, because most of the time he will have a bigger count by keeping it in his hand.

Keep a Near Card   In Example 2 I remarked that you want to keep the 7-7-6. The Six adds nothing to your meager score of 2, but is potentially valuable because it is in sequence with the Sevens. Here is another basic principle: When nothing better offers, save a near card.

Sometimes you have a close choice:

K 10 8 7 7 3   (Ex. 3)

You will of course keep the 8-7-7 and give the King. Shall you keep the Three, because it is low, or the Ten, because it is near the Eight? I would keep the Ten, but would not criticize a player who chose the Three.

Save a Run   Practically the law of the Medes and the Persians is that you save a run when you have it. Obviously this combination has the maximum opportunity to be promoted by the starter. Any of nine unseen cards (of the three other ranks) will add at least 5 points. Thus with:

K Q J 7 6 4   (Ex. 4)

the only question is what two of the three low cards to let go. If the crib is yours, give it 7-6 because they are near; if the crib is your opponent's, give 7-4 because they are wide.

The Double Run   If the run is doubled, so much the more reason for keeping it intact. The cash value of 8 points minimum, plus the great chance of improvement, is worth keeping even at the cost of giving the opponent's crib a pair or a fifteen. With:

$$Q\,Q\,8\,7\,6\,6 \qquad \text{(Ex. 5)}$$

give him the Queens, keeping your 10 points for a net gain of 8.

However, don't be wooden about this principle or any other. When you have a high score in six cards, and have to deplete it by any discard, consider and count all the possibilities. Once in a while you will be surprised to discover a case where you must break a double run.

$$K\,Q\,Q\,J\,5\,5 \qquad \text{(Ex. 6)}$$

To keep the double run, giving your opponent's crib the Fives, nets you 6 points. But if you give him the K-J, you keep 12 points and give him nothing.

On your own deal you would happily lay away the Fives, scoring 8 in hand and 2 in crib. The prospects of improvement kept intact this way are worth the 2 points sacrificed.

This matter of potential improvement weighs in many close choices.

$$J\,10\,10\,9\,6\,6 \qquad \text{(Ex. 7)}$$

Your opponent dealt. If you give him the pair of Sixes, you keep 8 for a net of 6. If you give him the J-10, you keep 6 and give nothing. The net is the same. Then give him the pair, for your overall chances of improving by the starter are better that way.

Treasure a Five The starter is more likely to be a tenth card than any other given rank, since there are twenty tenth cards in the deck. Hence a Five is to be treasured; it may become a fifteen. Furthermore, the crib is found to contain a tenth card more often than not. You may give a score if you give your opponent's crib a Five. By the same token, give a Five to your own crib if you can afford to do so.

About the only hand with which you should consider giving your opponent's crib a Five is a double run plus a Five and another odd card:

$$9\,8\,8\,7\,5\,A \qquad \text{(Ex. 8)}$$

Give the 5-A and take your chances, keeping your 12 cash points rather than reduce the hand to 6 points in order to hold the Five.

THE PLAY

Picking a Lead   It is a pleasant notion, in picking a lead, to balk your opponent's making a fifteen. The only way you can surely do this is to lead a card lower than a Five-spot. But the very low cards are best saved to eke out a go. Hence the proverbial saying that the best lead at Cribbage is a Four.

Not having a Four, or being unwilling to spare a Four, lead the card that has the best prospect of countering with a score if your opponent makes a score. Having a pair, lead from it, so that if he makes a pair you can make a pair royal. Having to lead an odd card, lead that which will let you counter with a run if he makes a fifteen. Thus:

9 8 5 5   (Ex. 9)

Lead the Eight. You have no defense against a pair, but if he makes fifteen with a Seven, you play the Nine to make a run.

The lead of a tenth card is much better than its reputation. The case against it has always been that he can make a fifteen with a Five—but if he has a Five, he is just too lucky anyhow! But if he responds to your lead with a high card, saving his lower cards for a go, you may score a go by playing your highest card. Having two or three tenth cards, you are probably better off to lead one of them, even if you have a Four.

The most dangerous leads are the Eight and Seven unless you have the card to make a run if he makes a fifteen. From:

9 7 6 4   (Ex. 10)

(having given your opponent's crib a K-Q) lead the Seven. But from:

8 8 4 2   (Ex. 11)

(having given your opponent's crib a K-Q) lead the Four.

Playing On and Off   The same considerations govern your

response to your opponent's lead. Play "on" toward a run if you have the card to prolong it, otherwise play "off."

9 9 6 3   (Ex. 12)

This is your hand after you have given your own crib the Q-5. Opponent leads an Eight. Respond with the Six, for if he plays the Seven to peg 3, you can come back with 9, scoring 4 for run and probably 1 for go. Obviously it would not be good to respond to the lead with a Nine, for he might play a Ten, scoring 3.

Q 10 5 3   (Ex. 13)

You gave your crib 9-6. Your opponent leads an Eight. You do not play on with the Ten, for if he makes the run with a Nine you cannot make a counterscore. Play off with the Queen.

Anticipate a Tenth Card   The last example illustrates a general principle: When you cannot make a score and do not wish to play on, play a high card by preference, saving low cards to squeeze out a go. But like all others, this principle has its exceptions. If avoidable, don't hike up the count where your opponent can score a go by playing a tenth card. For example:

10 9 9 8   (Ex. 14)

Opponent leads a Four. If you mechanically play the Ten, and he comes back with a tenth card, you have only yourself to blame! You could have responded with a Nine, and then you are sure of a second play.

K 3 3 2   (Ex. 15)

This is your hand, and your opponent opens a Ten. Again the mechanical play of the King may give your opponent a go. His lead makes it fairly probable that he has another tenth card in his hand. The right response is a Three.

Playing to the Score   Suppose that both you and your opponent need only about 7 points for game. If you are the dealer at this juncture, you must realize that your only chance to win is probably to peg out, for he counts first and can

probably make at least 7 in hand and pegging together.
Therefore you should save the cards best for pegging, regardless of how you butcher your count. Thus:

Q 9 9 8 7 5   (Ex. 16)

The normal discard to your own crib is the Q-5. But in this
desperate situation it is better to lay away the Q-9. Save low
cards and all possible different ranks. If your opponent leads
a Four, play on with the Five, hoping he will play a Six. If
you can peg a run of four, you can then win by making a pair
or fifteen later, since you are always sure of 1 for go or last.

Conversely, if you are the nondealer in this situation, and
have enough in hand to go out, play off at all costs, even
scorning the pairs and fifteens you might make. With the
above hand give the crib the Q-5; lead a Nine. If the dealer
pairs, you make a pair royal and may then go out by pegging.
If he plays a Six to peg 2, play your other Nine—don't risk
giving him a run with the Eight or Seven.

SHOWING

Count in Order   There is art even in the mechanical business
of counting your hand. As a courtesy to opponent, you should
indicate the separate scoring combinations, instead of announcing the flat total. This is the more incumbent if you
adopt the rule of muggins, as most players do.

The standard order of counting the points is: fifteens, runs,
pairs, flush, his nobs or his heels. Suppose that your hand is:

◇ J 6 5 4   Starter: ◇ 9   (Ex. 17)

The customary way of counting goes something like this:
   "Fifteen two, fifteen four, fifteen six, run makes
   nine, and one for his nobs—ten."
It is not necessary to point out the separate combinations of
fifteens. Nor need you itemize the count of those multiple
combinations having standard names. Thus with:

10 9 9 8   Starter: 6   (Ex. 18)

you say, "Fifteen two, fifteen four, and double run makes
twelve."

Multiple Combinations Here are the standard combinations that you may properly identify by name and count as a unit. The values given are the total for runs and pairs; fifteens, if any, are extra, and are counted separately.

	Value
PAIR ROYAL: three of a kind, as K-K-K	6
DOUBLE PAIR ROYAL: four of a kind, as Q-Q-Q-Q	12
DOUBLE RUN: run of three with one card duplicated, as K-K-Q-J	8
TRIPLE RUN: run of three with one card triplicated, as J-J-J-10-9	15
QUADRUPLE RUN: run of three with two cards duplicated, as 10-10-9-8-8	16
DOUBLE RUN OF FOUR: run of four with one card duplicated, as Q-J-10-9-9	10

LAWS OF CRIBBAGE

1. Number of Players Two or three, or four as partners. Best two-hand.

2. The Pack Fifty-two cards.

3. Rank of Cards K (high), Q, J, 10, 9, 8, 7, 6, 5, 4, 3, 2, A.

4. The Draw Lowest card deals. Players drawing cards of the same rank must draw again.

5. The Shuffle and Cut The dealer has the right to shuffle last. The player at his right cuts. The cut must leave not less than four cards in each packet.

6. The Deal (*two-handed*) Each player receives six cards, dealt one at a time. Players deal alternately during the game. The loser of a game deals first for the next game.

7. The Crib Each player looks at his six cards and lays away two of them to reduce his hand to four. The four cards laid away together constitute the crib, which belongs to the dealer but is not exposed or used until after the play.

8. The Starter After the crib is laid away, the nondealer cuts the pack and the dealer turns up the top card of the lower packet. This card, placed face up on the pack, is the starter. If the starter is a Jack (called "his heels") the dealer pegs (scores) 2 points at once. The starter is not used in the play.

9. The Play   After the starter is turned, the nondealer lays one of his cards face up on the table. The dealer similarly exposes a card, then the nondealer again, and so on—the hands are exposed card by card, alternately except for go's, as noted below. Each player keeps his cards separate from those of his opponent.

As each plays he announces the total of pips reached by the addition of his card to those previously played. For example, the nondealer begins with a Four, saying, "Four." The dealer plays a Nine, saying, "Thirteen." The Kings, Queens and Jacks count 10 each; every other card counts its pip value (Ace being 1).

10. The Go   During the play the running total of cards may never be carried beyond 31. If a player is unable to add another card without exceeding 31, he says, "Go," and his opponent pegs 1. But the player gaining the go must first lay down any additional cards he can without exceeding 31. Besides the point for go he is then entitled to any additional points he can make through pairs and runs. If a player reaches exactly 31, he pegs 2 instead of 1 for go.

a. The player who called "Go" must lead for the next series of play, the count starting at zero. The lead may not be combined with any cards previously played to form a scoring combination, the go having interrupted the sequence.

b. Playing the last card of all pegs 1 for go; consequently the dealer is sure to peg at least 1 point.

11. Pegging   The object in play is to score points by pegging. In addition to scoring for go, a player may score for the following combinations:

a. Fifteen: For adding a card that makes the total 15, peg 2.

b. Pair: For adding a card of the same rank as that played last previously, peg 2. (Note that face cards pair only by actual rank, Jack with Jack, but not Jack with Queen.)

c. Triplet (also called "Threes or pair royal"):   For adding the third card of the same rank, peg 6.

d. Four (also called "double pair" or "double pair royal"): For adding the fourth card of the same rank, peg 12.

e. Run (Sequence):   For adding a card which forms, with those played last previously, a sequence of three or more, peg 1 for each card in the sequence. (Runs are independent of suits, but go strictly by rank, e.g., 9-10-J is a run, but 9-10-Q is not.)

f. It is necessary to keep track of the order in which cards are played to determine whether what looks like a pegging formation is interrupted by a foreign card. Examples: Cards are played in this order: 8, 7, 7, 6. The dealer pegs 2 for fifteen, and the opponent pegs 2 for a pair, but the dealer cannot peg for a run because of the extra seven-spot. Again, cards are played in this order: 9, 6, 8, 7. The nondealer pegs 2 for fifteen on his first play, and 4 for a run on his second play. The cards were not played in sequential order, but form a true run with no foreign card.

12. Counting the Hands When play ends, the three hands are counted in order: nondealer (first), dealer's hand, crib. This order is important, for toward the end of a game the nondealer may "count out" and win before the dealer has a chance to count, even though the dealer's total would have exceeded that of his opponent.

The starter is considered to be a part of each hand, so that all hands in counting comprise five cards. The following are the basic formations of scoring value:

a. Fifteen: Each combination of cards that totals 15 counts 2.

b. Pair: Each pair of cards of the same rank counts 2.

c. Run: Each combination of three or more cards in the sequence counts 1 for each card in the sequence.

d. Flush: Four cards of the same suit in hand (not crib) count 4. Four cards in hand or crib of the same suit as starter count 5. (No count for four-flush in crib not if same suit as starter.)

e. His Nobs: Jack of same suit as starter counts 1.

13. Combinations   In the above table the word "combination" is used in the strict technical sense. Each and every combination of two cards that make a pair, of two or more cards that make 15, of three or more cards that make a run, counts separately. For example, a hand (with starter) of 8, 7, 7, 6, 2 scores 8 points for four combinations with a total of 15: the Eight with one Seven, and with the other Seven; the Six-Two with each Seven in turn. It scores 2 for a pair, and 6 for two runs of three—8-7-6 using each Seven in turn. The total is 16.

14. Muggins (optional)   Each player must count his hand (and crib) aloud and announce the total. Should he overlook any score, his opponent may say, "Muggins," and then himself score the points overlooked.

15. Game   Game may be fixed at either 61 points or 121 points. Play ends the moment either player reaches the agreed total, whether by pegging or counting his hand. If the non-dealer "goes out" by count of his hand, the dealer may not count either his hand or crib in the effort to escape lurch.

Each game counts 1 for the winner, but if the loser fails to pass the halfway mark (fails to reach 31 with a game of 61, or 61 with a game of 121) he is lurched, and the winner scores two games.

16. The Cribbage Board   Scoring by pencil and paper is very inconvenient in Cribbage. A special device is therefore used, the cribbage board (see illustration). This is a wooden or composition tablet with four rows, of thirty-one holes each, divided into two pairs of rows by a central panel. There are usually four or two additional holes near one end, called game holes. With the board come four pegs, usually in two contrasting colors.

The board is placed between the two players, and each takes two pegs of the same color. (The game holes are provided to contain the pegs before the start of a game.) Each

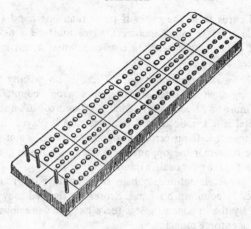

time a player scores he advances a peg along a row on his side of the board, counting one hole per point. Two pegs are used so that the rearmost can be jumped ahead of the foremost, its distance from the latter showing the increment in score. The custom is to "go down" (away from the game holes) on the outer rows and "come up" on the inner rows. The game of 61 is "once around" and 121 is "twice around."

IRREGULARITIES

17. Misdeal There must be a new deal by the same dealer if the cards are not dealt one at a time, if any hand receives the wrong number of cards, if a card is found faced in the pack, if a card is exposed in dealing, or if the pack is found imperfect.

18. Wrong Number of Cards If one hand (not crib) is found to have the wrong number of cards after laying away for the crib, the other hand and crib being correct, the opponent may either demand a new deal or may peg 2 and rectify the hand by drawing out excess cards or dealing additional cards from the pack to supply a deficiency. If the crib is incorrect, both hands being correct, the nondealer pegs 2 and the crib is corrected by drawing out excess cards or dealing added cards from the pack. If more than one hand (including the crib) is found incorrect, there must be a new deal, and if either player held the correct number in his hand, he pegs 2.

19. Erroneous Announcement There is no penalty for announcing a wrong total of cards or a wrong count, but the error must be corrected on demand. If an error in announcing the total is not noticed until the next card is played, it stands as announced. If an error in counting a hand is not noticed by the time that the opponent commences counting, or until the cut for the next deal, it stands.

No player is entitled to help from another or from a bystander in counting his hand. Scores overlooked may not be taken by the opponent unless there has been previous agreement to enforce muggins.

20. Erroneous Play A player who calls go when able to play may not correct his error after the next card is played. A player who gains a go and fails to play additional cards when able may not correct his error after the next card is played. In either case the card or cards erroneously withheld are dead as soon as seen by the opponent, and the offender may not play them or peg with them, and the opponent of the offender pegs 2 for the error.

21. Error in Pegging If a player places a peg short of the amount to which he is entitled, he may not correct his error after he has played the next card or after the cut for the next deal. If he pegs more than his announced score, the error must be corrected on demand at any time before the cut for the next deal, and his opponent pegs 2.

THREE-HANDED CRIBBAGE

Draw for the first deal; thereafter the deal rotates to the left.

Deal five cards to each player, one at a time, and one card to the crib. Each player lays away one card to the crib, which belongs to the dealer. Eldest hand cuts for the starter.

When a player calls go, the next hand must continue play

if able, and if he does play, the remaining hand must then play if able. If the first hand after the go cannot play, the second hand does not play. In any case the point for go is won by the hand that played the last card.

All other rules of play and scoring are as in two-handed Cribbage. The hands are counted in order to the left, beginning with eldest hand and ending with the crib. Game is usually fixed at 61.

FOUR-HANDED CRIBBAGE

Draw for partners and the first deal. Deal five cards to each player, one at a time. Each player lays away one card to the crib, which belongs to the dealer. Rules of play are as at three-handed Cribbage.

Scores made by partners are amalgamated in a running total. One player for each side should be appointed to keep the score. Game is 121.

PITCH

TEN THINGS EVERY WINNING PITCH PLAYER MUST KNOW

1. If you are never set back, you are not bidding enough.

2. Don't bid Four without the Jack in your hand.

3. Don't depend on the Queen for high or Four for low.

4. High, Low, and Jack are made by the deal; game is made by the play.

5. Try to know which opponent will stand for a boost, and bid one more against him.

6. You can often catch an opponent's Ten, but don't count on saving your own.

7. If an opponent usually pitches his high trump, then switches suits, lead your high trump when you get the lead.

8. When you are at the pitcher's right, lead a new suit.

9. Don't always trump when you can; have a reason.

10. Everyone is the low man's partner.

PITCH (SETBACK)

Pitch is our American version of the old English game All Fours. It is played under many different names, and with some variations in local rules, but I have selected the modern game that has become most popular.

Since Pitch is a "short game"—not all of the pack is dealt—the number of cards in play varies with the number of players. This fact must be taken into account in the bidding. I will deal primarily with the four-handed game. The strategy is much the same at three-handed, five-handed, and six-handed, but the probabilities change as to what is high and what is low.

HAND VALUATION

Trump Length The average expectation is that you will hold 1½ cards of each suit. But you can't actually hold 1½ cards—you must have one or two. A two-card length is therefore not a suit to be picked as trump with any expectation that it will furnish a long card. Any blank Ace or A-x is obviously worth a bid of one, but an A-J or A-2 is not intrinsically worth a bid of two. Compelled to open the Ace, you leave the lower card at the mercy of adverse higher cards. While an A-J has some prospect of taking 2 points (no opponent having a guarded King or Queen), you cannot afford to bid 2 with only this in hand. And an A-2 is worse than, say, an A-7, because with the latter you might pick up low on the pitch, while with an A-2 you contribute low to any opponent that has a second trump and leads it.

A three-card length is, on the average, as long as or longer than any other player's holding in the suit. You are entitled to assume that Jack or low in a three-card holding can be saved. The crux of the matter is that, having pitched, you still have a guard in case an opponent left with a high trump leads it. Such holdings as an A-J-x and A-3-2 are worth a bid of two.

Freak lengths of four or more trumps of course give added protection to your own Jack or low, and—more important—afford a strong prospect of capturing game. Thus an A-9-8-7 will make two more often than not, capturing game through the 4-point Ace plus what the long trumps gather from the opponents.

Any five or six trumps should be assumed to win the game point automatically. Of course, you will meet exceptions. But that is true of any rule of valuation or bidding that you can formulate. Pitch being a "short game," more deals will depart widely from the average probabilities than will hit them on the nose. That is why I incline to avoid saying, "The odds are . . ." The odds are easy to calculate and are of little use because they are only a starting point. I prefer to say, "You should assume . . ." thus and so, basing the advice not only on the abstract odds but also on the practical experience of what works. You have to be satisfied to win on net, not to win every time.

What Is High? Assume that there is only a 50-50 chance that a King will prove to be high, the Ace being undealt. It is not a bidding value unless combined with another half chance. Assume that the Queen is unlikely to be high, and not worth counting even as a plus value in a close question of bidding.

With the ♠ K-8-2 you should bid one; the guarded Deuce alone being fairly sure, and there is a chance the King will be high. A bid of two is not recommended, but is a fair gamble if hard pressed. With the ♠ K-8-3 and nothing else you have a good pass, but should venture one if "on the spot" (discussed later).

What Is Low? In your hand nothing above Deuce should be assumed to be low. The point here is that you have the problem of saving it; add to this problem any doubt as to whether your Three or higher is actually low, and the card is scarcely countable as a point.

The more comfortable situation is to hold trump tops that warrant the assumption you will catch low from an opponent. Assume that any A-K, led right out, will do so. Also, an A-Q-4 or better may be assumed to be worth 2 points if you can afford to lead the Queen after pitching the Ace.

What of the Jack? The Jack is very simple to reckon. Never assume you will gather the Jack unless you see it in your hand, adequately guarded. One third of the time, otherwise, it will not be in play, and when it is you cannot expect to drop it with less than an A-K, possibly an A-Q.

The Game Point It must be admitted that the vagaries of the game point are unforeseeable. Anything can happen, and everything does.

On two successive deals I have seen a player win the game point with a count of 8 and lose it with a count of 34. The average expectation is that there will be about 40 points in the cards, and that 16 points or more will be a plurality. But the total varies widely from deal to deal.

The big factor is, of course, the number of Ten-spots in play. On the average, there should be two. When the number is more or less than two, the total of points in the deal is practically sure to be way above or way below average accordingly.

The best assurance of capturing the game point is trump length, high side cards, or both, so that you have a prospect of winning at least three tricks. Having such length or strength, count at least a 50-50 chance to win the game point, combining this with any other 50-50 chance as a positive bidding value. For example: the ◊ K-9-6-2 is a fair two-bid.

Count your low as sure. There is a 50-50 chance that the King is high, plus a 50-50 chance for the game point.

The only other type of hand affording a biddable prospect of winning the game point is one of fair strength with a Ten that probably can be saved. For example:

♠ A 7 5   ♡ K 10   ◇ 3   ♣ ————   (Ex. 1)

♠ Q J 8   ♡ A 10   ◇ 3   ♣ ————   (Ex. 2)

It is true that "one Ten does not make the game." It is also true that one Ten often does! At all events, gathering a Ten plus your high trumps gives you an edge that can be overcome, as a rule, only by the falling of two other Tens to one opponent.

THE BIDDING

Bid 'Em Up! It cannot be overemphasized that waiting for sure hands to bid loses heavily in the long run.

Don't be an idle spectator while other players bid on skinny hands and bob up with 3 or 4 points by the accidents of the deal and play. The winning game is the aggressive game. By that I don't mean you should go to the other extreme, and overcall with three or four merely because you are annoyed at the other fellow's two-bid. Be aggressive when the bidding situation calls for optimism, and conservative where you have nothing to gain by taking risks.

The Opening One-Bid An opening bid of one rarely takes the contract. Why is it made at all? The answer is: to make it a little more expensive for the other fellows. Having an Ace, open the bidding as a matter of course.

If two players pass ahead of you, you are "on the spot." Bid one on "a hope and a prayer" rather than let the dealer have it for one. In many circles the "spot" never arises; eldest hand bids automatically.

The Higher Opening Bid If you are dealt better than a simple one-bid, keep in mind that you are not going to have a second chance to bid. Go the limit. This advice is easy to follow when you pick up something like:

♣ A K Q J 10 2   (Ex. 3)

♠ A K J 10 ♡ —— ♢ 3 ♣ 2   (Ex. 4)

With either hand bid four. The first is virtually ironclad. The second offers such good odds in your favor that a lesser bid would be cowardly.

But with borderline hands you have to distinguish two zones of bidding.

For any bid you need at least one point in hand; high, low, or Jack. For a second point there is always the chance of taking game. Hence there is a margin for aggressive bidding in bids of one and two.

A bid of three usually, and a bid of four always, assumes that you will take the game. Here you have no leeway. In this range, therefore, be conservative to the extent of looking at countable values. Don't stretch the normal minimum requirements.

As eldest hand, bid two (intending Spades) with any of the following. These are good solid bids of two:

♠ A J 6 ♡ K ♢ 6 4 ♣ ——   (Ex. 5)

♠ A 9 2 ♡ —— ♢ K 6 ♣ 3   (Ex. 6)

♠ K 9 7 2 ♡ —— ♢ —— ♣ A 4   (Ex. 7)

♠ K 8 6 4 2 ♡ 7 ♢ —— ♣ ——   (Ex. 8)

Sporty bids of two in this position are:

♠ J 10 3 2 ♡ 2 ♢ 8 ♣ ——   (Ex. 9)

♠ J 10 3 ♡ K ♢ —— ♣ K 10   (Ex. 10)

Overcalling: Be Bold Either Example 9 or 10 is a good overcall of two if one has been bid ahead of you. Here is a hand on which, as the dealer, I bid two and made it:

♠ J 10 9 ♡ J ♢ 6 ♣ 3   (Ex. 11)

When a one-bid has been made ahead of you, you are fighting something tangible by stretching a "one and a half" bid to two. Sometimes, though, especially as the dealer, you can see that a pass would be better, for the reason that you might take a point at the other fellow's trump. Just change one card in the foregoing hand:

♠ J 10 9   ♡ J 3   ◊ 5   ♣ ———   (Ex. 12)

I would have passed. Rather than risk the two-bid, I would have hoped that the pitch would be a Heart, in which case I would very probably make the Jack.

Paradoxically, the prospect of making a borderline three-bid is increased if two has been bid ahead of you. The reasons for this are: (a) The two-bid indicates, usually, a length of at least three, leaving this hand less room to hold stoppers against your trump suit. (b) The bid also indicates some high cards, which will fall to you if you have a good trump suit, thus aiding you to capture the game point. In other words, the stronger a hand is at its own trump, the weaker it is likely to be at any other, except as an unwilling contributor of game cards.

Suppose you are dealt:

♠ A J 7 3   ♡ 9   ◊ 4   ♣ ———   (Ex. 13)

As eldest hand you would bid two. Three would be an unwise stretch. But suppose you are the dealer, and two players have bid ahead of you, one and two. Now you should bid three without a qualm! Counting high and the Jack sure, you now have increased prospects both of catching or saving low and of making game by trumping outstanding Aces.

The Slam Bid   Obviously you cannot bid slam—four—without the Ace and Jack in hand, together with assurance of saving or dropping low. This means holding at least the King too, or the Two with at least four trumps. Even then, such a hand as:

♠ A K J 7   ♡ ———   ◊ 6   ♣ 8   (Ex. 14)

is a borderline case, for you might not take the game point. Why risk the slam bid when three is practically ironclad? Well, the answer is that you don't voluntarily bid a slam unless there is a "smudge" incentive. Whether to overcall a three-bid with this hand, otherwise, depends on the score.

Bidding to the Score   Inevitably the normal principles of bidding are often interfered with by special situations with the score. If one player stands at 10 (with 11-point game), who is going to let him play a one-bid? And if he has bid more, who is not going to stretch to the utmost to overcall?

Likewise, when your own score is low, and two or three others are around 7 to 9, you are impelled to bid high, trying to catch up, rather than wait for a better hand next deal. Here you incline to stretch—and one cannot say, on the odds, that you are wrong. As Pitch is usually scored, either you win or you lose; if you must lose, it makes no difference whether your score is 10 or zero. All experience goes to show that when you are ahead, with a score of 7 or more, you can afford to be conservative and wait for a solid hand, but when you trail with a score of 6 or less, you have got to bid what you have to the limit or more, because if you wait you will need two good hands in a row.

For the sake of your morale, however, you had better set yourself some rock-bottom minimums for "stretching," beyond which you will never go whatever the urgency. Just where you draw the line is apt to depend on what you know of your opponents—particularly of their sharpness in snaring the "gambler's point."

THE PLAY

The Pitch   From a suit headed by an Ace, King, or Queen there is no reason for failing to pitch the top card. A low lead is called for only when your suit is headed by the Jack. This card, as also low and a Ten, you try to make by ruffing, or as a long card, rather than by force of rank.

There is one situation, however, where you should pitch the Ten. You have made a routine one-bid on a J-10-x. The Jack is safe unless an opponent has a higher trump, adequately guarded, and saves it precisely to catch your Jack. Should this menace exist, you put the danger hand in a predicament by pitching the Ten. Shall he save his top to try for the Jack—with the great chance against him that you will run in the Jack on a ruff—or take the Ten toward the game point? Even though he diagnoses the situation exactly, he can rarely afford to hold up.

Later Trump Leads   With both an Ace and a King, continue with the King after pitching the Ace. This is the best chance either to catch or save low. With an Ace-Queen continue with the Queen if the King falls under the Ace, or if you can possibly afford to do so anyway.

With less top strength the normal procedure is to lead a second trump as early as possible, when you started with three or more. The more adverse trumps you knock together, the less chance you leave the opponents to ruff the high cards you hope to snare. A switch after pitching the Ace is logically limited to some such monstrosity as a holding of an A-J only (bid of one or two) or an A-J-2 (bid of two) or an A-7-2 (bid of two).

This being so, the opponents will often do well to continue trumps after an Ace pitch and switch. Since the pitcher surely lacks the King and probably the Queen, an opponent having one of these cards should usually lead it at the first opportunity. He may thereby pick up the Jack or low, and in any case he depletes the pitcher's game-snaring trumps. Almost a convention of defense is the rule that a defender who had a doubleton high trump must quickly lead his singleton top, thereby unblocking in case another defender had three trumps and can snare low from the pitcher.

The Right of Ruff The right to ruff a plain-suit lead, even when able to follow suit, chiefly affects the capture of the game point. What can happen is illustrated in the following deal:

Example 15

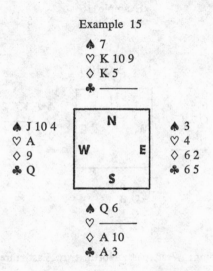

The bidding: West, one; North, pass; East, pass; South, two.

Trick 1. South pitches the ◇ A. East of course plays the ◇ 6, trying to save low.

Trick 2. South leads the ♠ Q, on which East makes his ◇ 2.

Trick 3. East leads the ♡ 4. South trumps with the ◇ 10, but North overtrumps with the ◇ K. North wins the rest. South is set back, as he took only high.

Needing the game point for contract, the Bidder should have trump length or strength sufficient for two trump leads, in order to bail out all but the exceptional trump lengths against him. Even with trump length he may have to play astutely to safeguard the game, as is shown below.

Safety Discarding   When able to discard a low plain card on a cheap trick, the Bidder should usually do so in preference to trumping. Otherwise his low loser might go on a fat trick won by another hand. For example:

Example 16

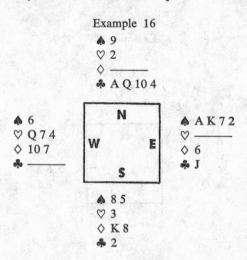

♠ 9
♡ 2
◇ ——————
♣ A Q 10 4

♠ 6
♡ Q 7 4
◇ 10 7
♣ ——————

♠ A K 7 2
♡ ——————
◇ 6
♣ J

♠ 8 5
♡ 3
◇ K 8
♣ 2

The bidding: West, pass; North, two; East, three; South, pass.

East hopes to take game as well as high and low. His bid is in part impelled by his singleton Club Jack, which will give North his contract if North's suit is Clubs.

Trick 1. East pitches the ♠A.

Trick 2. East cashes his ♠K.

Trick 3. East leads the ♣J. This lead is picked, rather than the ◇ 6, on the general principle of leading a plain card higher than a Ten, in order to prevent an adverse Ten from being saved easily. North is in with the ♣A.

Trick 4. North leads his ♡2. East discards the ◇6 and West wins with the ♡Q. East wins the last two tricks and scores high, low, and game.

Now observe what might happen if at Trick 4 East ruffed. At Trick 5 he leads his ◇ 6 and South puts up the ◇ K. West drops the ◊ 10 and North the ♣ 10, to give South game and so set East back. It is true that by ducking the lead of the ♡ 2, East risked letting the ♡ 10 (if in play) go to an opponent. But one hand (North) will have contributed nothing to this trick, whereas all three opponents may be able to fatten a losing Diamond lead by him.

This example shows the safety discard at its most uncertain —second hand after the lead. Where the bidder plays third or fourth to the trick, he can see more clearly whether the trick is going to be fat or lean.

Defensive Ethics As in other cutthroat games where there is temporary partnership against the Bidder in the play, Pitch presents questions of ethics. How far should you go to set the Bidder, with the effect of helping another player toward the game?

The practical code prevalent among Pitch players is that preventing any player from reaching game is the paramount concern on every hand. If the Bidder is high, everyone must co-operate against him. But if one of the defenders has a higher score than the Bidder, and could go out in the current deal, blocking him is more important than defeating the bid. This fact is of course taken into account in the bidding.

TWO-HANDED PITCH

In two-handed play, low is credited to the player who held it, regardless of which player won it in a trick. Game is 7 points. Typical trump holdings good for a bid of two are:

A 4	K 3
Q 2	10 6 3
A J	9 6 2

From such holdings as the Q2 and K3, pitch the low trump in case your opponent holds the blank Ace. He will thereby have high, but by saving your own high trump you may snare game.

LAWS OF PITCH, OR SETBACK

1. Number of Players Two to seven; most often played by three to five players, most popular for four. Each plays for himself.

2. The Pack Fifty-two cards.

3. Rank of Cards A (high), K, Q, J, 10, 9, 8, 7, 6, 5, 4, 3, 2.

4. The Draw High deals and has choice of seats; other players may sit where they please, and in case of any question the higher card drawn has preference.

5. The Shuffle and Cut Any player may shuffle, the dealer last, and the player to the dealer's right cuts, leaving at least five cards in each packet.

6. The Deal Three cards at a time, in rotation, beginning with eldest hand, until each player has six cards. After each hand the deal passes to the left.

7. Object of the Game To be the first player to reach a total of 11 points. Points are scored as follows:

   a. High   1 point for holding the highest trump in play.

   b. Low   1 point for winning the lowest trump in play.

   c. Jack   1 point for winning the Jack of trumps in play.

   d. Game   1 point for winning in tricks scoring cards to the greatest value, each Ten counting 10 points, each Ace 4, each King 3, each Queen 2, each Jack 1.

   e. If the trump Jack is not in play, no one counts it. If two or more players tie for game, no one counts the point for game.

8. The Bidding Eldest hand bids first. Each player in rotation has one chance to bid or pass. The possible bids are one, two, three, or four (without naming a suit). A bid of four is called *slam, smudge, shoot the moon,* etc.

9. The Play The pitcher (highest bidder) leads to the first trick. The suit of the card he leads (pitches) becomes the trump suit. On a trump lead each other hand must follow suit if able; on any other lead a player may either follow suit or trump, as he prefers. When unable to follow suit, a player may play any card—he need not trump. The player of the highest trump, or the highest card of the suit led if the trick contains no trump, wins the trick and leads first to the next trick.

10. Scoring   When all six tricks have been played, the points due each player are ascertained. Usually a score is kept with pencil and paper. Each player except the pitcher always scores whatever points he makes. The pitcher scores whatever points he makes if his score equals his contract; but if he has not scored as many points as he bid for, he is set back by the amount of his bid (the number of points he bid is deducted from his score). Thus a player may have a net minus score, being "in the hole," in which case his score is shown on the score sheet with a ring around it.

The first player to reach a plus score of 11 points wins the game. The pitcher's score is counted first, so that if he and another player reach 11 on the same hand, the pitcher wins even though the other player has a higher total score. If two players other than the pitcher could reach 11 on the same hand, the points are counted in this order: High, Low, Jack, Game.

11. Smudge   A player who smudges and who makes his contract by winning all 4 points wins the game immediately, unless he was in the hole before he made his bid, in which case he receives only the 4 points. If he fails to make the bid, he is set back 4 points and also loses the equivalent of two games.

IRREGULARITIES

12. Misdeal   It is a misdeal if an Ace, Jack or Deuce is exposed in dealing. Since the deal is an advantage, a misdeal loses the deal.

13. Revoke (failure to follow suit or trump when able to follow suit)   A play once made cannot be withdrawn, so a revoke stands and play continues to the end. If the pitcher revokes, he cannot score and is set back the amount of his bid, while each other player scores what he makes. If any player except the pitcher revokes, all players except the revoker score what they make (including the pitcher, even if he does not make his bid). The revoking player cannot score, and has the amount of the bid deducted from his score.

14. Error in Bidding   An insufficient bid, or a bid out of turn, is void and the offender must pass in his turn to bid.

15. Error in Pitching   Once the pitcher plays a card, the trump cannot be changed.

a. If a player pitches before the auction closes, he is assumed to have bid four and play proceeds; except that any player in turn before him who has not had a turn to bid may himself bid four and pitch, whereupon the card illegally pitched, and any card played to it, must be withdrawn.

b. If the wrong player pitches after the auction is closed, the pitcher may require that card and any card played to it to be withdrawn; and, when first it is the offender's turn to play, the pitcher may require him to play his highest or lowest card of the suit led or to trump or not to trump; except that if the pitcher has played to the incorrect lead, it cannot be withdrawn and the pitcher must immediately name the trump, which he must then lead the first time he wins a trick.

16. Settlement   The winner of the game receives one counter from each other player whose score is one or more, and two counters from each other player whose score is zero or who is in the hole. (Variant. Some play that the winner receives an additional counter from each player for each time that player has been set back.)

GLOSSARY

ABOVE THE LINE *Bridge*. The place on the score sheet where premiums are scored.

ACES UP *Poker*. A hand of two pairs including Aces.

ADVERSARY Any opponent; one playing against the highest Bidder.

ADVERTISE 1. *Poker*. Make a bluff intended to be exposed. 2. *Gin*. Discard a card to induce an opponent to discard another of same or near rank.

ANTE *Poker*. 1. A bet made before the deal. 2. Contribution to a pot which at the start belongs equally to all players.

AUCTION The period of the bidding.

BACK TO BACK *Stud Poker*. Said of the hole card and first upcard when they are a pair.

BAIT 1. bête. 2. advertise.

BALKING CARDS *Cribbage*. Cards selected by the nondealer to be laid away to the crib and which have the least chance of making scores.

BALANCED HAND *Bridge*. One that contains no void or singleton.

BANKER *Blackjack*. Dealer against whom all others bet.

BASE Four (Canasta) or five (Samba) natural matching cards—a base for a canasta.

BASE COUNT, BASIC *Canasta, Samba*. The total of all bonuses.

BATE bête.

BELOW THE LINE *Bridge*. The place on the score sheet where the trick score is entered.

BET   Any wager on the outcome of play or of a game, such as that the bettor holds the winning hand.

BÊTE (pronounced bate)   1. Beaten; having failed to make contract. 2. A forfeit paid by a loser or by a transgressor of a rule of correct procedure.

BETTING INTERVAL   Period during which each active player in turn has the right to bet or to drop out.

BICYCLE   The lowest possible hand in Lowball, consisting of 5-4-3-2-A.

BID   An offer to win a certain number of tricks or points in play; to make a bid.

BIDDABLE SUIT   *Bridge*. A player's holding in a suit that meets the systemic requirements for a bid.

BIDDER   1. Any player who makes a bid. 2. The player who makes the highest bid and assumes the contract.

BIDDER-OUT   *Pinochle*. The rule that the Bidder counts first, when the object is to win 1000 or other previously fixed number of points.

BIDDING   The auction; the period during which bids are made; competing in the auction.

BID OVER   Overcall.

BLACKJACK   The combination of an Ace and a face card or Ten, counting 21.

BLACK MARIA   *Hearts*. The Queen of Spades.

BLACKWOOD CONVENTION   *Bridge*. A system of cue bidding to reach slams, invented by Easley Blackwood.

BLANK A SUIT   Discard all cards held in that suit.

BLANK SUIT   Absence of any cards of that suit from the hand.

BLIND   1. *Poker*. A compulsory bet made before the deal; an ante. 2. Widow.

BLITZ   Shutout.

BLUFF   *Poker*. A bet on a hand that the player actually does not believe is the best.

BOOK   *Bridge*. The number of tricks a side must win before it can score by winning subsequent tricks; usually six tricks.

BORDERLINE BID   *Bridge*. A bid on a hand that barely meets the systemic requirements.

BOX   *Gin*. One deal; the bonus for winning a deal.

BREAK *Gin.* Discard a card from a combination. Also called split.

BURN A CARD Expose and bury it, or place it on the bottom of the pack.

BURY A CARD 1. Place it in the middle of the pack or among the discards so that it cannot be readily located. 2. *Pinochle.* Discard it, after taking the widow.

BUSINESS DOUBLE *Bridge.* One made for the purpose of exacting increased penalties.

BUST 1. A hand devoid of trick-taking possibilities. 2. *Blackjack.* Draw cards totaling more than 21.

BUY Draw from the widow or stock; cards so received.

CALL 1. Declare, bid, or pass; *Bridge.* Any pass, double, redouble, or bid. 2. *Poker.* Make a bet exactly equal to the last previous bet.

CANASTA A meld of seven or more cards. Natural canasta, one using no wild cards, as distinct from mixed canasta.

CASH Lead and win tricks with established cards.

CHIP A token used in place of money; to place chips in the pot.

CLEAR Establish a card or suit by forcing out adverse higher cards or stoppers.

CLEAR A SUIT Drive out all adverse cards that can win tricks in the suit.

CLOSE CARDS *Cribbage.* Cards near in rank, as Seven and Nine.

COFFEE HOUSING Talking and acting so as to mislead opponents as to one's cards.

COMBINATION 1. Group of cards of scoring value (Cribbage); any group of cards. 2. Two cards that can become a meld by addition of a matching third card (Gin).

COME-ON 1. *Bridge.* Signal to partner to lead or continue a suit; echo. 2. *Gin.* A discard selected for purpose of advertising.

COMPLETED TRICK One to which every hand has played a card.

CONCEALED HAND   *Canasta.* Melding out by yourself with a canasta, having previously melded no card.

CONDONE   Waive penalty for an irregularity.

CONTRACT   The obligation to win a certain minimum number of tricks or points.

CONVENTIONS   Advance agreement between partners on how to exchange information by bids and plays.

COUNT   1. Score; determine or total the score. 2. Numerical total of certain cards, as deadwood in Gin, cards played in Cribbage. 3. Base values.

COUNTER   A card having a point value when taken in a trick.

COUNT OUT   Go game, especially by accumulation of points during play of a hand.

CRIB   *Cribbage.* The extra hand formed by the players' discards, belonging to the dealer.

CRIBBAGE BOARD   A device for scoring.

CROSSRUFF   *Bridge.* Alternate trumping of each other's plain-suit leads by the two hands of a partnership.

CUE BID   *Bridge.* One that systemically shows control of a suit, especially by possession of the Ace or a void.

CUT   Divide the pack into two packets and reverse their order.

DEAD CARD   One which cannot be used in play or which has already been played.

DEADWOOD   1. *Poker.* The discard pile. 2. *Gin.* Unmatched cards in a hand.

DEAL   1. Distribute cards to the players; the turn to deal. 2. The period from one deal to the next, including all incidents of making the trump, bidding, melding, discarding, playing, showing, and scoring.

DEALER   1. The player who distributes the cards in preparation for play. 2. Banker.

DECK   1. All the playing cards with which a game is played; also called pack. 2. *Canasta.* (rarely) the discard pile.

DECLARATION   1. Call; bid; naming of a trump suit or game; the auction. 2. The trump suit or game as named in a bid.

DECLARER 1. *Bridge.* The player who plays both his hand and the dummy. 2. Bidder (2).

DEFENDER *Bridge.* An opponent of declarer.

DEFENSIVE BID *Bridge.* 1. One made by an opponent of the opening Bidder. 2. One made to prevent opponents from winning the contract cheaply.

DEFENSIVE STRENGTH *Bridge.* Cards that are expected to win tricks against an adverse contract.

DEMAND BID *Bridge.* One that systemically requires partner to keep the auction open or to make a responsive bid.

DEUCE Any two-spot.

DISCARD 1. Lay aside excess cards in exchange for others from the stock or the widow; a discarded card or cards. 2. Play a plain-suit card not of the same suit as the lead.

DISCARD PILE Cards previously discarded.

DISCOURAGING CARD *Bridge.* Any played that indicates no desire to have the suit led or continued.

DISTRIBUTION Division of cards among the hands, especially as to the number of each suit held by each hand.

DOUBLE *Bridge.* A call which has the effect of increasing the trick values and penalties in case the last preceding bid becomes the contract.

DOUBLE BÊTE *Pinochle.* The penalty suffered by a Bidder who has elected to play the hand and has lost.

DOUBLE PAIRS ROYAL *Cribbage.* Four of a kind.

DOUBLE RUN *Cribbage.* A hand comprising a run of three cards with one rank duplicated.

DOUBLETON An original holding of two cards in a suit.

DRAW 1. Pull cards from a pack spread face down, to determine seats, first deal, etc. 2. Receive cards from the stock to replace discards.

DROP Withdraw from the current deal.

DUMMY *Bridge.* Declarer's partner; the hand laid down by him and played by declarer.

ECHO *Bridge.* A signal comprising the play of a higher card before a lower card of the same suit.

80 KINGS *Pinochle.* A meld of four Kings, one of each suit.

ELDEST HAND   The player at the left of the dealer.

ENCOURAGING CARD   One played that indicates a desire to have the suit led or continued or indicates strength in it.

ENTRY   A card with which a hand can eventually win a trick and so gain the lead.

ESTABLISHED SUIT   One that can be cashed in its entirety without loss of a trick.

EXIT   Get out of the lead; compel another hand to win a trick.

EXPOSED CARD   One played in error, inadvertently dropped, or otherwise shown not in a legitimate manner and therefore (in most games) subject to penalty.

FACE CARD   Any King, Queen, or Jack. (The Ace is not a face card.)

FALSE CARD   One selected for play, when there is a choice, to mislead opponents as to the contents of the hand.

FIFTEEN   *Cribbage.* A combination of cards totaling 15 in pip values; the score of 2 for such a combination.

FILL   *Poker.* Draw cards that improve the original holding.

FINESSE   An attempt to make a card serve as an equal to a higher-ranking card held by an opponent.

FISH   Advertise.

5-POINT CARD   *Canasta.* Any Seven, Six, Five, Four, or black Three, each valued at 5 points.

FLUSH   1. *Poker, Cribbage.* A hand with all cards of one suit. 2. *Pinochle.* A meld of the A, K, Q, J, 10 of trumps.

FOLD   *Poker.* Withdraw from the current deal, as signified by turning one's cards face down.

FOLLOW SUIT   Play a card of the same suit as the lead.

FORCE   1. Compel a player to trump if he wishes to win a trick. 2. *Bridge.* Make a bid that systemically compels partner to respond. 3. *Canasta.* Discard a card which the next player is compelled by the rules to pick up.

FORCING BID   Demand bid.

40 JACKS   *Pinochle.* A meld of four Jacks, one of each suit.

FOUR OF A KIND   Four cards of the same rank, as, four Aces.

FREE BID   *Bridge*. One made voluntarily, not under any systemic compulsion.

FREE DOUBLE   *Bridge*. The double of an adverse contract which is sufficient for game if made undoubled.

FREE RIDE   *Poker*. Playing in a pot without having to ante or bet.

FREEZE THE PACK   *Canasta*. Discard a wild card, thereby increasing the difficulty of taking the discard pile.

FULL HOUSE   *Poker*. A hand comprising three of a kind and a pair.

GIN   *Gin*. A hand completely formed in sets, with no deadwood.

GO   *Cribbage*. A call signifying that the player cannot play another card without exceeding 31; the score of 1 point to opponent when go is called.

GO OUT   1. Get rid of all cards in the hand, as in Gin, Canasta. 2. Reach the cumulative total of points necessary for game.

GRAND SLAM   *Bridge*. The winning of all thirteen tricks by one side.

GROUP   Cards forming a valid meld; especially three or four of a kind, as distinguished from a sequence.

GUARDED   *Bridge*. Accompanied by as many small cards of the same suit as there are higher cards outstanding, as Q, x, x.

HARD   *Blackjack* not including an Ace.

HIS HEELS   *Cribbage*. A Jack turned as a starter; the score of 2 to the dealer for this turn-up.

HIS NOBS   *Cribbage*. A Jack of the same suit as the starter, in hand or crib; the score of 1 point for such a Jack.

HIT   1. *Gin*. Discard a card that the next player can use. 2. *Blackjack*. Deal another card to (a player).

HOLD UP   *Bridge*. Refuse to win a trick with.

HOLE CARD   *Stud Poker*. The first card received by a player, which is dealt face down.

HONORS   1. High cards, especially if they have scoring value.

2. *Bridge.* The five highest trumps, or, if there is no trump, the four Aces.

IMPERFECT PACK   One from which cards are missing, in which a card is incorrectly duplicated, or which has become so worn that some cards are identifiable from the back.

INFORMATION   Disclosure of holdings, intentions, and desires between partners through the legitimate channels of bidding or play.

INFORMATORY DOUBLE   *Bridge.* A systemic double made primarily to give information to partner.

INITIAL MELD   *Canasta.* The first made by a side.

INSIDE STRAIGHT   *Poker.* Four cards needing a card of interior rank to make a straight, as 9-8-6-5.

INSUFFICIENT BID   One that is not legally high enough to overcall the last previous bid.

INSURANCE   *Blackjack.* A bet that dealer will not get a natural, when he has an Ace showing.

IN THE HOLE   Minus score, so-called from the practice of marking a score as minus by drawing a ring around it.

IN THE MITT   *Pinochle.* Received in the deal, as 100 Aces in the original hand.

JACKPOT   *Poker.* A deal in which everyone antes; usually in such a deal a pair of Jacks or better is required to open.

JOKER   An extra card furnished with the standard pack, and used in some games as the highest trump or as a wild card.

JUMP BID   *Bridge.* A bid of more tricks than are legally necessary to overcall a bid.

KICKER   *Draw Poker.* An extra card kept with a pair for a two-card draw.

KITTY   1. A percentage taken out of the stakes to pay expenses or admission fees. 2. A pool to which bets are paid and from which royalties are collected; a pool that shares like a player in winnings and losses of certain Pinochle bids. 3. Widow.

KNAVE   The Jack of a suit.

KNOCK 1. *Gin*. Signify termination of play by laying down one's hand. 2. *Poker*. Signify disinclination to cut the pack, or to bet, by rapping on the table.

LAST 1. *Cribbage*. The point for playing the last card. 2. The score for winning last trick, as in Pinochle.

LAY AWAY 1. *Pinochle*. Discard after taking up the widow. 2. *Cribbage*. Give cards to the crib.

LAY OFF *Gin*. Get rid of cards on an opponent's meld.

LEAD Play first to a trick; the card so played.

LIGHT In debt to the pot.

LIMIT *Poker*. The maximum amount by which a player may increase a previous bet.

LIVE CARD One still in the hands or stock or otherwise available; one that is not dead.

LONG CARD One left in a hand after all opponents have exhausted the suit.

LONG SUIT A holding of more than four cards in a suit; the longest holding in any suit in a hand.

LURCH *Cribbage*. The winning of a game when the opponent has not reached the halfway point.

MAKE The contract; the trump suit; name the trump suit or game.

MAKE UP Gather and shuffle the pack for the next deal.

MARRIAGE *Pinochle*. A meld of the King and Queen of a suit.

MATCHED, MATCHING Corresponding in kind, said of cards that may legally be melded, as in Gin, Canasta.

MELD A combination, set, or group of cards of value in scoring or in getting rid of one's cards; show or announce such a combination.

MINOR MELD *Canasta, Samba*. Any meld less than a canasta.

MISDEAL Any departure from the laws of correct procedure in dealing.

MIXED CANASTA A meld of seven or more of a kind, including wild cards.

MUGGINS *Cribbage*. The right of a player to take points overlooked by his opponent.

NATURAL   1. Without the use of any wild card. 2. A combination that wins at once; in Blackjack, a face card (or Ten) and an Ace.

NATURAL CANASTA   A meld of seven or more cards, none wild.

N-S, E-W   Compass points, used to designate the four players in a game, as Bridge. (Note: compass designations are often used also in three-handed and two-handed games.)

OFFENSIVE STRENGTH   *Bridge.* Cards that are expected to win tricks at one's own contract.

ONCE AROUND   Game fixed at 61, when scored on a Cribbage board.

100 ACES   *Pinochle.* A meld of four Aces.

OPEN   1. Make the first declaration or the first bid. 2. *Poker.* Make the first bet, especially in a jackpot. 3. *Stud Poker.* Face-up on the table. 4. Make the first lead of a suit.

OPENERS   *Poker.* A holding that entitles a player to open a pot.

OPENING BID   The first bid of the auction.

OVERCALL   Make a bid legally sufficient to supersede the last previous bid.

OVERRUFF, OVERTRUMP   Play a trump higher than one previously played to a trick.

OVERTRICK   *Bridge.* Any won by declarer in excess of his contract.

PACK   1. The deck of cards. 2. *Canasta, Samba.* The discard pile.

PAINT   *Hearts.* Discard a Heart on a trick won by another player.

PAIRS ROYAL   *Cribbage.* Three of a kind.

PART SCORE, partial   *Bridge.* A trick-score total of less than game.

PASS   1. A declaration signifying that the player does not wish to make a bid, or that he withdraws from the current deal. 2. *Hearts.* The cards exchanged among the original hands after the deal.

PASS OUT A DEAL   Abandon the deal after all players pass.

PAT HAND   The original hand when it refuses to discard and draw, as in Draw Poker.

PEG   *Cribbage*. A marker used for scoring on a Cribbage board; win points, especially in play.

PENALTY CARD   *Bridge*. An exposed card that must be played at first legal opportunity.

PICTURE CARD   Face card.

PINOCHLE   A meld of a Queen of Spades and Jack of Diamonds.

PITCH   The opening lead, which fixes the trump suit.

PLACES OPEN   Outstanding cards that will improve a hand.

PLAIN SUIT   Any card that is not trumps.

PLAYED CARD   One gathered in a trick; one legally construed to be played.

PLAYING TO THE SCORE   Modifying normal strategy of bidding or play when one side is close to game.

PLAY OFF   *Cribbage*. Play a card of rank far enough from that of previous cards so that opponents cannot make a run.

PLAY ON   *Cribbage*. Play a card that may enable an opponent to make a run.

POINT COUNT   A method of valuing a Bridge hand by assigning relative numerical values to the high cards.

POT   The aggregate of chips or money at stake in a deal, consisting usually of contributions from each active player.

PRE-EMPTIVE BID   *Bridge*. A high opening bid, made to shut out adverse competition.

PRIZE PILE   *Canasta*. The discard pile when frozen.

PSYCHIC BID   *Bridge*. One made without the cards to support it, for the purpose of misleading the opponents.

QUITTED TRICK   One that has been turned face down.

RAISE   1. *Poker*. Put more chips in the pot than are necessary to meet the previous bet. 2. *Bridge*. Bid an increased number of tricks in a declaration previously bid by partner.

REBID   *Bridge*. A bid made by a player who has previously bid.

REDEAL   A new deal by the same dealer, usually after a misdeal.

REDUCE   *Gin*. Lower the count of one's deadwood by discarding high cards; reducer, a low card.

RE-ENTRY   A card with which a hand can eventually regain the lead after having lost it.

RESPONSE   *Bridge*. A bid made in reply to a bid by partner.

REVOKE   Fail to follow suit when able; fail to play a card as required by a law of correct procedure or by a proper penalty.

ROTATION   The movement of the turn to deal, bid, or play. In modern practice this is to the left, or clockwise.

ROUNDHOUSE   *Pinochle*. A meld comprising a King and a Queen of each suit.

ROYAL FLUSH   *Poker*. An Ace-high straight flush.

RUBBER   The winning of the first two out of three games by one side.

RUFF   Play a trump on a plain-suit lead.

RUN   A sequence of three or more cards of the same suit, as in Gin and Samba.

SACRIFICE BID   *Bridge*. One made without the expectation that the contract will be fulfilled, for the purpose of saving greater loss.

SAFE DISCARD   *Gin, Canasta*. One that the next player surely or probably cannot use or pick up.

SAMBA   Seven cards of the same suit in sequence.

SCHNEIDER   Shutout.

SCORE   1. The counting value of specific cards or tricks. 2. The accumulated total of points won by a player or a side. 3. Score sheet.

SECOND HAND   Second in turn to call or play.

SEQUENCE   Two or more cards of adjacent rank, as 8-9-10.

SET   1. A group of cards of scoring or melding value, as in Canasta, Gin. 2. *Bridge*. Defeat the contract.

SETBACK   A deduction from a player's accumulated score; a variant name for certain games, as Pitch.

SET MATCH   *Bridge.* Play with unchanging partnerships.

SHORT SUIT   *Bridge.* A holding of less than four cards in a suit.

SHOW   1. Meld; expose. 2. *Cribbage.* Count the hand.

SHOWDOWN   *Poker.* The facing of all active hands to determine the winner of a pot.

SHUFFLE   Mix the cards in the pack preparatory to dealing.

SHUTOUT   *Gin family.* Winning of a game when the opponent has not scored a point.

SHUTOUT BID   Pre-emptive bid.

SIDE STRENGTH   High cards in plain suits.

SIGNAL   Any convention of play whereby one partner informs the other of his holdings or desires.

SIGN-OFF   *Bridge.* A bid that asks partner to pass or to close the auction as soon as possible.

SINGLE BÊTE   *Pinochle.* A forfeit paid by a bidder who concedes loss of the hand without play.

SINGLETON   An original holding of one card in a suit.

60 QUEENS   *Pinochle.* A meld of four Queens, one of each suit.

SKUNKED   Shutout.

SLAM   The winning of all the tricks by one side.

SLUFF or SLOUGH   Discard in playing.

SMALL SLAM   *Bridge.* The winning of twelve tricks by one side.

SMEAR   Discard a counting card on a trick won by partner. Also, schmier.

SMUDGE   *Pitch.* A bid to win all four points.

SOFT   *Blackjack* including an Ace that may be counted as 1 or 11.

SPLIT   1. *Gin.* Discard a card from a combination or set. 2. *Bridge.* Play, second hand, one of equal honors, as K-Q, or Q-J.

SPLIT A PAIR   *Blackjack.* Divide two equal cards originally received, to make two separate hands.

SPLITTING OPENERS   *Poker.* In a jackpot discarding part of the combination that qualified the hand to open (in an effort to better the chances of improvement).

SPOT CARD   Any of ranks 10, 9, 8, 7, 6, 5, 4, 3, 2.

SPREAD   1. Open; show. 2. A contract that can be fulfilled without playing. 3. Any meld.

STAND   Accept the cards already dealt without drawing, discarding, or redealing, as in Blackjack.

STAND-OFF   A tie; cancellation of a hand or bet by an indecisive result.

STARTER   *Cribbage.* The card cut by nondealer and turned up by dealer prior to the play.

STAY   *Poker.* Remain in the pot without raising; meet a bet; call; see.

STOCK   An undealt portion of the pack, which may be used later in the same deal.

STOP CARD   *Canasta.* Any wild card or black Trey, so-called because when discarded it stops the next player from taking the discard pile.

STOPPER   A holding by which a hand can eventually win a trick in a suit led by an adversary.

STRAIGHT   *Poker.* A hand of five cards in sequence, but not all in the same suit.

STRAIGHT FLUSH   *Poker.* A hand of five cards in sequence in the same suit.

SUFFICIENT BID   One high enough legally to supersede the last previous bid.

SWEEPSTAKE   *Hearts.* A method of settlement; the pot is won only by a player who is clear.

SYSTEM   *Bridge.* An agreement between partners on the requirements for various bids and tactical procedure in various situations.

TABLE STAKES   *Poker.* A method of placing a limit on betting.

TAKE-ALL   *Hearts.* The winning of all the counting cards by one player.

TAKEOUT   *Bridge.* The bid of a different declaration from that bid by partner.

TAKEOUT DOUBLE   Informatory double.

TENACE   A holding of two cards in a suit, lacking one or more cards of intervening rank, as with 10-A. Perfect tenace lacks one intervening card; imperfect tenace lacks two or more. Major tenace is A-Q; minor tenace is K-J.

10-POINT CARD   *Canasta.* Any K, Q, J, 10, 9, or 8, each valued at 10 points.

TENTH CARD   Any of pip value 10, as a face card at Cribbage.

THIRD HAND   Third in turn to call or play.

THREE OF A KIND   Three cards of the same rank, as three Aces.

THROW OFF   1. Discard. 2. Smear.

TOUCHING CARDS   Cards in sequence.

TRAP   Advertise.

TREY   Any three-spot.

TRICK   A round of cards during the play, one card being contributed by each active hand; the packet of such cards when gathered.

TRUMP CARD   Any of the trump suit, or one arbitrarily designated as a trump by the rules of the game.

TRUMP SUIT   One selected under the rules of the game to have the special privilege that every card in this suit ranks higher than any nontrump card in trick winning.

TURN-UP   A card turned face-up, after the deal, to fix or propose the trump.

TWICE AROUND   Game fixed at 121, when scored on a Cribbage board.

TWO-SUITER   *Bridge.* A hand containing five or more cards in each of two suits.

UNBALANCED HAND   *Bridge.* One that contains a singleton or void.

UNDERCUT   *Gin.* Show a hand that counts the same or less than the opponent's after he has knocked.

UNDER THE GUNS   *Poker.* Said of the first player in turn to bet.

UNMATCHED CARD   *Gin* family. Any that is not part of a set; deadwood.

UPCARD   1. *Stud Poker.* One properly dealt face up. 2. *Gin.*

The first card turned up from the stock after the deal; the uppermost card of the discard pile.

VOID Blank suit.

VULNERABLE *Bridge*. Said of a side that has won a game toward rubber.

WHITEWASHED Shutout.

WIDE CARDS *Cribbage*. Those too far apart in rank to be likely to form runs.

WIDOW Extra cards dealt at the same time as the hands, and which usually become the property of the highest bidder. Also called the blind.

WILD CARD One that may be specified by the holder to be of any rank and suit.

WILD DISCARD *Gin*. Dangerous discard; one that may be used by the next player. (Note: seldom used to mean the discard of a wild card.)

x Any low card, as A x—Ace and one low card.